James For............. .................
written for the *New York Times*, the *Atlant...
other publications. A former clerk for Sup........ ......... Justice Sandra
Day O'Connor, he spent six years as a public defender in Washington,
D.C ......... he co-founded the Maya Angelou Public Charter School.

....his superb, shattering book probably made a deeper
impression on me than any other this year'
Jennifer Senior, *New York Times*

...ul book, written so well, that gives us the
...gins and consequences of where we are ... I can see
why [the Pulitzer prize] was awarded'
Trevor Noah, *The Daily Show*

...markable ... Forman's beautifully written narrative,
...iched by firsthand knowledge of the cops and courts,
nei... condemns black leaders in hindsight nor exonerates the
wh... ...ominated institutions ... He adds historical nuance to
the... ...y of "mass incarceration" told in ... *The New Jim Crow*'
Charles Lane, *Washington Post*

...sing ... [Forman's] moving, nuanced, and candid
... challenges another aspect of the "New Jim Crow"
th... ...e shows that some of the most ardent proponents of
...on-crime policies in the era that brought us mass
in... ...tion were black politicians and community leaders –
m... ...whom were veterans of the civil rights movement ...
...e correctives offered by Forman ... have consequences
...ot only for how we understand mass incarceration,
but for how we go about fixing it'
*New York Review of Books*

# LOCKING UP OUR OWN

## CRIME and PUNISHMENT in BLACK AMERICA

### JAMES FORMAN JR.

ABACUS

First published in the United States in 2017 by Farrar, Straus and Giroux
First published in Great Britain in 2018 by Abacus

1 3 5 7 9 10 8 6 4 2

Copyright © 2017 by James Forman, Jr.

The moral right of the author has been asserted.

A CIP catalogue record for this book
is available from the British Library.

ISBN 978-0-349-14368-2

Printed and bound in Great Britain by
Clays Ltd, Elcograf S.p.A.

Papers used by Abacus are from well-managed forests
and other responsible sources.

Abacus
An imprint of
Little, Brown Book Group
Carmelite House
50 Victoria Embankment
London EC4Y 0DZ

An Hachette UK Company
www.hachette.co.uk

www.littlebrown.co.uk

*To Ify and Emeka,*

*the loves of my life*

# Contents

Introduction                                                          3

PART I: ORIGINS

1. Gateway to the War on Drugs: Marijuana, 1975              17

2. Black Lives Matter: Gun Control, 1975                     47

3. Representatives of Their Race: The Rise of
   African American Police, 1948–78                          78

PART II: CONSEQUENCES

4. "Locking Up Thugs Is Not Vindictive": Sentencing, 1981–82   119

5. "The Worst Thing to Hit Us Since Slavery": Crack and
   the Advent of Warrior Policing, 1988–92                    151

6. What Would Martin Luther King, Jr., Say?:
   Stop and Search, 1995                                      185

   Epilogue: The Reach of Our Mercy, 2014–16                  217

   *Notes*                                                    241
   *Acknowledgments*                                          287
   *Index*                                                    291

# LOCKING UP OUR OWN

# Introduction

All of us in the public defender's office feared the Martin Luther King speech. Curtis Walker, an African American Superior Court judge in Washington, D.C., was famous for it. And today Brandon, my fifteen-year-old client, was on the receiving end.*

"Son, your lawyer here has been telling me some good things about you: how you dote on your little sister, how your football coach says you are a born leader, how some of your teachers believe you can do better. He says he has found a program for you that will help you with school, and that I should give you a chance at that and not lock you up."

Brandon had pleaded guilty to possessing a handgun and a small amount of marijuana—enough to use, but not to sell. I had argued for probation. Judge Walker told Brandon he was considering my proposal. But first he had some things to say.

"Mr. Forman says you need another chance. But let me ask you,

---

*Throughout this book I have changed the names of individual clients and the other lawyers and judges involved in their cases.

do you even realize how many chances you've already had? You might think you have it hard. But let me tell you, it was harder once. Black boys picked cotton once upon a time. Sat in the back of the bus— those who were lucky enough to even *be* on the bus, and not walking."

Judge Walker was getting into his rhythm now. He wasn't a preacher, but he sounded like somebody who had spent more than a few Sundays in the pews.

"Now you can go to school, study hard, live your dreams. It isn't easy—I know that. But it is *possible*. And people fought, struggled, and died for that possibility. Dr. King died for that, son. And what are you doing? Not studying! No, you are cutting class, runnin' and thuggin', not listening to your momma or grandmother. Instead, you want to listen to some hoodlum friends." By now, the judge was glaring at Brandon.

Out of the corner of my eye, I could see that Brandon was keeping his gaze steady on the judge. This was good. Judge Walker liked that. If Brandon avoided eye contact, Judge Walker would think he was being disrespectful.

"Well, let me tell you: Dr. King didn't march and die so that you could be a fool, so that you could be out on the street, getting high, carrying a gun, and robbing people. No, young man, that was not his dream. That was not his dream at all."

This was the speech I knew so well. The words changed a bit each time, but the theme stayed the same: Life is not easy for African Americans today, but it's better than it was, and you best stop being a thug and start taking advantage of the opportunities that others fought so hard for.

I was also familiar with the emotions etched on Judge Walker's face as he spoke—anger, frustration, and despair. I was a new public defender, but the judge had been around for a long time. He looked and sounded like somebody who was tired of lecturing black boys (and a few girls), but not so tired that he wouldn't try one more time. He was mad at Brandon, but he hadn't given up on him. He just seemed like a man with no good alternatives, confronting a problem that was too big for him to solve.

Judge Walker paused, took his eyes from Brandon, and started looking through the case materials spread out before him. His lecture done, he was taking his time imposing a sentence. Another good sign. Judge Walker was known for giving defendants a fair trial, but if you lost, look out. Defense attorneys called him "a long-ball hitter," referring to the lengthy sentences he imposed. But now he was hesitating. Maybe I had persuaded him that this was not an easy case.

I knew that probation was a long shot. The gun charge was serious. And worse, a report from the court's social worker had claimed that Brandon hung out with other kids who were involved in some recent neighborhood robberies.

But the robbery allegations were just rumors; Brandon hadn't been charged with that. As for the gun, well, Brandon lived in a terribly dangerous neighborhood, one where kids sometimes carried guns for self-defense. Most important, I had told Judge Walker, this was Brandon's first arrest, and he had great potential. His football coach and two of his teachers had written letters about his promise, his family was supportive, and he had recently enrolled in a tutoring program for at-risk students. And Brandon had pleaded guilty, accepted responsibility for his actions, and been remorseful. Juvenile court was supposed to offer second chances, and Brandon was a perfect candidate.

The prosecutor argued that Brandon should go to Oak Hill, D.C.'s juvenile detention facility. I had countered by pointing out what everybody knew: Oak Hill was a dungeon, with no functioning school, frequent incidents of violence, no counseling or mental health services worth the name, and no transition services for young offenders once they were released.[1] Brandon would miss months of actual school while serving his sentence, and it was possible that the principal wouldn't take him back once he returned to his neighborhood. If this happened, there was no good alternative school he could turn to.

Brandon fidgeted as we waited for Judge Walker to speak, and I tried to calm him by placing my hand gently on the back of his shoulders. I glanced behind me and offered what I hoped was a comforting smile to Brandon's mother and grandmother sitting in the first row.

They had never missed a court hearing, had always voiced their support for Brandon. Now all they could do was wait.

Judge Walker finally gathered the papers up into one stack and placed them back in the case file. When he spoke, the verdict was quick and painful. "Brandon," he said, "I believe you have potential, and I see you have supportive teachers and family. But none of that was enough to stop you from picking up a gun. Even if I believe that you had it because you were scared, you could have hurt somebody. Son, actions have consequences. Your consequence is six months at Oak Hill. After which I hope you make good on the hopes that your mother and grandmother have for you."

That was it. The bailiff, who had been sitting behind us, stepped forward to take Brandon to a cell in the courthouse. Brandon's mother gasped and started to cry. Judge Walker wouldn't like that—none of the judges did—but what could he do now? The courtroom clerk would probably help her out into the hallway. Or so I hoped. I had to go see Brandon.

The cellblock was just a few feet behind the courtroom, but it was a world apart. No majesty here, no wood paneling, no carpeting or cushioned seats. Just metal and concrete, housing black boys like Brandon. And make no mistake about it: they were all black. That day, Brandon's cell held three other black teens waiting for their cases to be called. The picture was the same in almost every D.C. courtroom, whether the accused were juveniles or adults. There were a few women and girls, but mostly men and boys. Nearly all—according to official records, more than 95 percent—were African American.[2]

This state of affairs was no secret. In 1995, the year Brandon came before Judge Walker, the Sentencing Project issued one of a series of increasingly alarming reports documenting blatant racial disparities in the criminal justice system. Nationally, one in three young black men was under criminal justice supervision.[3] In Washington, D.C., the figure was one in two.

Racial disparities were nothing new. But now they were being exacerbated by an experiment in punitive criminal justice the likes of which the world had never seen. Beginning in the early 1970s, America had adopted an array of increasingly tough approaches to crime, including aggressive street-level policing, longer sentences, and a range of lifetime punishments such as felon disenfranchisement.[4] The result? By 1995, a nation with only 5 percent of the world's population held almost 25 percent of its prisoners.[5] And an ever-growing proportion of these prisoners were black.

Brandon was now one of them.

He looked defiant when I arrived in the cellblock. I think he wanted to cry, but he definitely would not do that in front of the other kids. I told Brandon I would come to see him at Oak Hill and try to help him get through his six months. ("Do the time, don't let the time do you," the kids liked to say.)

At that moment, I hated Judge Walker and the entire court system. Most of all, I realized, I hated the Martin Luther King speech.

It would be one thing, I thought, for the judge to give Brandon this speech if he was going to put him on probation. In that case, a heartfelt lecture might have done some good. It might have been something that Brandon needed to hear, something that would encourage him to make the most of his second chance. But to invoke Dr. King while locking up another young black man? It was perverse. Surely Judge Walker had noticed that everybody in the cell a few feet away from him was black. Yet here he was, simply adding to the gross racial disparities in the criminal justice system. Where did he get off taking the moral high ground?

As I saw it, I was the person in that courtroom fighting for Dr. King's legacy—I was the one doing civil rights work. I had become a public defender so that I could confront racial injustice. Just one year before, I had been serving as a law clerk for Supreme Court Justice Sandra Day O'Connor. She had encouraged me to work for the Department of Justice or join a national civil rights organization such as the NAACP Legal Defense Fund. I remember her surprise when I told her that I wanted to defend poor people charged with crimes in the local courts of Washington, D.C.

When Justice O'Connor asked why I wanted to be a public defender, my answer was simple: This was the unfinished work of the civil rights movement. I was literally a child of that movement. My parents had met in the Student Nonviolent Coordinating Committee (SNCC, which everyone pronounced "Snick"), one of the major civil rights groups in the 1960s. My dad, born in 1928, was raised in Mississippi, where he ate dirt to feel full during the Great Depression. When he was eight years old, he failed to say "Yes, ma'am" to a store clerk, and white men in the store threatened to lynch him if his uncle brought him to town again.[6] Active in campus politics as a student in the 1950s, my dad joined the fledgling SNCC in 1961. As the group's executive director, he ran internal operations—everything from paying the bills to expanding staff to planning strategy for voting rights drives.[7] My mom had dropped out of Sarah Lawrence College to join SNCC's New York office in 1962. Six months later, she became a coordinator at the group's Atlanta headquarters, raising money and communicating with SNCC chapters at northern colleges.

Now, thirty years later, I was an African American clerking at the Supreme Court, beginning a professional life that would not have been possible without generations of sacrifice and struggle. But despite the gains of the civil rights movement, I knew that progress wasn't the whole story. The nation's prison population was growing darker. In 1954, the year of *Brown v. Board of Education*, about one-third of the nation's prisoners were black. By 1994, when Justice O'Connor and I were talking, the number was approaching 50 percent.[8] The criminal justice system, I told her, was where today's civil rights struggle would be fought. And my short time representing young men like Brandon had convinced me that I was right.

Thoroughly pissed off, I left Brandon and returned to face his family, who I knew were probably sobbing in the hallway of the courthouse. On my way, I passed back through the courtroom, where the judge, the court reporter, and the juvenile prosecutor were chatting, waiting for the next case to be called.

As I passed them, I noticed another racial reality. It wasn't only

Brandon and the other young men in the cellblock who were black. So was everybody in the courtroom—not just the judge, but the court reporter, the bailiff, and the juvenile prosecutor. So was the police officer who had arrested Brandon, not to mention the police chief and the mayor. Even the building we were in—the H. Carl Moultrie I Courthouse, named after the city's first black chief judge—was a reminder of the African American influence on D.C.'s legal system.[9]

This wasn't my first time in an all-black D.C. courtroom, but something—probably my anger at the Martin Luther King speech—made the reality stand out that day. When I got back to my office, I continued the racial tally. I had been to the detention facility that would be Brandon's new home more times than I wanted to count, and I knew that all the guards there were black, too. The city council that wrote the gun and drug laws Brandon had been convicted of violating was majority African American and had been so for more than twenty-five years. In cases that went to trial, the juries were often majority black. Even some of the federal officials involved in D.C.'s criminal justice system were African American, including Eric Holder, then the city's chief prosecutor.

What was going on? How did a majority-black jurisdiction end up incarcerating so many of its own?

Over time, I have come to see that this question, though particularly urgent in Washington, D.C., is of national significance. In September 2014, the Sentencing Project issued a report comparing the attitudes of whites and blacks regarding crime and criminal justice policy. It found that when Americans were asked, "Do you think the courts in this area deal too harshly or not harshly enough with criminals?" more whites (73 percent) than blacks (64 percent) said "not harshly enough." Media coverage of the report emphasized what the Sentencing Project called "the racial gap in punitiveness."[10] But the fact that almost two-thirds of blacks displayed such punitive attitudes received little notice. How could it be that even after forty years of tough-on-crime tactics, with their attendant toll on black America, 64 percent of African Americans still thought the courts were not harsh enough?

I wrote this book to try to answer such questions. Along the way, I have tried to recover a portion of African American social, political, and intellectual history—a story that gets ignored or elided when we fail to appreciate the role that blacks have played in shaping criminal justice policy over the past forty years.[11] African Americans performed this role as citizens, voters, mayors, legislators, prosecutors, police officers, police chiefs, corrections officials, and community activists.[12] Their influence grew as a result of black progress in attaining political power, especially after the passage of the Voting Rights Act in 1965.[13] And to a significant extent, the new black leaders and their constituents supported tough-on-crime measures.

To understand why, we must start with a profound social fact: in the years preceding and during our punishment binge, black communities were devastated by historically unprecedented levels of crime and violence. Spurred by a heroin epidemic, homicides doubled and tripled in D.C. and many other American cities throughout the 1960s. Two decades later, heroin would be eclipsed by crack, a terrifying drug whose addictive qualities and violent marketplace caused some contemporaries to label it "the worst thing to hit us since slavery."

Letters from black citizens, neighborhood association newsletters, and the pages of the black press from the past forty years reveal astonishing levels of pain, fear, and anger. In 1968, a group of black nationalists in D.C. called drug dealers "black-face traitors of our people who sell dope to our young boys and girls and make whores and thieves of them." A decade later, a black D.C. neighborhood association circulated a flyer promoting ways to defend homes from break-ins: the list included guard dogs, security alarms, wild snakes, and, for those with fewer resources, fishhooks strung around doors and windows to puncture the flesh of would-be burglars.[14] By the 1980s and 1990s, the files of D.C. Council members were crammed with letters from scared constituents, complaining that "we feel like prisoners in our homes, strangers on our own streets," and begging for more police action.[15]

As they confronted this devastating crime wave, black officials exhibited a complicated and sometimes overlapping mix of impulses.

Some displayed tremendous hostility toward perpetrators of crime, describing them as a "cancer" that had to be cut away from the rest of the black community. Others pushed for harsher penalties but acknowledged that these measures would not solve the crisis at hand. Some even expressed sympathy for the plight of criminal defendants, who they knew were disproportionately black. But that sympathy was rarely sufficient to overcome the claims of black crime victims, who often argued that a punitive approach was necessary to protect the African American community—including many of its most impoverished members—from the ravages of crime.

Many black officials advocated tough-on-crime measures in race-conscious terms. For example, some blacks opposed marijuana decriminalization because they saw it as tantamount to giving up on black youth—youth they had a responsibility to protect from the destructive impact of drug use. Others argued that blacks were entitled to expanded police forces and courts—state resources they had historically been denied. Some, like Judge Walker, believed they were protecting the legacy of the civil rights movement in the face of the black community's self-immolation.

In documenting the range of black responses to crime, this book repudiates a claim sometimes made by defenders of the criminal justice system: that African Americans protest police violence while ignoring violence by black criminals.[16] There is much to say to this critique—not least, "Of course we hold government to a higher standard than street gangs." But these pages suggest another response: African Americans have *always* viewed the protection of black lives as a civil rights issue, whether the threat comes from police officers or street criminals.[17] Far from ignoring the issue of crime by blacks against other blacks, African American officials and their constituents have been consumed by it.[18]

This book tells a story about what African Americans thought, said, and did. But in focusing on the actions of black officials, I do not minimize the role of whites or of racism in the development of mass incarceration. To the contrary: racism shaped the political, economic, and legal context in which the black community and its elected representatives made their choices. From felon disenfranchisement laws that suppress black votes, to exploitative housing practices that strip black wealth, to schools that refuse to educate black children, to win-at-all-costs prosecutors who strike blacks from jury pools, to craven politicians who earn votes by preying on racial anxieties, to the unconscious and implicit biases that infect us all, it is impossible to understand American crime policy without appreciating racism's enduring role.[19]

We witnessed another example of the enduring power of race-baiting in the 2016 presidential election campaign. Donald Trump, whose signature contribution to political debate had been his relentless propagation of the lie that Barack Obama is not an American citizen, ran the most racist presidential campaign since the arch-segregationist George Wallace's 1968 bid. While Latinos and Muslims were Trump's principal targets, African Americans were far from immune. In particular, Trump revived the "law and order" mantra that Republicans such as Goldwater, Nixon, and Reagan had once used to great effect, portraying America's black neighborhoods as killing fields whose only hope lay in aggressive policing. We don't yet know how this campaign theme will translate into policy over the course of the Trump presidency, but the prospect of more stop-and-frisk and less federal civil rights oversight of local police departments is ominous indeed.

These pages reveal the myriad ways in which American racism narrowed the options available to black citizens and elected officials in their fight against crime. For example, African Americans wanted more law enforcement, but they didn't want *only* law enforcement. Many adopted what we might think of as an all-of-the-above strategy. On one hand, they supported fighting drugs and crime with every resource at the state's disposal, including police, courts, and prisons. On the other hand, they called for jobs, schools, and housing—what many termed "a Marshall Plan for urban America." But because African Americans are a minority nationally, they needed help to win national action against poverty, joblessness, segregation, and other root causes of crime. The help never arrived. The requests for assistance came at a time when Reaganism was ascendant, the Great Society was under assault, and there was little national appetite for social programs—especially those perceived as helping blacks. So African Americans never got the Marshall Plan—just the tough-on-crime laws.[20]

Understanding African American attitudes and actions on matters of crime and punishment requires that we pay careful attention to another topic that is often overlooked in criminal justice scholarship: class divisions within the black community.[21] Although mass incarceration harms black America as a whole, its most direct victims are the poorest, least educated blacks. While the lifetime risk of incarceration skyrocketed for African American male high school dropouts with the advent of mass incarceration, it actually decreased slightly for black men with some college education. As a result, by the year 2000, the lifetime risk of incarceration for black high school dropouts was *ten times higher* than it was for African Americans who had attended college.[22]

These class dynamics drove elected officials toward a tough-on-crime stance in some predictable ways. For example, longer sentences for burglary are unsurprising, since they put (mostly poor) black burglars behind bars and leave (mostly middle-class) black homes protected. But class divisions influence criminal justice debates in black communities in less obvious ways as well: they explain, for example, why black elected officials have been much more likely to speak out against racial profiling (which harms African Americans of all classes) than against unconscionable prison conditions (which have little direct impact on middle-class or elite blacks).[23]

Finally, the incremental and diffuse way the war on crime was waged made it difficult for some African American leaders to appreciate the impact of the choices they were making. Mass incarceration wasn't created overnight; its components were assembled piecemeal over a forty-year period. And those components are many. The police make arrests, pretrial service agencies recommend bond, prosecutors make charging decisions, defense lawyers defend (sometimes), juries adjudicate (in the rare case that doesn't plead), legislatures establish the sentence ranges, judges impose sentences within these ranges, corrections departments run prisons, probation and parole officers supervise released offenders, and so on. The result is an almost absurdly disaggregated and uncoordinated criminal justice system—or "non-system," as Daniel Freed once called it.[24]

Although the existence of this diffuse structure is not news, we have yet to comprehend how the lack of coordination has contributed to the growth of our carceral system. In a tough-on-crime era, no single actor doubles or triples the incarceration rate. But as we shall see, if all the actors become even somewhat more punitive, and if *they all do so at the same time*, the number of people in prison and under criminal justice supervision skyrockets. Yet nobody has to take responsibility for the outcome, because nobody *is* responsible—at least not fully. This lack of responsibility is crucial to understanding why even reluctant or conflicted crime warriors (which some African Americans were and are) become part of the machinery of mass incarceration and why the system continues to churn even to this day, when its human toll has become increasingly apparent.

This book is an account of a city in crisis, where rates of crime and violence rose to unprecedented levels. It explores the acts and attitudes of African American citizens and leaders—of men and women like Judge Walker. When he locked Brandon up, I was furious. Yet in the course of my research, I encountered many people like the judge, and I have come to better understand their motives. I have tried to tell their story fairly, describing the relentless pressure they were under to save a community that seemed to be crumbling before their eyes.

This is also a book about my clients, men and women like Brandon. They, too, struggled with limited options. They made mistakes and sometimes harmed others. But they deserved better than the criminal justice system in which they were trapped.

# PART I

# Origins

# 1

# GATEWAY TO THE WAR ON DRUGS
## Marijuana, 1975

Every generation makes mistakes. Sometimes these errors are relatively harmless or easily fixed. But every so often, a misstep is so damaging that future generations are left shaking their heads in disbelief. "What were they *thinking*?" we ask each other. "How did they not see what they were doing?" We gaze out at the wreckage we've inherited, the failed policies and broken lives, and we think, *This was avoidable.*

The War on Drugs, including the turn toward ever more punitive sentencing, is likely to be judged that sort of mistake.

It is now widely recognized that the drug war has caused tremendous damage—especially in the low-income African American communities that have been its primary target. In 1995, the legal scholar Michael Tonry, an early critic of the War on Drugs, said it "foreseeably and unnecessarily blighted the lives of hundreds of thousands of young disadvantaged black Americans."[1] In the years since Tonry wrote those words, the consequences of the policies he denounced have only intensified. Blacks are much more likely than whites to be arrested, convicted, and incarcerated for drug offenses, even though blacks are no more likely than whites to use drugs.[2] And although blacks play a greater role in street-level drug distribution in most markets than do whites, the best research has shown that this doesn't explain all the racial disparities in incarceration rates.[3] Marijuana produces particularly blatant arrest disparities: in Washington, D.C., the black arrest rate for marijuana possession in 2010 was eight times that for whites, and in that same year, law enforcement in the city made 5,393 marijuana possession arrests—nearly fifteen arrests a day.[4]

All of which raises the question: Why would black people ever have supported the drug war?

Answering this question requires that we return to a time before the drug war achieved unstoppable momentum and before a massive increase in incarceration rates made America the world's largest jailer. In the early to mid-1970s, a majority-black city had the chance to say no to a policy that stigmatized many young blacks and diminished their life prospects. The choice that city made presaged the subsequent course of the tough-on-crime movement in black America.

"Hey, we didn't get our forty acres and a mule," said George Clinton, frontman of the funk band Parliament. "But we did get you, CC." CC was Chocolate City, and Chocolate City was Washington, D.C. There were other chocolate cities in the United States—"We've got Newark, we've got Gary, / Somebody told me we got L.A., / And we're working on Atlanta"—but D.C. was special. As Clinton put it, "You're the capital, CC."

The year was 1975, and D.C.'s black citizens, who made up 70 percent of the city's population, had good reason to celebrate. Since Reconstruction, Congress had denied the city's residents any meaningful role in their own governance. Southern Democrats controlled the District, and they had no interest in granting even a measure of self-determination to a city with so many black residents. South Carolina representative John L. McMillan ran the House of Representatives' District Committee during the 1950s and 1960s; an avowed racist, he viewed the District as his private plantation, stocking the local government with cronies who shared his antipathy toward blacks.[5]

But McMillan and other white supremacists were losing their grip on black people's fate. The election of black mayors across the country demonstrated how the nation was changing. In 1967, there was Carl Stokes in Cleveland, followed by Kenneth Gibson in Newark in 1970; then, three years later, Tom Bradley in Los Angeles, Maynard Jackson in Atlanta, and Coleman Young in Detroit.[6] And then D.C. got its turn. In 1973, Congress passed the Home Rule Act, set to take effect in January 1975.[7] Although it stopped well short of making D.C. fully autonomous, the Home Rule Act provided for an elected mayor with substantial executive authority—including control of the police department—and for a city council with significant legislative power.[8]

Elections were held on November 5, 1974. Two months later, on January 2, 1975, the nation's first black Supreme Court justice, Thurgood Marshall, swore in D.C.'s first elected black mayor in one hundred years, Walter E. Washington. (Before his election, Washington had been serving as an appointed mayor/commissioner, a mostly ceremonial position; even this limited status had infuriated Representative McMillan, who protested by sending a truckload of watermelons to Washington's office.) Marshall also swore in the city's first elected city council, eleven of whose thirteen members were black. Behind them on the stage, a police band played Marvin Gaye's "Let's Get It On." The District Building hosted a public reception, and the city's residents crowded in, congratulating their newly elected officials and collecting autographs on souvenir programs. President Gerald Ford delivered a statement through a representative, declaring that "the power that should have been in Washington all along is now back in Washington . . . the right of every citizen to have a voice in his or her government." So when Parliament released the album *Chocolate City*, it was only fitting that the title song's refrain was "Gainin' on ya," and that the cover art featured the Lincoln Memorial, the Washington Monument, and the Capitol Building all coated in chocolate. The song even opened with a playful prediction: "They still call it the White House, but that's a temporary condition too."[9]

In 1975, D.C.'s racial composition meant that except in Ward 3, the city's only majority-white district, any white candidate seeking a seat on the new city council needed a biography that could appeal to black voters. In Ward 1, which included the Shaw, U Street, and Columbia Heights neighborhoods, such a candidate emerged—someone who would spark one of the newly empowered city's first debates about criminal justice.

David Clarke was a graduate of the Howard University School of Law, where he had been one of a handful of white students. After earning his degree, he took a job in the Washington, D.C., office of Dr. Martin Luther King's Southern Christian Leadership Conference. A few years later, he opened his own private practice and quickly gained a reputation for representing the underdog. As one friend remembered, "If you got in trouble, everybody knew to go get David Clarke because you didn't have to pay him."[10]

When Home Rule arrived, Clarke jumped eagerly into the race for city council. His was the classic grassroots campaign: headquartered in his one-bedroom apartment, it made up in passion what it lacked in money. Ultimately, District voters were convinced by Clarke's authenticity, compassion, and civil rights pedigree, and on inauguration day he was sworn in as one of two white members on the city council.[11]

Once in office, Clarke turned his attention to what he regarded as a matter of pressing importance: the increasingly vigorous enforcement of marijuana laws by the Metropolitan Police Department (MPD). Marijuana arrests had jumped from 334 in 1968 to 3,002 in 1975—a 900 percent increase.[12] Moreover, 80 percent of those arrested were black, and having this arrest on their records could undermine their life chances, making it harder for them to obtain housing, jobs, public benefits, or student loans.

Clarke's election coincided with a national movement to decriminalize marijuana. Today, we connect the drug war with Richard Nixon, who, in 1971, famously announced "a new, all-out offensive" against drugs, the nation's "public enemy no. 1."[13] But Nixon's offensive was largely aimed at harder drugs; it is easy to forget that this same era saw substantial momentum for making possession of small amounts of marijuana a civil infraction (for which citizens would get a ticket) rather than a criminal offense (for which they could be arrested and jailed). This movement garnered so much support that by 1975, the widespread decriminalization of marijuana seemed wholly possible, even inevitable.[14]

Advocates of decriminalization came from many quarters. In 1970, the Controlled Substances Act had established the National Commission on Marihuana and Drug Abuse, an investigative body deemed "conservatively oriented" by *The Washington Post*. Over the following two years, the commission conducted dozens of hearings and authorized more than fifty research projects, with several members even trying marijuana for themselves.[15] Finally, in 1972, the commission released its highly publicized final report, titled *Marihuana: A Signal of Misunderstanding*. The report was far more sympathetic to marijuana than many observers had expected. "Experimental or intermittent use of this drug carries minimal risk to the public health," the report declared, "and should not be given over-zealous attention."[16]

The report was too permissive for President Nixon, who immediately rejected it.[17] But it gave a much-needed boost to decriminalization advocates at the state level, where they notched some victories. Oregon decriminalized marijuana in 1973; two years later, California, Colorado, Ohio, and Alaska followed suit. Support for decriminalization came from unlikely sources, including William F. Buckley and his staunchly conservative *National Review*, which in 1972 ran a cover story with the headline "The Time Has Come: Abolish the Pot Laws."[18] In 1977, President Jimmy Carter opened the door to federal legislation, asking Congress to decriminalize the possession of small amounts of marijuana. "Penalties against possession of a drug should not be more damaging to an individual than the use of the drug itself," Carter declared in a message to Congress.[19]

Despite this liberalizing shift in attitudes in parts of the country, the Washington, D.C., police did not let up, and they concentrated their attention on the city's black neighborhoods.[20] That 80 percent of those they arrested were black may not have been an egregious disparity in

**Marijuana Arrests**

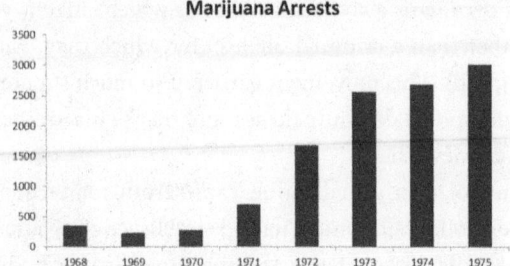

( Jerry V. Wilson, *The War on Crime in the District of Columbia, 1955–1975*
[Washington: U.S. Department of Justice, 1978], Table 7-21, page 77)

a city that was 70 percent black, but for David Clarke, the number
proved an important point. In overwhelmingly white states such as
Oregon and Maine, marijuana decriminalization was a question of civil
liberties and individual autonomy. But in majority-black Washington,
D.C., it was also a pressing matter of civil rights and racial justice.
That D.C.'s police force would dramatically increase marijuana arrests
at a time when the national momentum was moving toward lesser
penalties was, in a word, infuriating.

Luckily, Clarke found himself in the perfect position to effect
change: after his victory, he had been named head of the city council's
Committee on the Judiciary and Criminal Law, which most referred
to simply as the Judiciary Committee. He quickly took aim at the city's
marijuana laws: on March 18, 1975, Clarke unveiled a proposal to eliminate prison as a possible penalty for possession. Instead, anyone possessing less than two ounces of marijuana would be subject to a $100
fine.[21] (At the time, marijuana possession carried the same maximum
penalty as sale of the drug—a year in prison and a $1,000 fine. The max-
imum increased to ten years and $5,000 for any subsequent offense.)[22]
Clarke also proposed that police officers issue citations rather than
make arrests.

Clarke's bill would pass only if he could persuade his black colleagues (and Walter Washington, the city's black mayor) to view the
issue through a civil rights lens. So, on July 16, Clarke opened Judi-

ciary Committee hearings documenting the disparate racial impact of marijuana-related arrests and prosecutions in D.C. Several witnesses testified in favor of the bill, including D.C. Superior Court judge Charles Halleck. Halleck, a former prosecutor, had forsworn his tough-on-crime roots; according to *The Washington Post*, in the early 1970s he "grew a beard and moderately long hair and became, in the eyes of some, as pro-defendant as he had once been pro-prosecution."[23] Like Clarke, Halleck was white—but also like Clarke, he had directly observed the ways in which D.C.'s criminal justice system targeted young black men. He was particularly critical of the MPD for its selective enforcement of marijuana possession laws: the officers, he asserted, "routinely" stopped cars that contained more than one black male and proceeded to "jack up people that they search." If they found even one marijuana cigarette, Halleck said, the police would gleefully arrest an entire carful of young black men. "They look in somebody's ashtray and seize a roach," he testified. "That justifies an arrest."[24]

As additional witnesses spoke, it became clear that the selective enforcement of D.C.'s marijuana laws extended well beyond the police. The Washington Urban League presented research demonstrating that prosecutors were more likely to pursue cases involving black defendants and to dismiss cases involving whites. The disparities held even when controlling for variables such as employment and education: blacks with jobs were more likely to receive punishment than similarly employed whites, and black students fared worse than white ones.[25]

But the most devastating impact, witnesses agreed, was the lifelong stigma that came from a relatively minor offense. Invoking a story that remains familiar today, multiple witnesses testified to the collateral damage of a minor drug conviction—consequences that could be more debilitating and enduring than any sentence imposed by a judge. Dr. Vincent Roux, chairman of the D.C. United Way, noted that the burden of criminality haunted black men long after their arrests; he lambasted the criminal justice system for its "ability to almost destroy a person's life by a criminal record" and placed special emphasis on the system's "ability to prosecute and intimidate black men in particular."[26] Judge Halleck, for his part, argued that the ultimate effect of marijuana enforcement was to "stigmatize those young men with arrest records and criminal records." Even if the majority of such men avoided jail time, he continued, they still had to report their arrests and convictions on employment, housing, and school applications. A criminal record would often render young black men effectively unemployable, creating a downward spiral of criminality: some of these men, Halleck argued, would inevitably become "angry with the system," frustrated by their inability to find work. They "may go around and shoplift something"—and suddenly, from there, "they are off on the road to . . . wind[ing] up down at Lorton for long periods of time."[27] (For most of the period covered by this book, D.C. prisoners were held at Lorton Reformatory in Lorton, Virginia.)

Although racial justice was a prominent theme in the case for decriminalization, Clarke and his allies did not rest there. Their other central claim was that marijuana was much less dangerous than other drugs, and that criminalization was therefore a severe overreaction. Dr. Lester Grinspoon of the Massachusetts Mental Health Center sought to dispel what he called the "many myths about marijuana."[28] He told the council that marijuana was not addictive, that it did not cause psychosis or brain damage, that it was not a gateway to more serious drugs, and that it did not undermine an individual's drive to succeed.[29] Other experts were more equivocal about the health risks users faced, but all agreed that when it came to small amounts of marijuana, criminalization produced more harm than the drug itself. As Robert DuPont, the head of the National Institute on Drug Abuse, argued, there were many ways for the government to discourage marijuana use, but to do so through the criminal justice system, with its associated costs and stigmas, made no sense at all.[30]

By the end of the hearings, Clarke and his witnesses had offered a compelling case for why D.C. should join the growing number of states adopting a less punitive approach to marijuana. By abolishing criminal penalties for limited possession, the city council could take a firm stand for racial justice. It could save legions of black citizens from the lasting consequences of arrest and conviction, and it could adopt, instead, penalties that would be commensurate with the drug's actual risks. Passing Clarke's bill, it seemed, was the obvious choice. What could possibly stand in the way?

Heroin. As a nation, we've mostly forgotten about the devastation heroin wrought in urban America fifty years ago. When I talk in my law school classroom about the War on Drugs, my students usually assume that I'm speaking about the response to crack, which ravaged black communities in the 1980s and 1990s. A few students have first-hand memories of the crack epidemic; the rest have either read about it or seen it represented in movies and on TV. But when I tell them that heroin was to the '60s what crack was to the late '80s, I get blank stares. This amnesia comes at a cost: without taking heroin into account, one cannot understand African American attitudes toward the drug war.

Heroin had long troubled D.C.—a 1955 government report called the city's drug problem "serious and tragic and expensive and ominous"—but by the late 1960s, what had been a problem became an epidemic. Heroin began to devour the city's poor black neighborhoods. Studies at the D.C. Central Detention Facility (commonly known as the D.C. Jail) revealed the extent of the crisis: in the early to mid-1960s, less than 3 percent of new inmates were addicted to heroin, but beginning in 1967 the growth rate exploded, tripling by 1968, then tripling again by February 1969. By June 1969, an astonishing 45 percent of the men admitted to the jail were addicts.[31] In the city itself, the number of addicts rose from 5,000 in early 1970 to 18,000 by Christmas of that year. By 1971, there were about fifteen times more heroin addicts in Washington, D.C., than in all of England.[32]

These addicts were overwhelmingly likely to be young black men. Many had dropped out of high school; the former Urban League executive director Whitney Young warned that children as young as eleven or twelve were dying from heroin overdoses.[33] But the drug didn't simply destroy its users' own lives: each new addict was another person—strung out, unemployable, and often desperate—whose number one priority was securing the means to stay high. A study of Washington, D.C., and three other cities found that the average heroin addict committed more than three hundred crimes a year.[34] The devastation in these cities' poor black communities took many forms: as overdose deaths skyrocketed, parents buried their children; as fear of robberies and burglaries spread, residents stayed home with doors and windows bolted shut; as desperate young addicts resorted to stealing from their kin, families were forced to turn against their own.[35]

D.C.'s heroin epidemic produced two main responses. The first came from the government: a public health effort, heavy on treatment and light on law enforcement. This strategy was pioneered by Jerome Jaffe, the director of the Nixon administration's Special Action Office for Drug Abuse Prevention, who advocated "methadone maintenance," the practice of providing addicts with a free synthetic alternative to heroin in the form of 40- to 80-milligram "stabilization doses" of government-regulated methadone. Only a few addicts were expected to overcome their addiction; the real benefit was for the community, since the drug user who substituted methadone for heroin would no longer need to rob and steal to support his habit.[36] In D.C., Jaffe's disciple Robert DuPont set up maintenance centers around the city, and any adult who had been addicted to heroin for at least two years was eligible to receive daily stabilization doses from trained medical personnel.[37]

The second response to the epidemic was organized by local activists, neighborhood leaders, and community groups. Among the most prominent was a black nationalist named Hassan Jeru-Ahmed. Hassan—who preferred being referred to by his first name—was a tall, slender man who once made a living selling wigs. A high school dropout, recovering addict, and former federal prisoner, Hassan had been converted by his experience with addiction and crime into an unrelenting drug warrior.[38]

Like DuPont, Hassan viewed heroin as D.C.'s most urgent problem and methadone as part of the solution—but that was the extent of their agreement. For Hassan, methadone was useful only as a strategy for weaning addicts off heroin. He wanted it to be administered in exceedingly small doses—just enough to dull the pain of heroin withdrawal—for a few months at most.[39] But methadone *maintenance*, to Hassan, just meant substituting one addiction for another.[40]

In rejecting methadone maintenance, Hassan dismissed the core of DuPont's anticrime strategy. He didn't doubt that methadone users would commit fewer crimes, but he was loath to accept masses of black citizens strung out—and completely dependent—on government narcotics. "It would be a dreary eulogy," he declared, "to read in the future's history that America solved all problems except the drug problem and allowed her enemies to poison her to death through her youth."[41] In Hassan's view, criminality was a symptom of addiction and methadone maintenance merely a surface treatment. The far better strategy was to cure the disease. Hassan's claim resonated widely in black D.C.; as William Raspberry, the first African American columnist for *The Washington Post*, argued, "The guy who was sick on heroin is just as sick on methadone. The streets may be a little safer, but the addict is scarcely better off."[42]

Hassan founded the Blackman's Development Center (BDC) in May 1969, and it quickly became one of the most active antidrug organizations in the city. The BDC worked closely with Hassan's other organizations, the United Moorish Republic and the Blackman's Volunteer Army of Liberation (Hassan called himself the army's "commanding officer"); at its peak, the BDC had more than seven hundred members, many of them ex-addicts like Hassan.[43] The BDC's anger at DuPont and his Narcotics Treatment Administration (NTA) was rooted in America's history of racial subjugation. Hassan and his colleagues believed that whites *wanted* blacks to be addicted to narcotics, because it made them passive; in the BDC's eyes, methadone maintenance was a thinly veiled attempt to keep black people oppressed. In a series of posters plastered all over the city, the BDC condemned heroin addiction as "SLAVERY 1969."[44] At any one of the organization's

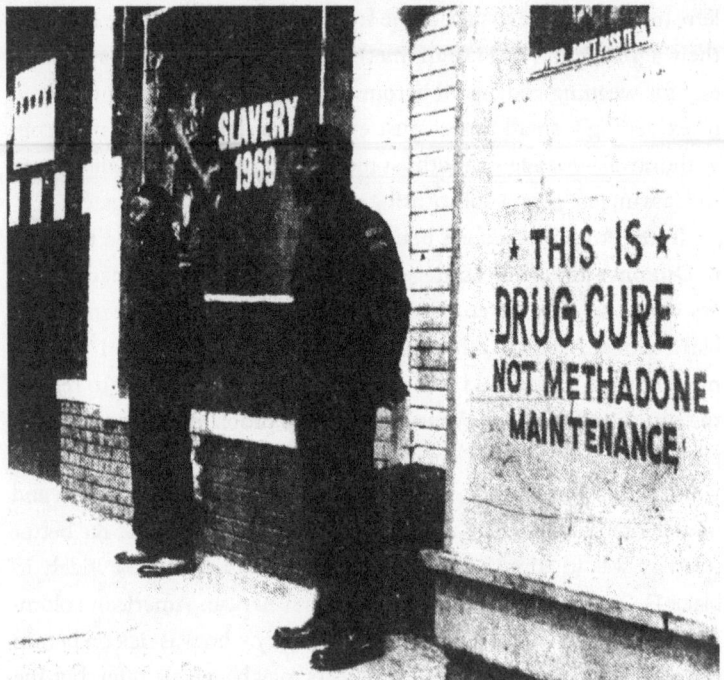

Members of the Blackman's Development Center outside one of the group's offices, 1969 (Gary Lindsay, "Black Man's Army in War Against Drug Abuse," *The Washington Afro-American*, October 11, 1969)

three field offices, users could find a place to live during their initial detox periods and then enter longer-term educational and counseling programs. THIS IS DRUG CURE read a sign outside one office, NOT METH-ADONE MAINTENANCE.[45]

DuPont and Hassan also diverged when it came to the question of drug dealers. DuPont had little to say about them: he figured that his methadone maintenance plan would cause the heroin market to dry up. But the BDC had no interest in a heroin substitute: it wanted drugs off the street altogether, and that meant going after the people who had brought drugs to the street in the first place. The ultimate enemies were the white dealers—many with Mafia connections—at the top of the country's drug distribution networks. As one call-to-arms BDC poster asserted, "The only people that can break white-face dog mafia . . . selling illegal heroin and other dope to our school children, our families is OURSELVES."[46]

The other enemy came from within the community: black street dealers. These men were vilified for their complicity in the white-controlled system of racial exploitation. On this point, a BDC flyer could not have been clearer: "We must deal with the black-face traitors of our people who sell dope to our young boys and girls and make whores and thieves of them for white-face dog dealers." Since America had never cared for its black poor, it was up to D.C.'s honest, law-abiding black residents to protect their community, to "take care of" the race traitors in their midst by calling Hassan's anonymous hotline. "Anywhere that you see them let us know we will deal with them ourselves," the flyer read. "They will be personally warned just once. If they do not stop immediately . . . WE WILL STOP THEM!!!"[47]

While drug sellers were among the most reviled figures in the black community, heroin users were hardly free from scorn. Hassan's BDC showed little tolerance for users, especially those who committed crimes to sustain their habits. The organization warned them to stop and offered them a chance at treatment. Those who declined the offer were frequently reported to the police or roughed up. Marion Barry, the city's future mayor, shared Hassan's impatience with heroin addicts. In 1967, he had founded Pride, a program designed to help unskilled D.C. youth find jobs. While speaking to Carrol Harvey, a D.C. government official, Barry expressed doubts about allowing users to enroll: "Goddamn junkies would steal from their mothers," he said. "I don't know whether we should let them in the program."[48]

Although Hassan advocated punitive action against drug sellers, it is important to remember that he also called for root-cause solutions to the heroin epidemic (improving schools, fighting racism) and an ethic of black responsibility that valued hard work, education, and self-discipline. In this respect, he represented the "all of the above"

Flyer, Blackman's Development Center, 1969

approach to addressing drug use and crime.[49] Accordingly, the BDC extended job training and drug treatment programs with one hand and turned drug dealers over to the police with the other. (Hassan was, in the words of one federal prosecutor, a "gutsy" informant.)[50]

In Hassan's view, the police were not doing enough to protect black neighborhoods from the drug trade. "We look around us and there is a man down the block selling narcotics and he sells it to schoolchildren," Hassan recounted, but the police would often refuse to take action, citing "technicalities" and "red tape."[51] The BDC, which was not hampered by the Constitution or by bureaucracy, believed that it had a mandate from the community to stop the drug traffic by any means necessary.[52] Its members were familiar with the city's corners and alleys, with the nooks and crannies of D.C.'s drug marketplace. So when the city's police officers failed to do their jobs, a shadow force was prepared to step in.

There are not many Hassans around today. But though his virulent antidrug rhetoric is no longer in fashion, it was common back in the 1970s—and not just in D.C. Similar language was heard in Detroit, which, like D.C., was overwhelmed by rising crime and addiction.[53] At a prayer breakfast celebrating the inauguration of Coleman Young, Detroit's first black mayor, Judge Damon Keith urged Young to tackle the crime epidemic: "Your administration will have to devise a means of ridding this city, root and branch, of the criminals who are committing murders, rapes and assaults on the people of this city." For Keith, this included going after "the drug pusher," who "must be exposed and brought to the bar of justice."[54] When Young followed Keith to the podium, he brought the majority-black audience of more than two thousand people to its feet with a promise to do just that. "I issue an open warning right now to all dope pushers, to all rip-off artists, to all muggers: it's time to leave Detroit."[55]

Some of the nation's most effective black antidrug activists were based in Harlem, New York, where church leaders, community groups, and the local black press demanded a more hard-nosed response to that city's heroin crisis. The leader of Harlem's antidrug coalition, profiled in Michael Fortner's book *Black Silent Majority*, was a firebrand of a minister named Oberia Dempsey.[56] Unlike Hassan, Dempsey did not embrace the "all of the above" approach: "The *only* answer to the narcotic problem in America is law enforcement," he proclaimed in a letter to the *Amsterdam News*, New York's leading black paper. Rev. Dempsey demanded that the city, state, and federal governments dispatch more officers to help get heroin off the street and impose much longer sentences for both users and sellers. He also called on the government to "erect health camps, or citizens conservation camps, throughout the country, far away from cities, and take every known addict and thug off the streets." In Dempsey's vision, society would rehabilitate offenders through incarceration, locking them away "for a period of ten years, or more, and provid[ing] the proper help, to help the unfortunates help themselves."[57] In the meantime, law-abiding blacks needed to arm themselves. After being stabbed above the eye near his home in 1971, Dempsey called on the residents of Harlem to carry weapons in order to "ward off these hoodlums."[58]

Dempsey tapped into rich veins of anger and fear. And he wasn't alone. In 1973, in the midst of a crime wave that paralleled D.C.'s in both swiftness and severity, the New York–based NAACP Citizens' Mobilization Against Crime demanded that the government lengthen "minimum prison terms for muggers, pushers, and first degree murderers." That same year, the *Amsterdam News* advocated mandatory life sentences for the "non-addict drug pusher of hard drugs." The paper's editors defined drug dealing as "an act of cold, calculated, premeditated, indiscriminate murder of our community."[59]

In all three cities, one of the more common—and, in retrospect, striking—aspects of antidrug rhetoric was its militant character. This was a black nation fresh off the battlefields of Selma and Watts; few doubted that blacks were a minority tribe under continual assault. Under such conditions, many viewed drug dealers as the enemy within, a fifth column that had to be identified and eliminated. When a black teenager he mentored died of a heroin overdose, the Harlem-based writer Orde Coombs captured the era's outrage:

> We know that the people who make millions every year from our children's misery are white. But, we also know that no white man comes into our Harlems to sell his packets of doom. That dirty work is done by Black men and women who . . . have no qualms about sell-

ing out our future so that their present can be made flashy with an air-conditioned, two-toned Eldorado.[60]

Having lost faith in law enforcement, Coombs advocated taking up arms against drug dealers on a national scale. "Those of us who fight for our children's lives know what we have to do," he wrote in 1970. "We must walk through our Harlems and find the Black pushers and kill them in their burgundy jump suits." Coombs was anguished to find himself endorsing black-on-black vigilante justice, but he saw no other choice. "If after all our talk about Black pride, we cannot be responsible for ourselves, we cannot rid our neighborhoods of death," he wrote, "then we should cease, forever, all talk about a Black nation."[61] Or as a civil rights activist explained to the black columnist William Raspberry, "the pusher, as the conscious agent of those who would destroy black people, is a dangerous enemy and must be destroyed."[62]

David Clarke understood heroin's toll. But as he saw it, that had nothing to do with marijuana, which had caused no such harm. Indeed, he used the example of heroin and other hard drugs as a foil. Marijuana, he argued, was not a gateway to harder drugs; it was a drug of a different kind and didn't warrant the same criminal justice response.

One of his fellow council members, however, saw things differently. Douglas Moore led the charge against Clarke's proposal, picking up right where Hassan had left off. (By 1975, Hassan and his Blackman's Development Center were no longer a political force; the organization was in decline as a result of allegations of anti-Semitism combined with questions about its finances.) To abandon the fight against marijuana, Moore argued, would be to abandon the black community. In his eyes, the simple misstep of marijuana experimentation carried dramatic risks for blacks, and especially for poor black youth: a life of addiction, crime, and degradation.

Like Clarke, Moore came to the D.C. Council from the civil rights movement. But unlike Clarke, who had been affiliated with King's relatively moderate Southern Christian Leadership Conference, Moore represented the more radical tradition of black nationalism. Like many nationalists of his era, Moore had left the United States in the 1960s, stopping first in France and then settling in the Democratic Republic of the Congo, a nation of special interest for black activists. (Patrice Lumumba, the Congo's Pan-Africanist prime minister, was a venerated figure for the black left, especially after he was assassinated—with, many believed, the CIA's assistance.) When Moore returned to the United States in 1966, he decided to live in D.C., home to Howard University, his alma mater. Again, his geographic choice was unsurprising: with its majority-black population, D.C. was becoming increasingly attractive to a generation of educated, politicized blacks, a generation tired of living in white-dominated environments.[63] In addition, Moore saw D.C. as a domestic front in the global black nationalist struggle. Despite their majority status, the city's blacks still lived as second-class, economically marginalized citizens, and the District itself was fighting to secure independence. "I saw that the situation here was the same as in Africa," Moore told the *Washington Post* reporter Juan Williams. "In Africa the blacks are in the bad houses, the bad schools, just like in Washington."[64]

Moore quickly found his political home in the Black United Front, the coalition founded in 1968 by Stokely Carmichael. (Carmichael himself had moved to D.C. after leaving the Student Nonviolent Coordinating Committee, which he had helped lead into the Black Power era.) The two men soon became political allies and close friends; Moore even officiated at Carmichael's marriage to Miriam Makeba, the South African singer and civil rights activist. When the newlyweds left for Guinea in 1969, Moore assumed leadership of the Black United Front. Wearing a dashiki, a black leather coat, and sunglasses, Moore became a well-known local activist, and few were surprised when he decided to run for a seat on the inaugural city council.[65]

Moore campaigned as a champion of the city's black poor, promoting self-determination and control of local institutions and actively opposing efforts by white outsiders to tell D.C.'s blacks how to govern themselves. When it came to criminal justice, Moore wanted to increase the number of blacks and women on the police force, and he openly challenged the racial and class biases pervading the system. "All too frequently," he argued, "whether and how long a person is imprisoned is dependent not on guilt or the nature of the crime, but on the race and socio-economic status of the alleged offender."[66] Moore's reformist spirit won him the endorsement of the Prison Campaign Committee, a group of inmates at the D.C. Jail. "We are using the same criteria in picking candidates, as the court system uses in determining our sentences," wrote the group's leader. "And that is by looking at a person's record."[67] Ultimately, Moore's message resonated outside the prison, too: of the seventeen candidates for the two at-large council seats, he received more votes than everyone but Marion Barry.[68]

Months later, when David Clarke recommended the partial decriminalization of marijuana, Moore used his new platform to launch a withering critique of the proposed legislation. He rejected Clarke's claims that the law would help blacks, arguing that America had never been concerned about drug use in the black community. This argument arose from a central paradox of the African American experience: the simultaneous over- *and* under-policing of crime. In 1968, for example, in the wake of racial turmoil on a national scale, the Kerner Commission found that many blacks believed that "the police maintain a much less rigorous standard of law enforcement in the ghetto, tolerating illegal activities like drug addiction, prostitution, and street violence that they would not tolerate elsewhere."[69] In Moore's eyes, the issue of marijuana decriminalization was gaining traction because white kids were now using the drug—and getting arrested—more often. These young whites were the true objects of Clarke's legislation, Moore claimed, as "people don't want them to get criminal records because they want them to become young judges and lawyers."[70]

Moore's hard-eyed skepticism was common among a certain segment of black activists who viewed their self-proclaimed white allies with suspicion. For example, in 1970, the black poet, singer, and activist

Gil Scott-Heron had ridiculed white activists, such as members of Students for a Democratic Society (SDS):

> The irony of it all, of course
> Is when a pale face SDS motherfucker dares
> Look hurt when I don't call him brother and tell him to go find his
>     own revolution
>
> . . .
>
> He is fighting for legalized smoke, or lower voting age
> Less lip from his generation gap at home and fucking in the street
> Where is my parallel to that?
> All I want is a good home for my wife and children
> And some food to feed them every night.[71]

There was, of course, a significant difference between David Clarke and the "pale face SDS motherfucker" in Scott-Heron's poem: unlike the self-centered SDS member, Clarke advocated for decriminalization explicitly out of concern for black lives. Still, black leaders had experienced enough disappointment to have developed a healthy suspicion of even the most left-leaning white ally. As Stokely Carmichael had once joked, "I'm going to tell you what a white liberal is. You talking about a white college kid joining hands with a black man in the ghetto, that college kid is fighting for the right to wear a beard and smoke pot, and we fighting for our lives."[72]

In addition to questioning Clarke's motives, Moore claimed that decriminalization would only hinder blacks' attempts to achieve equality. In his eyes, marijuana use was both a symptom of racial oppression—blacks who used the drug were "suffering from the stresses of white racism"—and, just as important, a cause.[73] Drug users, Moore believed, were in no position to undertake the work of rebuilding their individual lives, let alone that of collectively mobilizing against racism. Again, this belief was prevalent among members of the black left during the 1970s. After two Howard University students died from apparent drug overdoses in October 1971, students, professors, and local activists organized a series of antidrug activities. "Black people don't have the time or the resources to waste themselves in a world of distorted reality," said Professor Lovinger Bowden, the head of the university's Speech and Communication Department, at one of the events. "We cannot pull ourselves together if we are on 'Cloud Nine.' "[74] In 1975, Maynard Jackson, Atlanta's first black mayor, used the same logic to oppose decriminalization in his city: "You cannot lead a movement when the army is asleep. We need nothing that debilitates us, tears us down. We cannot change anything when we do not have weapons in hand—not guns and knives—but your brains and discipline."[75]

Stokely Carmichael took the argument one step further, casting drugs as a deliberate attempt by fearful whites to tranquilize black opposition. "Fighting against drugs is revolutionary because drugs are a trick of the oppressor," he told an audience of Morehouse College students in 1970. "The political consciousness of our people is rising, and in order to dull the political consciousness of our people, the oppressor sends more drugs into the community."[76] If Moore shared Carmichael's conspiratorial suspicions, he didn't say so during the marijuana debate; still, he agreed that drugs hobbled black Americans. Instead of a community rendered impotent and ignorant by drugs, Moore sought collective action: "I want a strong, virile black thinking population."[77]

At Clarke's Judiciary Committee hearings, the witnesses aligned with Moore's point of view spoke passionately about the burdens of drug use and addiction, especially as borne by the city's youth. Theirs was an echo of the argument Hassan had adopted in his fight against heroin; no matter how effectively Clarke's allies documented the havoc that drug enforcement wreaked on the black community as a whole, young users remained the weak link in their case for reform. After all, nobody was willing to defend the right of adolescents to get high. Don Freeman, on behalf of a group called Community Research, argued that "even mild regular use of marijuana during the crucial years of adolescence does represent a potentially serious concern."[78] Paul Quander, an assistant principal at H. D. Woodson High School, asked, "Is the city council going to legislate permissiveness and expect our young children to retain a place of usefulness in society?"[79] Furthermore, in the light of broader racial inequalities, decriminalization looked like another roadblock to black success. White children, Moore noted, had good schools and "a lot of opportunities to think." Black children lacked these advantages, and the evils of their situation would only be compounded by drug use. Once again echoing Carmichael and Jackson, Moore declared, "It would seem to me to be a social crime to depenalize marijuana so as to make it possible for more black children who cannot think already to keep them from thinking."[80]

Among those who agreed with Moore, no one offered more significant testimony than Superior Court judge John Fauntleroy. Like Moore, Fauntleroy was sensitive to the plight of poor and working-class blacks. Raised in segregated Washington, D.C., he had graduated from Armstrong Technical High in 1937, where he had trained in printing. Though he was unable to find work in that field, Fauntleroy was resilient and talented, and he eventually landed a clerical job with D.C.'s largest employer: the federal government. Later, he enrolled in night classes at Robert H. Terrell Law School, a program that, despite its brief nineteen-year life span, managed to educate a generation of local black lawyers.[81] In 1967, after twenty years in private practice, Fauntleroy became one of D.C.'s first black judges. He used the bench as a pulpit, arguing for the rehabilitation of juvenile offenders and challenging the "keep them out of sight, keep them out of mind" attitude that he saw as prevalent in the city.[82] In one high-profile incident, he stirred controversy in D.C.'s legal community by criticizing the city's respected Public Defender Service (PDS) for failing to hire black lawyers.[83] Charles Ogletree, the renowned Harvard Law professor, was a first-year lawyer at PDS at the time; he remembers Fauntleroy as a "very conscientious and highly regarded jurist," admired by public defenders and prosecutors alike.[84]

So here we have a barrier-breaking black judge who, like Moore, was outspoken on issues of racial discrimination, particularly in relation to the city's youth. And yet, also like Moore, Fauntleroy was unswayed by Clarke's insistence that decriminalizing marijuana would benefit the black community. Instead, he believed that the fragile state of affairs for black teenagers in D.C.'s poor neighborhoods was an argument *for* prohibition.

White teenagers could use marijuana without jeopardizing their futures, Fauntleroy explained. After getting high, they could always "return to enjoy the comforts of the suburbs." But poor black teenagers in the inner city had no room for error. Lacking a middle-class cocoon to shield them from the consequences of marijuana use, those "who have been born in frustration, who have suffered economic deprivation, who have lived in substandard housing, who may have come from families receiving welfare payments, who have no automobiles, etc.," might never recover from youthful rebellion. Such kids, Fauntleroy concluded despairingly, will "have a difficult time securing any job, and having been truants from school, will more or less drop out upon reaching the age of sixteen." So even if decriminalizing marijuana might save a black adolescent from getting arrested, it all but guaranteed more serious problems down the line: drug use, school failure, and crime.[85]

In his testimony, Fauntleroy even cited a case in which a group of stoned high school students decided to rob their counselor: they broke into his home, beat him and his wife with a pistol, and took their money, television, and stereo. The students were now facing life imprisonment in Fauntleroy's courtroom. If drugs had been less available, the judge suggested, such suffering could have been avoided.[86]

Whereas Fauntleroy supplied social arguments against decriminalization, the city's black clergymen added ethical and spiritual imperatives. As head of the Committee of One Hundred Ministers, Andrew Fowler was among D.C.'s most powerful religious figures. Fowler opposed Clarke's bill because of the harm marijuana caused to the individual user and to the black community as a whole. Marijuana was habituating, Fowler argued; it had negative psychological effects, including anxiety and impaired judgment; and it often led to crime. (Fowler did not cite any research to support these assertions, opting instead to claim authority from his thirty-plus years of direct experience as a local pastor.) Drawing from Matthew 25, Fowler told the members of the city council that to decriminalize marijuana would be to abandon the city's downtrodden. "As a result of marijuana some people are hungry, some are thirsty, some are strangers, some are naked, some are sick and some are in prison," he said.[87] The city's poorest souls needed deliverance, he argued, and the proposed legislation offered just the opposite: a legalized Hell. "We urge you to stand in the breach," he said, speaking to the council on behalf of D.C.'s Christians. "The judgment of God is against us otherwise."[88]

In addition to arguing that marijuana was harmful in itself, black pastors insisted that it was a gateway to harder drugs. This was the thrust of testimony by Samuel George Hines, who spoke before the city council on behalf of the Second Precinct Clergymen's Association, a group of thirty local ministers. Perhaps Hines and his colleagues had not read *Marihuana: A Signal of Misunderstanding*, which, three years earlier, had found that marijuana actually was not a gateway drug. Or perhaps they had read the report but found its conclusion at odds with their own experiences with drug users. In either case, speaking out of concern for the city's impressionable youth, Hines railed against the argument that marijuana use was innocuous. If such an attitude prevailed, he argued, "Innocent young people could be lured into harmless 'fun' that could lead to deeper drug involvement."[89]

The fear that the marijuana high might eventually become insufficient, causing the user to seek a more powerful high, was nothing new. Hassan had raised this concern in 1970, arguing that young people who smoke marijuana can be "induced to take heroin," since "they have been told to 'try this pill; it will get you high faster and keep you there longer.' "[90] And drug sellers could be counted on to push ever more serious products: as Fauntleroy emphasized in his testimony, a dealer on the street typically had more than one drug in his inventory. To tempt a marijuana user with harder drugs—including "heroin, amphetamines, LSD, angel dust, and other drugs"—was simply good business.[91]

David Clarke and the witnesses who supported decriminalization took great pains to emphasize that they were not promoting marijuana use. But Moore scoffed at these disclaimers, maintaining that the city's young black men, whose lives he championed, would interpret the city council's actions differently. "I can hear young people quoting [the new law] all across the city," he declared. "They'll be saying, 'You can have two ounces now, Blood, because it is legal.'" This was simply intolerable to Moore, whose views on drugs were straightforward: "Black men don't need crutches of marijuana or heroin."[92]

Moore was also unmoved by Clarke's harm-reduction arguments. He didn't want D.C.'s black communities to be places where young people who smoked marijuana had to pay a fine instead of going to jail; he wanted young people not to smoke pot in the first place. He wanted the city's black youth off drugs, in school, and in the workforce. "I have three black boys," Moore told Clarke's committee. "I don't think black folks have any purpose in taking any kind of drugs."[93]

The city council did not heed Moore's call—at least not at first. On October 8, 1975, by an 8–4 vote, it gave preliminary approval to Clarke's proposal. But before it could become law, the proposal would need to be voted on a second time—per the provisions of the Home Rule Act—and then signed by the city's new mayor, Walter Washington. From Washington's desk, the bill would go to the congressional House District Committee for a thirty-day waiting period. Unless Congress rejected the law, it would go into effect.

Charles Diggs, one of the founders of the Congressional Black Caucus and the chair of the District Committee, did not much like Clarke's bill. However, like virtually all blacks in Congress, he was deeply protective of the District's newly acquired right to self-governance. "Diggs Tests Veto Views on Pot Bill," ran a *Washington Post* headline, speaking to the congressman's ambivalence. Ultimately, though, while Diggs let city leaders know that he did not support the law, there is no evidence to suggest that he attempted to block its passage.[94]

But others did rise up in opposition. Having failed to prevent the bill's initial approval, the city's ministers redoubled their efforts in order to thwart its final passage. This time, they made it clear that their opposition did not exist solely on the moral plane—it could have real political efficacy, too. Indeed, the black church was among D.C.'s most powerful political constituencies. As Moore himself noted, the institution with the greatest influence over the city's votes was not among the usual suspects: "it is not the Board of Trade, it is not the Democratic or Republican Party; it is not even the labor unions." Rather, he said, "[i]n a city with a weak party structure, it is the black church that has control over most people."[95]

Fowler, Hines, and the rest of the city's black clergymen claimed that the majority of D.C.'s citizens shared their opposition to Clarke's bill.[96] The available opinion data, though limited, supports their contention. In the midst of the council's deliberations in 1975, the Bureau of Social Science Research asked residents of D.C. and its suburbs whether they agreed that "marijuana use should be made legal, with age and other controls, like those for alcohol."[97] This was not the precise issue before the council (Clarke's proposal would have kept marijuana illegal but reduced penalties to a citation and a fine), yet the results were significant nonetheless. Released in the midst of the city council debates, they revealed that while white D.C. voters supported legalization by a hefty fourteen-point margin, the numbers for black voters were flipped: only 43 percent supported legalization, with 51 percent opposed and 6 percent undecided.[98]

The clergymen worked diligently to make sure that black opinion remained firmly in the prohibitionist camp. Before the bill's initial passage, a group of 150 ministers had rallied at the District Building. There, one minister had gone so far as to warn city council members that they, the pastors, would meet them "at the polls."[99]

Now they turned up the heat, targeting Sterling Tucker, the chair of the city council. On October 21, a group of fifty ministers met with Tucker and asked him to table the legislation rather than allow it to come up for a final vote.[100] The fifty-one-year-old Tucker was an ambitious politician with a reputation for getting along with diverse constituencies (he headed the local chapter of the moderate, business-friendly Urban League in the 1950s and also served a brief stint in 1968 as a cochair of the more radical Black United Front).[101] Tucker's willingness to negotiate led to complaints that he lacked firm convictions. As a friend of his told a reporter in 1974, "In a tough fight, a politician wants to know who will be on my side and they aren't quite sure of him because he keeps his options open with everyone."[102]

The ministers had already proved themselves to be a formidable constituency. In the last election, they had endorsed Mayor Washington as well as eleven of the thirteen victorious candidates for city council, including Tucker himself. If he wanted to stay in office, Tucker needed to keep the votes these ministers carried—and the survey results from the Bureau of Social Science Research indicated that those votes would not go to a politician in favor of decriminalization. Especially not when the city's ministers had made it clear that they were more than willing to turn black dissatisfaction into political expression.

Tucker also had reason to fear that even if the bill passed, Mayor Washington would veto it.[103] Washington had kept silent while Clarke's proposal was before the council, but he had deep connections with the city's religious leaders.[104] If Tucker had opposed the ministers only to have Washington side with them, not only would he have risked his career, but his efforts would have come to naught. In the end, the ministers prevailed; just hours after their meeting with Tucker, the council chair tabled the bill, an action that doomed it for the current legislative session.[105] As of Tuesday evening, October 21, Bill 1-44, the Marijuana Reform Act of 1975, was dead.[106]

Our standard accounts of the War on Drugs are powerful and indispensable, but we need to supplement them in order to understand why the majority-black city of Washington, D.C., remained committed to marijuana prohibition. After all, this was not a story in which a white majority, acting out of indifference or hostility to black lives, imposed tough criminal penalties that disproportionately burdened a black minority. Quite the opposite: the leaders of the decriminalization effort were white, and the only available poll suggests that white citizens largely supported Clarke's bill. No: it was blacks who killed marijuana decriminalization in D.C.[107]

But why? There are a number of reasons—all of them essential to understanding the drug war's role in creating a new, and racially charged, system of punishment.

We must start with the fact that decriminalization's leading opponents—people like Judge Fauntleroy and Doug Moore—were among the black community's most dogged defenders. They were committed race men, not Uncle Toms. During the formal political debates, and in their public lives more generally, these leaders regarded themselves as the guardians of the black community, and especially of its young people, whom they were determined to protect from the dangers of drug use. Their opposition to decriminalization was not simply an expression of what the law professor Randall Kennedy has called the "politics of respectability"—the practice by which respectable blacks seek to expel the criminal element from their midst or shun them as disreputable embarrassments to the race.[108] Instead, it illustrates what might be termed the politics of responsibility.

The rising crime rates of the late 1960s, and the heroin epidemic in particular, explain why their sense of responsibility to the black community led them to oppose decriminalization. Heroin's rampage had taught black leaders and constituents a clear lesson in the social realities of drug use. Addiction, they had learned, could spread exponentially, and its consequences were not exclusively personal: drug use could decimate families, schools, even entire neighborhoods. The libertarian approach to drugs—"What I put in my body is my business"—would therefore find little purchase in black communities. Additionally, the specter of heroin raised the stakes of the "marijuana as gateway drug" argument: since heroin had destroyed communities so quickly, the thinking went, even the slightest risk that marijuana might lead a user to heroin was not one that policymakers could afford to take. As Rev. Andrew Fowler had cautioned the members of the D.C. Council, "The young users of marijuana will be easily susceptible to the harder drugs." These youth, he warned, "have no guardian but you."[109]

But if decriminalization's opponents felt responsible for the fate of black D.C., why didn't they appreciate the damage that continued criminalization would do to that very community? The answer lies in one of this book's central arguments: Mass incarceration is the result of small, distinct steps, each of whose significance becomes more apparent over time, and only when considered in light of later events. The decision not to decriminalize marijuana in 1975 exemplifies this phenomenon. Opponents of Clarke's bill minimized the harms of criminalization by stressing that most arrestees did not end up with convictions and that almost none went to prison.[110] As unimaginable as that sounds today, it was true at the time. Those who joined the 1975 debate also were unaware that in the years to come, criminal convictions—and even arrests without convictions—would lead to increasingly serious collateral consequences. In short, because D.C.'s debate over marijuana decriminalization took place before the full-scale drug war was launched, decriminalization's opponents could not foresee the eventual impact of their victory on the young blacks they were trying to save.

Racial distrust was also a key factor in D.C.'s decision. The champions of marijuana reform—Judge Halleck and, most important, David Clarke—were white. Although several black city council members (including Marion Barry) voted in favor of the bill, they were not the face of the legislation or at the foreground of the debate.

The racial identity of the bill's primary supporters was particularly troubling in the era of post–Home Rule politics. After living under Congress's thumb for a century, D.C.'s residents had finally begun to wriggle free; in their campaigns for office, many of the city's politicians had run on platforms stressing independence from the white political establishment. Some candidates, like Doug Moore, had gone further, directly criticizing members of the black elite for refusing to stand up to white power brokers. In this context, not everybody was quite ready to believe a group of white men who claimed that they were seeking to help black youth avoid the stigma of criminality.

But why were whites the face of the movement? Between 1973 and 1975, D.C. police arrested more than eight thousand black people for marijuana possession.[111] One might have expected them or their family members to serve as witnesses or public voices in the debate over decriminalization. But though they were referenced in the abstract, there were no flesh-and-blood black victims of the nascent drug war making the case for Clarke's proposal. In this respect, too, the war against marijuana anticipated events to come. As the tough-on-crime movement gathered force, those who had been arrested or convicted rarely participated in debates over criminal justice policy, in D.C. or nationally. They rarely told their stories. And their invisibility helps explain why our criminal justice system became so punitive.

# 2

# BLACK LIVES MATTER
## Gun Control, 1975

On January 4, 1975, two days after the mayor and city council took their oaths of office, the city's largest black paper—*The Washington Afro-American*, popularly known as the *Afro*—led with a crime story above the masthead on its front page. "Pastor Robbed of $1100 at Gunpoint," the headline declared. Below the masthead was a second headline: "New Council Discusses City's Future." The challenge that violent crime would pose to D.C.'s recently elected government was visible from the beginning.

The pastor was Rev. Leon Lipscombe, and the robbery was brazen. Two men had interrupted his wife, Ida, as she was outside washing windows. They flashed a gun, then hustled her into the house, where they found Rev. Lipscombe. The robbers pushed the couple upstairs to their bedroom, tied them to the bed, and covered them with a blanket. Then they ransacked the house, leaving with jewelry, watches, and the $1,100 holiday bonus Rev. Lipscombe had just received from his congregation.

Lipscombe's status as a church leader made the robbery newsworthy,

## Pastor robbed of $1100 at gunpoint

"It is the symptom of our times, but not beyond redemption. Each of us must say it is up to me to make the difference," said Rev. Leon G. Lipscombe, while rebuking an incident in which he lay face down, bound by hands and legs while his home was being robbed.

Rev. Lipscombe, 46, is the pastor of the Ulric AME Church, 3419 18th Place S.E. He and his wife, Ida, along with their son and a home repairman were robbed at

gunpoint this past Monday morning at the Lipscombe home at 2400 Alabama Ave. S.E.

Recalling the morning, Rev. Lipscombe said it all began when his wife went outside at about 9 o'clock to wash the windows.

While washing the windows, he said, his wife was approached by two men who asked if she was the "Rev.'s wife" and then forced down off the ladder at gun point and taken to the rear. One of the home

where the robbers gained entrance to the house.

"When they knocked at the door, I heard footsteps but I thought it might have been my wife accompanied by my son. When I opened the door they showed a gun over her shoulder and in my face and said 'both of you lay on the floor and don't make a move, or I'll blow your brains out.'"

Once in the house, the minister said

they inquired as to whether or not there were any weapons in the home. Then at gun point they forced both up the stairs and into the bedroom.

"They made us get face down on the bed, then tied our hands and our feet and covered us with a blanket. They were very polite," he emphasized, "to if it were a set up. One of them told the other one, 'Don't

(Continued on Page 2)

## Washington Afro-American

AND THE WASHINGTON TRIBUNE

| 83rd YEAR  NO. 34 | JANUARY 4, 1975 | 16 PAGES  20 CENTS |

## New council discusses city's future

By Gail Hauser
And Gerard Burke
AFRO Staff Writers

It has been more than 100 years since Washington residents had the right to elect their own city officials.

That right was obtained in 1974 when District voters embraced the Home Rule Charter than-President Richard M. Nixon had signed into law in December, 1973.

That Home Rule Charter provides for a city government consisting of a mayor plus eight city council persons from each ward and four at-large city councilpersons. These new city government officials were sworn in Thursday.

The AFRO asked D.C.'s newly elected city council persons two basic questions:

(1) What will your priorities be as a member of the city council and (2) do you feel a sense of historical importance as a member of the first elected governing body for the District in more than 100 years?

STERLING TUCKER, CITY COUNCIL CHAIRMAN: "One of the things we'll be trying to do is to establish a mechanism to plan for more than one year at a time both in terms of planning and budget.

"As an example, we have $60,000 million in transportation monies available to D.C. but it's for highways. That money need not be limited to highways. We've got to get people to and from work and to

and from stores.

"But we don't have an overall master plan in transportation. If we get an overall master plan, people will tolerate a few high-speed roadways if they know these will not be the only things they'll be getting."

The chairman also raised housing, establishment of a strong economic base, and education as being high on his priority list.

"The historical impact will come later," Tucker said, "as we come to understand the power of the government, as we start passing laws, as we begin to find out what we can do.

"What is important for us is not to operate in the same manner as before. We've got to act with the authority we

have and also use the responsibility that authority requires."

DAVID A. CLARKE, WARD ONE: "Home Rule means two things; it means change and it means doing it ourselves.

"It means change in housing to assure adequate shelter, in the delivery of services to clean our streets and make life liveable, in taxes to take the burden off the poor, and in public safety and law enforcement to imbue law and order with justice.

"And Home Rule means doing it ourselves by looking to ourselves to answer the questions, even those which cannot be

(Continued on Page 2)

*(The Washington Afro-American, January 4, 1975)*

but the crime itself was hardly an aberration. Between 1960 and 1969, the District's murder rate tripled, attracting widespread attention from national politicians who invoked rising crime in a majority-black city as part of their effort to discredit both the Johnson administration and liberalism more broadly.[1] In 1964, just as crime in D.C. began to rise, the Republican presidential candidate Barry Goldwater said that D.C. was "the one city which should reflect most brightly the president's concern for law and order, for decent conduct. Instead it is a city embattled, plagued by lawlessness, haunted by fears." As the historian Michael Flamm points out, "left unsaid—but understood—was Washington's image and reputation as a heavily African American city."[2] Goldwater's strategy was called out by NAACP executive secretary Roy Wilkins, who said that "every utterance touch-ing on [the crime] issue by the Republican nominee and his vice presi-dential running mate has had ill-concealed racial overtones, undertones, and just plain out-and-out tones."[3] Richard Nixon picked up where Goldwater left off: "D.C. should not stand for disorder and crime," he declared.[4]

White conservatives weren't the only ones raising the issue. The city's two leading papers, *The Washington Post* and *The Washington Star*, reported frequently on the crime crisis, with such headlines as "New Report on D.C. Crime: Profile of a Frightened City" and "The Guns of D.C.: Dodge City on the Potomac" (the latter by a young reporter named Carl Bernstein).[5] Although crime was concentrated in the city's poorest neighborhoods, it seemed that nobody was immune, a point made clear when Mississippi senator John Stennis was shot during a robbery. On January 30, 1973, Stennis was confronted at gunpoint out-side his home by two young black men who took his wallet, twenty-five cents, and his Phi Beta Kappa key. Though he didn't resist, the young men clubbed Stennis to the ground and shot him. A senseless and sickening assault on a victim of such prominence would have earned headlines at any time. But coming when it did, after a decade of rising crime and violence, it provided more than a momentary jolt.

Even stalwart liberals began to reassess core principles. Writing in *The Washington Star*, Milton Viorst described being home alone a few nights after the Stennis shooting. The doorbell rang, and when Viorst approached to answer, he saw two black faces. "I remember saying to myself, 'Baby, it looks like this is it.'" His fear, Viorst admitted, was based on race: "If you want to call that racism, go ahead." Still, he an-swered the door. As it turned out, the visitors only wanted directions. Viorst's relief at surviving the encounter was matched by his sadness and anger at how the Stennis assault—"so random, so purposeless, so unexplainable"—had changed him. Afraid to answer his own door just because the faces on the other side were black? What had hap-pened to him? That's what rampant crime does, he concluded.

[I]t is not just the people who are shot, stabbed, raped or robbed who are hurt. All of us are hurt—because we abandon our cities at night and lock ourselves into our homes, without feeling secure. We are terrorized by each other, especially when our colors are different. Crime has polarized us far more effectively than Jim Crow ever did.[6]

While the crime crisis affected the entire city, black D.C. was hit hardest. On a visit to the District in 1963, Malcolm X had identified street crime as a grave problem, and he told reporters gathered at National Airport that he planned to launch a series of blacks-only meetings to examine the issue.[7] And the problem wasn't limited to D.C.: crime was spiraling out of control in black communities across the country.[8] In Philadelphia, murder rates nearly doubled in the 1960s; in Boston, Detroit, and New York, they more than doubled; Cleveland's more than tripled.[9]

Criminologists remain divided on the causes of the rise in crime in D.C. and nationally. Some cite the postwar baby boom (young people commit more crimes than older ones do). Others blame the heroin epidemic, and still others point to lead emissions from automobiles (lead poisoning is associated with impulsive behavior in young adults, and emissions rose steadily for decades before the federal government banned leaded gasoline). But whatever the reason, the stark fact remains: D.C. had become a much more dangerous place in the 1960s, as residents witnessed the largest decade-long crime wave ever recorded, then or since.[10]

What made the crime surge so lethal, many agreed, were guns—especially handguns. In 1974, when the number of killings in D.C. set a new record, more than 60 percent of the 407 murders involved firearms.[11] Indeed, gun violence had become the leading cause of death for D.C. males under the age of forty.[12] The national trends were similar: as the murder rate spiked in the 1960s, so too did the number of homicides involving firearms.[13] In addition, robberies, including armed robberies, had increased since the early 1960s at a higher rate than any other crime, and by 1973, more and more of those armed robberies involved handguns instead of knives or other less lethal weapons.[14]

In the summer of 1975, as David Clarke and Doug Moore were locking horns over marijuana's impact on the black community, the D.C. Council was also debating what would be the most sweeping gun control measures in any American city. As we shall see, the marijuana and gun control debates in D.C. would follow an astonishingly similar trajectory. In each case, city leaders faced a perceived threat to the black community—drug use and abuse in one case, gun violence in the other. And in each case, they faced the same question: Is the criminal law the best way to respond?

We do not typically think of drug policy and gun policy in similar terms. The distinction between them is reflected in our politics: liberals generally object to antidrug measures but favor restrictions on guns, while conservatives normally take the opposite positions. The distinction is also reflected in our language: when we criminalize drugs, we call it a "war on drugs," but when we do the same thing with guns, we name it "gun control." Of course, there are good reasons to regard the issues differently—even the most ardent drug warrior would concede that guns pose a more direct and lethal threat to public safety than does any narcotic. But despite such differences, guns and drugs—and our response to them—have commonalities that we rarely acknowledge. Those commonalities would help shape the direction of American crime policy at the dawn of the era of mass incarceration.

In 1975, virtually every part of the city's black community was consumed by the crime epidemic. The *Afro* pressed for action, launching a series of editorials urging the city's leaders to "make it so that crime doesn't pay."[15] Under such headlines as "Why Not an Anti-Crime Drive?" the paper declared, "It is becoming increasingly shocking, discouraging and frightening to residents of the District of Columbia to turn on the radio or television or pick up the newspaper, daily or weekly, and learn that one of their neighbors has been a victim of

*'We must make it so crime doesn't pay'*

(*The Washington Afro-American*, January 18, 1975)

crime."[16] The editorial was accompanied by a cartoon depicting the city's black leaders gathered around a conference table, working under black shadows labeled "Growing crime menace."

Neighborhood newsletters took an increasingly urgent tone, pleading with residents to "join in the fight against crime" and to contact the local police precinct "[i]f you notice anything strange or any suspicious-looking strangers walking through our streets."[17] A coalition of churches and neighborhood groups organized a crime-prevention seminar featuring Mayor Washington.[18]

Even Howard University, with its proud history as a training ground for the black elite, was under siege. Its campus newspaper, *The Hilltop*, lamented that "deaths and crime again greeted this year's homecoming" and ran an editorial cartoon featuring a drawing of a black man: "Wanted: Brother for Crimes Against Brother." Twenty-five years before Chris Rock unleashed his famous routine complaining that "niggers" (shiftless, lazy, and criminal) were making things miserable for "black people," *The Hilltop* made the same distinction in crime reports like this: "Wednesday, October 25th Sister Velencia Abner, a resident of Frazier Hall, was robbed of $10 by a Black man (nigger) holding a silver plated .38."[19] Crime conferences were a regular feature of campus life, including a daylong session keynoted by Alvin Poussaint, a leading black psychiatrist and the author of *Why Blacks Kill Blacks*.[20]

Some D.C. residents fortified their homes, installing burglar bars and replacing single locks with multiple deadbolts.[21] Others took up martial arts such as kung fu and judo—the owner of one of the city's most popular studios claimed to have trained more than four thousand students in recent years.[22] For those who couldn't attend a class, an *Afro* columnist offered readers a primer: "If an attacker has you by the shoulders or throat with both hands, chances are he is not concentrating on his midsection. A sharp kick to the groin, preferably with pointed toes, proves extremely effective." Then the columnist advised, "Don't stand around to finish him off. Run like hell!"[23]

Under such conditions, it is hardly surprising that many residents decided to stay at home when possible. National polls showed fear of crime increasing among all segments of the population, and polls that included a racial breakdown almost invariably showed blacks as more fearful than whites.[24] In an Urban League poll, two-thirds of respondents from low-income areas reported that they were "afraid to walk in their own neighborhoods." A commission established by Mayor Washington found that 20 percent of men in D.C. and an astonishing 45 percent of women said they never went out alone at night.[25]

(*The Hilltop*, Howard University, October 27, 1972)

But no amount of caution seemed to work. One local activist was shot in the head and killed while walking to a neighborhood association meeting to discuss fighting crime.[26] A crime researcher was robbed at gunpoint while walking to Capitol Hill to present his findings to a Senate committee.[27] A fourteen-year-old boy named Kenneth Washington was killed by a stray bullet as he rode in a *Washington Post* truck delivering the morning paper.[28] Even churchgoing was no longer safe, as worshippers discovered when purse snatchers began targeting them as they walked home from services. When the *Afro* declared that it was "time to end this self-destruction," and that "we must begin to make things hot for the would-be criminals," few could be found who disagreed.[29]

> The problem of guns for black people is simply this: We have so many, that we are killing, injuring and robbing ourselves to the brink of chaos.
>
> —John Wilson, D.C. Council, Ward 2, 1975[30]

John Wilson had not campaigned for public office as a crime fighter. Born in 1943 in the tiny town of Princess Anne on Maryland's rural Eastern Shore, Wilson had been raised by his grandparents. By high school, he had grown into a funny, handsome basketball star, more interested in romance than in studying (in his yearbook, he asked to be remembered for "his way with the girls").[31] Wilson entered college in 1961, but books couldn't match the urgency of the civil rights movement, and he soon left to join SNCC, the Student Nonviolent Coordinating Committee. SNCC was considered the most aggressive of the major organizations working in the South. As former president Jimmy Carter (a Georgia native) once said, "If you wanted to scare white people in Southwest Georgia, Martin Luther King and the Southern Christian Leadership Conference wouldn't do it. You only had to say one word—SNCC." Wilson fit right in, and during the mid-1960s he traveled from Maryland to the Deep South, where he registered voters, organized sit-ins, and was arrested many times.[32]

In 1969, Wilson did what fellow activists like Doug Moore, Stokely Carmichael, and Marion Barry had done a few years earlier. He moved to Washington, D.C., a place *Jet* magazine called "one of the next urban meccas for civil rights refugees."[33] And in 1973, when the Home Rule Act set the stage for an elected city council, Wilson faced a choice common to movement veterans: Having won the right to vote and hold office, should they join the system or continue to press for change from the outside? Calling himself a "realist," Wilson chose the inside track; at thirty-one years old, he ran for office in Ward 2, the city's most racially and economically diverse district, and won.[34]

But Wilson couldn't avoid the issue of crime. Nor did he want to; after Kenneth Washington was killed delivering the paper, Wilson kept a copy of the news story nearby.[35] Like his fellow council members, he belonged to a class of black elected officials emerging nationwide. Their candidacies were premised on the notion that they would be different from the white politicians who came before them. No longer would the concerns of black citizens fall on deaf ears. No longer would the police refuse to enter black neighborhoods. (As the NAACP's Roy Wilkins recalled from his childhood in Kansas City, the police took the view that "there's one more Negro killed—the more of 'em dead, the less to bother us."[36]) Gone were the days when one black man could kill another and receive a pardon on the grounds that "this is the case of one negro killing another—the old familiar song—'Hot supper; liquor; dead negro.' "[37]

John Wilson needed an answer to the crime crisis, and gun control was the logical choice. By modern standards, his proposal was absurdly ambitious. If you raise the topic of "gun control" over dinner today, most people will think you mean tighter background checks, smaller ammunition clips, and restricted access for people with mental illnesses. But things were quite different forty years ago, and Wilson's proposal indicates just how much has changed: the council member wanted to ban the sale, purchase, and possession of all handguns and shotguns in the city. Current gun owners would be obligated to turn in their weapons, and anyone who failed to do so would face possible prison time for a first conviction and a mandatory prison term for a second. As Wilson explained, "People think I want to take everybody's gun away—and they're perfectly right."[38]

Wilson offered his gun control bill in the same year that David Clarke was pressing for marijuana decriminalization. Both legislators argued that their proposals would help blacks most of all. But compared with Clarke, Wilson had an important advantage: the vocal support of black crime victims.[39]

## Black Victims Speak

On April 4, 1975, seven years to the day after Martin Luther King's assassination, Richard Ware, recently retired after a long career with the State Department, woke up to a parent's worst nightmare: a call informing him that his son was dead. Richard Ware III, an assistant manager at 4 Guys Grocery on Alabama Avenue, had been on his way to the bank to deposit the store's cash from the day. Before he could get there, two armed men demanded his money. When he hesitated, they shot and killed him.

Some parents turn inward after such a tragedy. For Ware, it was a call to action. Just two months after his son's death, he and his wife began circulating a petition demanding "that the Mayor and the City Council take action to halt the slaughter in our streets." When a council committee held a public hearing on Wilson's gun control legislation, Ware was among those who testified.

"Let's put first things first," he said. "My family wants to live free of fear. Free to walk the streets without concern about who is in front of or behind us."[40] Ware reported that more and more of his friends were afraid to go outside, even in the middle of the day. The racial dimension of the city's gun violence was especially troubling to him. As he pointed out, both his son and his son's murderer were black—and this was hardly unusual. At the time of the Ware murder, 85 percent of those killed by guns in the District of Columbia were black, and so were a similar percentage of murder suspects. Violence within the black community, both in D.C. and across the country, was taking a horrifying toll. Nationally, the black homicide rate was seven to eleven times higher than the white homicide rate.[41]

How, Ware asked, could this be happening now? Under slogans like "Black Pride" and "Black Is Beautiful," many African Americans in the late 1960s and early 1970s had begun celebrating the black aesthetic, black culture, and black solidarity. "It is ironic," Ware lamented, "that as black men have more frequently called each other brother, there has been an increase in black killing black."[42]

Ware was not the only one to note the bitter irony, as a cartoon from *Ebony* magazine indicates (note the poster advertising a James Brown concert—his song "Say It Loud—I'm Black and I'm Proud" had become one of the anthems of the Black Pride movement).

"Right on, brotherman. Now if you'll just quietly raise that other arm . . ."

(*Ebony* magazine, July 1973)

For Ware and Wilson, reducing the number of guns in circulation was critical to bringing safety to the city's streets. "All of this terror," Ware said, "is caused by the man with the gun. We must fight him or die. The key to overcoming him is simple—take his gun. He is nothing without his gun."[43]

Victims like Ware had an important ally: the black church. As we have seen, D.C.'s black religious leaders were effective opponents of marijuana decriminalization. Although organized church groups did not take a stand in the gun control debate, individual ministers played important roles—none more so than Rev. Walter Fauntroy. The pastor of New Bethel Baptist Church, Fauntroy had become D.C.'s first elected representative to Congress in 1971.[44] Gun control was one of his signature issues in the House, and on the local level, he was a lead witness in favor of D.C.'s legislation.[45]

Testifying before the D.C. Council, Fauntroy said that he was "tired of handgun funerals." Guns, he said, had taken not only the lives of national heroes like Martin Luther King, Jr., but also those of countless others whose names had already been forgotten. Fauntroy emphasized that the issue was not simply an abstraction for him: "As a minister and activist in the civil rights movement, I have officiated at the funerals of numerous citizens who would be alive today had we a law banning the manufacture, sale and possession of handguns."[46] Fauntroy hoped that prohibition would change how Americans—especially the city's youth—viewed guns: "From Wyatt Earp to the Godfather, we mislead our young people who think they can secure their manhood through the barrel of a gun."[47]

Other ministers joined Fauntroy in using their personal experiences to advocate for gun restrictions. Rev. Stanford Harris, of Capitol Hill's Ebenezer United Methodist Church, told the council that he spoke on behalf of a coalition of ministers, "at least two of whom have had guns pointed at their faces and bodies." He also spoke for his congregation, which included many senior citizens "who have suffered the trauma and fear of assaults with handguns." Finally, Rev. Harris said, he spoke for himself: he, too, had lost a son to gun violence. He told the council "of the utter despair and continuing psychic pain brought to my family when our twenty-two-year-old son had his brains brutally torn to pieces by a handgun in the hands of another young man."[48]

## A Harder Edge: Mandatory Minimums

Alongside empathy for Rev. Harris and other victims' relatives lay outrage at those who pulled the triggers. That anger found its political expression in the demand for tougher criminal penalties—especially for any crime involving guns. Fauntroy proposed that anybody caught selling a gun would face a five-year maximum sentence, while those convicted of illegal possession would face up to two years.[49] This wasn't tough enough for John Wilson, who felt that mandatory minimum sentences were required. The current sentencing laws, he complained, were "largely disobeyed and ignored by the judges and prosecutors."[50] According to U.S. Attorney Earl Silbert, only 7.6 percent of those convicted of illegal gun possession in 1974 had received jail time; the rest had received suspended sentences, probation, or fines.[51] The Washington Post's William Raspberry seconded Silbert's criticism, complaining about a D.C. judge who had imposed jail time in only one out of seventy-three cases in which a defendant had been convicted of a gun offense.[52] This needed to change, said Wilson, who hoped to force judges to impose prison time. He also wanted to strip prosecutors of the ability to plea-bargain in gun cases. As he put it, under his proposal, "people would know that if caught with a gun they will have to serve 10 to 12 months, no ifs, ands, or buts."[53]

Wilson's accusation that judges and prosecutors were disobeying the law was, in one sense, unfair: discretion is built into every part of the criminal justice system, and judges and prosecutors do nothing wrong when they seek or impose something less than the maximum. But whatever its merits, Wilson's complaint was growing ever more common in the 1970s, and his solution exemplified what was becoming the standard response in American criminal justice: When you want to stop people from doing something, take away discretion and impose more prison time.

The racial impact of such proposals was obvious—nobody doubted that blacks would be the ones locked up. Wilson acknowledged as much, saying, "Anyone who has been to court knows that at least 95 percent of the people arrested for carrying a deadly weapon are black."[54] But he was prepared to pay that price. In an open letter to other city leaders, he stressed that the criminal element was a minority victimizing the majority: "We must begin to realize that a very large majority of the residents of this city . . . are being terrorized by a small group of people who have no respect for anyone." Though few in number, this group presented a huge threat. Left unchecked, Wilson said, the criminal element will "limit our mobility, our safety and our economic and social growth." He was aware that his tough stance might be construed as antiblack—the comedian and activist Dick Gregory, for example, had recently said that "crime in the streets" was "America's new way of saying 'nigger.'" In language that would have made Richard Nixon or Barry Goldwater proud, Wilson offered this rejoinder: "'Respect for law' can no longer be considered code words for bigotry."[55]

Wilson wasn't alone. After a three-day conference on "black crime" at Howard University, the *Afro* editorialized that toughness was in order. Reflecting on the city's rapid deterioration—"peaceful, safe and agreeable" areas had been "radically transformed into an environment of fear and fright"—the paper concluded that "the courts and the judges should take harsher views on convicted offenders and mete out tough and longtime sentences."[56] It was the only way, said the editors, to "stop this small minority of criminal element from its path of destruction."

## A National Movement

Even with this tough talk, gun control advocates knew that there were limits to what D.C.—or any city—could do to keep guns off the streets. As Fauntroy admitted, "Even strict enforcement would hardly make a dent in the problem, because the heart of the matter is in the thousands of guns that come pouring into the District every month from control-free havens in North Carolina, South Carolina, and elsewhere."[57] Still, supporters of Wilson's legislation persevered, for they saw themselves as the vanguard of a national movement. During Fauntroy's testimony, Clarke told him, "I feel that decisive action by the new City Council of our Nation's capital will, I think, start the momentum in the nation for a sane handgun control policy."[58] Richard Ware shared Clarke's belief that others were paying attention to D.C.—especially, Ware thought, other blacks. He said, "To a black man, the city of Washington is a significant symbol." As "the one major city in the U.S.A. with a majority black population and an elected government with a black majority . . . [w]hat happens in D.C. is watched by all U.S.A. blacks and nonblacks alike."[59]

Gun control supporters had reason for optimism. Opinion polls showed growing public support for firearms restrictions, especially after the assassinations of John and Robert Kennedy in the 1960s. African American public opinion on gun control was shifting rapidly, too, and black elected officials around the country had begun to champion gun control initiatives.[60] The two leading advocates from the black political class were Atlanta mayor Maynard Jackson and Detroit-based congressman John Conyers. Their motivations paralleled those of Wilson and his colleagues in D.C.: Atlanta had earned the bleak designation of the nation's "murder capital," and Detroit was right behind it. As Jackson told the *Atlanta Daily World*, the city's leading black paper, "We are living in an armed camp—an illegally armed camp. It is my job to stop the killing."[61] Calling gun control his "most urgent" priority, Conyers used his position as chair of the House Judiciary Committee's Subcommittee on Crime to push a legislative package that included a ban on handguns.

Testifying before Conyers's subcommittee, Jackson described the burden of being the chief black elected official in a city where so many blacks were being shot. "The black-on-black homicide rate is one of the worst disgraces we have in the country," he told Conyers. Jackson ultimately grounded his argument in an appeal for racial empathy: "I, as a black man, and a black American, and as a mayor of this city, plead with you on behalf of all Atlantans black or white to do something and please do it now."[62]

Jackson's rhetoric, however, obscured one significant fact about gun crime: it wasn't equally distributed throughout black America. Rather, it was concentrated among the poorest blacks, who were forced into living conditions that generated violence. Few black Americans would disagree with the Detroit psychologist who said in 1973, "Living in a frustrating, stress-inducing environment like a ghetto every day of your life makes many people walking powder kegs."[63] This understanding led some community leaders to insist that gun control would not succeed, because it failed to address crime's root causes. In Chicago, Rev. Russ Meek, a black anti-gun-control activist, countered Conyers's proposal by arguing that Congress should "attack the social causes of crime and not the ownership of weapons."[64]

It bears emphasis that black supporters of gun control like Jackson acknowledged "the social causes of crime" and insisted that they had not abandoned the struggle against inequality and racial injustice. But they also argued that restricting guns was a useful step, even if it didn't solve the entire problem. "Black Americans are economically oppressed," Jackson said in his congressional testimony, "but while we address that, while we fight with all that we have for a fair shake for Americans, all Americans, including black Americans, in housing, in employment, in the delivery of health service . . . while we are doing this we must address the additional problem of the presence of handguns." Erma Henderson, the first black woman on Detroit's city council, also supported Conyers's proposal but insisted that it must be part of a larger effort to improve conditions in black communities. "If we do not ease the tension of racism and economic disaster," she warned, "gun control laws will not work."[65]

In the D.C. Council, Wilson wanted to be ready for the "root causes" argument. To prepare for his committee's public hearing, he drew up a list of possible objections to gun restrictions, followed by what he planned to say in response. Under the heading "Gun Controls Do Not Attack the Root Social and Economic Causes of Crime," Wilson wrote, "Of course they don't. But they will reduce the effects of crime." And D.C.'s black citizens, Wilson thought, couldn't wait for America to address root causes. As he said in his prepared response, "[W]aiting until society solves its root social and economic problems, when right now we can reduce the loss of life, the bodily harm, and the loss of property that result from crime and accident, makes no sense."[66]

In one of its many editorials endorsing gun control, the *Afro* commended Wilson's approach. "Every time the subject of high crime comes up, there are those who blame racism, oppression, poverty, self-hatred, discrimination and joblessness," the paper noted. "[O]f course, all those things play a part in the crime picture, and we never are going to rid the cities of crime to any substantial degree until those annoying conditions and the forces which create them are improved or corrected." And yet, the editors concluded, "if a gun control bill will help, then let's have a gun control bill, and let's have it as soon as possible."[67]

## Opposition: Guns for Self-defense

One unique feature of the continuing gun control debate is that a gun may be the only dangerous item that can plausibly be viewed as a solution to the very danger it presents. Nobody argues that the solution to cocaine addiction is more cocaine. But guns can be defended on just those grounds. And in D.C., council member Doug Moore was there to mount the defense. In the summer of 1975, Moore was combating David Clarke's marijuana decriminalization initiative by arguing that it would do more harm than good to D.C.'s black community. That same summer, Moore fought a similar campaign against gun control.

While Wilson argued that protecting blacks required getting rid of guns, Moore claimed the opposite: Blacks needed guns for self-defense. Since the government could not be counted on to protect black citizens against violence, Moore said, gun ownership was the only way for blacks to achieve the equal protection promised by the Fourteenth Amendment.[68] But guns weren't merely a form of individual protection, according to Moore. They were also a tool of collective self-defense against violent whites. If D.C. was to give up its guns, he argued, that would "make it difficult for the people of this city—many of whom are black—to defend themselves" against gunslinging vigilantes from neighboring majority-white states. Moore warned that people "from Maryland and Virginia or New York or any other state would come and say, you know they took all the guns in D.C. and so we are on our way in."[69] Coleman Young, Detroit's first black mayor, shared Moore's concern. Said Young, "I'll be damned if I'll let them collect guns in the city of Detroit while we're surrounded by hostile suburbs and the whole rest of the state . . . where you have vigilantes practicing in the wilderness with automatic weapons."[70]

To modern ears, Moore's and Young's claims may sound outlandish. But they shouldn't. These officials were expressing views rooted in a black political and intellectual tradition that Nicholas Johnson has called "the black tradition of arms."[71] In this tradition, guns were both a practical tool for black self-defense and a symbol of black self-determination.

After the Civil War, blacks were frequently terrorized in southern states, with courts and law enforcement often serving as accomplices. The Fourteenth Amendment—which, as Moore stressed, promised blacks equal protection of the law—was, in part, a response to this violence.[72] Many Reconstruction legislators argued that the Fourteenth

Amendment was necessary to ensure that recently freed slaves would receive state protection from private violence. In 1866, for example, the New Hampshire Republican Daniel Clark asked, "Is the negro not entitled to his life as clearly and fully as the white man?" If the answer is yes, Clark continued, then "has he not a right just as good to have it protected by law?"[73]

The promise of equal protection, however, was one of the many casualties of Reconstruction's defeat. Violence played an essential role in the tyranny that whites imposed on blacks throughout the Jim Crow South. Senator Ben "Pitchfork" Tillman boasted of how he and other white supremacists used force and violence to steal elections: "We have done our level best. . . . We have scratched our head to figure out how we can eliminate the last one of them. We stuffed ballot boxes. We shot them [Negroes]. WE ARE NOT ASHAMED OF IT."[74] Whites also used violence to deprive blacks of property and material possessions. As Ta-Nehisi Coates has argued, Jim Crow was as much about plunder as about separation. "When we think of white supremacy," he writes, "we picture Colored Only signs, but we should picture pirate flags."[75] Just so. And the pirates had guns.

Keeping blacks subjugated required that they be unarmed. Alabama's law was typical: "Any freedman, mulatto, or free person of color in this state" was forbidden "to own fire-arms, or carry about his person a pistol or other deadly weapon."[76] Blacks caught breaking the law were subject to incarceration—which, in the early twentieth century, often meant being sold into debt servitude and forced to work in conditions that approximated slavery. According to Douglas Blackmon, "In an era when great numbers of southern men carried sidearms, the crime of carrying a concealed weapon—enforced almost solely against black men—would by the turn of the century become one of the most consistent instruments of black incarceration."[77]

During Reconstruction, blacks fought state repression with the very tool the state wished to deny them: the gun. After members of white rifle clubs in South Carolina tried to deter blacks from voting in an 1876 election, black citizens signed a public petition declaring, "We tell you it will not do to go too far in this thing. Remember there are 80,000 black men in this state who can bear Winchester rifles and know how to use them."[78]

Guns remained essential to black self-defense into the twentieth century. Beginning in 1917, a series of violent racial conflicts erupted in many northern cities. Labeled "race riots" by the white press, they are more accurately described as organized white-on-black violence. As the historian David Krugler explains, "African Americans were not so much *rioting* as fighting back, counterattacking, repelling violence; above all, *resisting.*"[79]

D.C.'s armed response was led by its black World War I veterans, most of whom had fought in the 368th and 372nd Infantry regiments.[80] Upon their return, these men found that racial segregation had become more entrenched under the leadership of Woodrow Wilson, the same president who had sent them off to war. Wilson restored segregation in federal government agencies and buildings, where screens were put up to separate black and white workers, and in 1915 he showed the racist film *The Birth of a Nation* in the White House.[81] When the Boston newspaper editor Monroe Trotter led a black delegation to Washington to complain about Wilson's policies, the president is alleged to have told them, "Segregation is not humiliating, but a benefit, and ought to be so regarded by you gentlemen."[82]

In 1919, when a white mob mobilized to attack blacks in D.C., the city's black veterans were prepared to defend themselves and their families. As a military intelligence agent wrote in a confidential memo shortly before the fighting, "these officers and soldiers returning to their homes in Washington have told their grievances and . . . have boasted of their ability to handle guns and of their determination to use the arms in their possession rather than submit to unjust treatment."[83] Meeting at the intersection of Seventh and T Streets, NW, black drivers assembled a convoy and headed to Baltimore, returning with trunks full of weapons. The fighting with the white mob lasted five days, and although black casualties were higher, the two sides were more closely matched than was true in other cities.

The resistance by D.C.'s black veterans earned the praise of the NAACP leader James Weldon Johnson, who said, "The Negroes saved themselves and saved Washington by their determination not to run, but to fight . . . fight in the defense of their lives and their homes. If the white mob had gone unchecked—and it was only the determined effort of black men that checked it—Washington would have been another and worse East St. Louis." *The Messenger*, a publication cofounded by the labor organizer A. Philip Randolph, cited D.C.'s armed resistance as evidence that a "New Negro" had arrived. D.C.'s fighting blacks were hailed as an alternative to old-guard black establishment leaders like Booker T. Washington and W.E.B. Du Bois, whom the paper lampooned for encouraging blacks to "be modest and unassuming" and to "forget our grievances."[84]

THE "NEW CROWD NEGRO" MAKING AMERICA SAFE FOR HIMSELF

(*The Messenger*, 1919)

The same refrain was heard throughout the twentieth century. From the anti-lynching activist Ida B. Wells ("A Winchester rifle should have a place of honor in every black home, and it should be used for that protection which the law refuses to give") to Malcolm X ("It is lawful for anyone to own a rifle or a shotgun and it is everyone's right to protect themselves from anyone who stands in their way to prevent them from obtaining what is rightfully theirs"), the list of African Americans who invoked gun ownership as a tool of racial self-defense reads like a Who's Who of black America.[85]

The black tradition of arms was especially familiar to someone like John Wilson, who had spent much of the 1960s in SNCC. Southern-born SNCC members such as Fannie Lou Hamer spoke openly about their guns: "I keep a shotgun in every corner of my bedroom and the first cracker even look like he wants to throw some dynamite on my porch won't write his mama again."[86] SNCC members from the North took note of how well armed their hosts were. Remembering his years in the South, my father, James Forman, wrote, "self-defense—at least of one's home—was not a concept new to Southern blacks in 1963 and there was hardly a black home in the South without its shotgun or rifle."[87] SNCC's Julian Bond agreed: "Almost everybody with whom we stayed in Mississippi had guns." Although these guns were principally for hunting, Bond noted that "they were there for other purposes, too."[88] Soon the SNCC workers adopted the practices of their hosts. The historian Clayborne Carson estimates that by the end of the summer of 1964, almost all SNCC fieldworkers were armed.[89]

By the late 1960s, blacks got a reminder about why they might want to hold on to their weapons: Longtime gun control opponents suddenly became interested in restricting access to guns when blacks began to brandish them publicly and politically. In California, for example, elected officials—including Governor Ronald Reagan—rushed to enact strict gun control laws after members of the Black Panthers (the full and neglected name of the group being the Black Panther Party for Self-Defense) armed themselves. The sponsor of the gun control

bill, Don Mulford, denied that race had played a role, but black legislators knew better. As one of them pointed out, Mulford had dropped his
opposition to gun control only after "Negroes showed up in Oakland—
his district—with arms."[90] The next year, Congress passed its first gun
control legislation in thirty years. Though the law was generally weak,
Congress did try to limit the availability of one class of guns: inexpen-
sive, poor-quality handguns called Saturday night specials.[91] The
journalist Robert Sherrill wasn't the only one to conclude that a law
singling out guns favored by the poor was a law "passed not to control
guns but to control blacks."[92]

D.C.'s black nationalists, including Doug Moore, Stokely Carmichael, and the Black United Front (BUF), certainly saw it that way. On
April 5, 1968, the day after Martin Luther King was assassinated, as
grief turned to rage in D.C. and other cities, Carmichael and SNCC
held an emergency press conference at the New School for Afro-
American Thought, located just north of Fourteenth and U Streets.
"When white America killed Dr. King last night, she declared war on
us," said Carmichael. Later in his statement, he added, "There no
longer needs to be intellectual discussion. Black people know that they
have to get guns."[93] In November of the same year, Carmichael told a
crowd of more than nineteen hundred at Howard University that they
must "be willing to live, to fight, and kill for one's own people."[94]
Meanwhile, the BUF, led by Carmichael and Moore, protested local gun control proposals; in August 1968, the group resolved that
"D.C. gun-control legislation is a white racist means of taking away
from black people an instrument of self-defense."[95] The next month, both
neighboring Maryland counties—Montgomery and Prince George's—
rejected gun control measures, leading the BUF to reiterate its opposition to gun control. Both Montgomery and Prince George's counties
were majority white at the time, and using an argument that Moore
would deploy again seven years later, the BUF said that it made no sense
for "68 percent black Washington" to adopt gun control "while the
surrounding 95 percent white suburbs with no similar gun control
legislation are actively being urged to arm and are arming."[96]

Twelve to One

The D.C. Council vote wasn't even close. Though the force of distant and recent history was behind him, Moore couldn't persuade even one of his colleagues that blacks in D.C. should be allowed to continue to bear arms. In 1976, by a 12–1 vote, D.C. passed one of the nation's strictest gun control laws. It wasn't the all-out ban Wilson had initially proposed, but it went a long way in that direction. The city council required current owners to register their handguns and prohibited residents from acquiring new ones; these rules were backed by a ten-day jail sentence for violators.[97] Nor had Moore been able to win the battle for public opinion. Although D.C.'s blacks were less supportive of gun control than were whites—a result likely attributable to the black tradition of arms—majorities of both groups were in favor.[98]

Though Moore was the lone vote against gun control on the D.C. Council, he did have allies around the country. A few shared his view that blacks needed guns for collective self-defense. For example, Chicago's Rev. Russ Meek said that gun control efforts unfairly targeted blacks while whites retained their guns. "Gun control is race control," Meek argued.[99]

Most black gun control opponents emphasized individual self-protection. When Maynard Jackson pressed for gun control in Georgia, State Representative Billy McKinney led the opposition. McKinney, one of the first black police officers in Georgia, said that with violence rising, "I carry a gun all the time for protection."[100] Meek, who had been featured in *Ebony* magazine for his work teaching "black karate" at Malcolm X College, agreed.[101] He told Conyers's committee that even he needed protection against street thugs: "I don't intend to try to fight off a sawed-off shotgun or a pistol or a sawed-off rifle with a karate chop or a broom."[102] Given long-standing black attitudes about self-defense, these arguments resonated: when a 1968 CBS poll asked, "Do you think people like yourself have to be prepared to defend their homes against crime and violence, or can the police take care of that?"

blacks were more likely than whites to say they would need to defend their homes themselves.[103]

The self-defense argument had a particular meaning for some black women. "Being single and alone, I feel that I should have the right to some type of protection," said Georgia representative Betty Clark of DeKalb County when she opposed Maynard Jackson's handgun ban in the state legislature.[104] Doug Moore often invoked the issue of women's safety, arguing that gun restrictions put them especially at risk: "[I]f you are going to take all the guns away, you are going to tell me that every single woman in this city is going to be left to the mercy of the criminals, the rapers, the robbers or even the nasty tempered husbands."[105] Moore said he wanted to institute programs around the city, including in schools, to teach women how to shoot, and on the second day of the hearings, he shared a story about how gun training had worked for a female resident.[106] According to Moore, "a lady was raped and the police never found the man. The husband decided to teach her how to shoot and the same criminal came back to rape her again. She killed him."[107]

But Moore and the other dissenters were just that—dissenters. By the mid-1970s, the black political establishment definitively favored significant gun restrictions, including handgun bans. Conyers claimed that he sensed growing support for gun control among black citizens as well, and the 12–1 vote for gun control in D.C. supports Conyers's view that things had changed.[108]

But why? What caused a hundred-year-old black tradition of arms to fade so quickly?

There are two major reasons. First, the black tradition of arms grew out of a history of white-on-black violence. As Randall Kennedy explains, "[n]othing has more eroded confidence in the criminal justice system than the long history of willful refusals to punish white anti-black vigilantes."[109] Though hardly a thing of the past, white racist violence was being replaced by a new threat to black life. Around the country, black papers that once detailed lynchings and attacks on civil rights workers now devoted banner headlines to the stories of people like Rev. Lipscombe and his wife, tied down and robbed in their home. Richard Ware's son, a black grocery store employee shot while being robbed by other blacks, had come to represent violent crime in black America. Testifying before D.C. lawmakers, Ware said, "In my youth, blacks were often killed by whites; today blacks are more generally killed by blacks."[110] The argument that blacks need guns to protect themselves against the majority had lost its relevance to men like Ware. As he argued, "The greater fear by blacks should be about the potential for racial suicide rather than genocide."[111]

The second answer concerns a shift in political power. Guns developed a special meaning in African American communities in response to racist governments that ignored—and sometimes even abetted—black death. But for all the brave rhetoric, few thought that sitting up with your shotgun was the best option.[112] It was what you did when you had no other recourse. Recall Ida B. Wells's famous words: "A Winchester rifle should have a place of honor in every black home, and it should be used for that protection *which the law refuses to give*."[113] But what if the law didn't refuse? What if police came when called? What if the government actually tried to protect black lives?

When Richard Ware testified before the D.C. Council, he was looking up at a dais populated by lawmakers whose very existence repudiated the racism that had fostered the black tradition of arms. Many of these officials, including John Wilson, had pledged their youth to defeating Jim Crow—a challenge that had seemed impossible when they started. But now they'd won, and they were the ones in charge. They promised to provide police protection to a community so long denied it. And they weren't the only symbol of change. The John Wilsons of politics had their counterparts in policing, many of whom joined the call for handgun control. Increasing numbers of black Americans were willing to place their trust in these new leaders—even if that meant disarming.[114]

Understood in this light, D.C.'s gun control law was a civil rights triumph. It had been just twelve years since SNCC's Ella Baker had famously declared, "Until the killing of black men, black mothers' sons, becomes as important to the rest of the country as the killing of a white mother's son—we who believe in freedom cannot rest until this happens."[115] Baker's outrage had been prompted by the loss of civil rights workers James Chaney, Michael Schwerner, and Andrew Goodman in Mississippi in 1964. Schwerner and Goodman were whites from the North, and their disappearance generated substantial press attention and an extensive search for their bodies. Many SNCC workers complained that when blacks disappeared, nobody paid attention. These complaints were validated during the search for the missing workers, when authorities happened upon the bodies of two black men along Mississippi riverbanks whose deaths had never been investigated.[116] Little more than a decade later, John Wilson and his colleagues could reasonably declare that, at least in D.C., the killing of black men mattered.

## Gun Control, or the War on Guns?

Still, we should celebrate this achievement with caution. After all, Wilson and his colleagues expressed their concern for black life by resolving to lock up those who sold or possessed guns. As passed, D.C.'s law imposed only a ten-day sentence on violators, but Wilson and Fauntroy had sought greater punishment. They failed to get it due to a quirk of D.C. law. When Congress granted the District some measure of autonomy in the early 1970s, it imposed a moratorium on the city council's ability to change local criminal law. After much debate, the city's lawmakers concluded that they could enact gun control legislation consistent with this restriction, but only if they refrained from tacking substantial prison time onto the proposal.[117] In 1979, when the moratorium on criminal legislation expired, the city immediately toughened its laws (this is the subject of chapter 4).

Black lawmakers outside of D.C. didn't have to wait: they could, and did, seek longer sentences for gun crime without delay. Some, like Atlanta's Maynard Jackson, argued that illegally possessing a gun should bring a mandatory minimum penalty. Jackson cited as a model a 1975 Massachusetts law that imposed a one-year mandatory sentence for illegal possession, saying, "Now, I don't know whether this is a liberal or conservative or moderate position, in fact, I don't give a hoot, but I'll tell you this, Mr. Chairman, if minimum mandatory sentences will work, especially in this area, I am for it."[118]

Alongside Jackson's call for mandatory minimums for gun possession, there emerged a related proposal that attracted support from great numbers of black legislators, including both advocates and opponents of handgun bans: mandatory prison time for people who commit crimes while armed with a gun.[119] In D.C., Doug Moore found a rare point of agreement with Wilson and Fauntroy. "I believe we should have stricter penalties" for armed criminals, Moore said. "I may have to go to law school to be able to do it, but I want to make it so hard that anyone who uses a gun in a robbery or anything that he is going to get the maximum."[120]

Even Detroit's mayor, Coleman Young, saw mandatory minimums for gun crimes as a reasonable compromise: a way to fight crime without forcing law-abiding black citizens to disarm.[121] In 1976, Michigan passed a two-year mandatory add-on sentence for defendants convicted of possession of a firearm in the commission of a felony.[122] Young's view—that private citizens should be able to keep guns in their homes while criminals who use them should face harsh sentences—was in line with the beliefs of many black citizens. In nearby Chicago, two-thirds of black residents told pollsters that citizens should be allowed to own firearms; the same percentage said that courts did not deal harshly enough with criminals who use guns.[123]

Ultimately, the gun control debate mirrored the marijuana fight in form and outcome. In both cases, elected officials and other community leaders identified an issue plaguing the community, focused on its racial dimensions, and led a political response that emphasized prohibition. In both cases, prohibition was backed with law enforcement and an escalating series of criminal penalties.

As we shall see, the impulse to impose ever-tougher sentences would prove difficult to restrain. And this remained true even when the punitive measures adopted in D.C. and elsewhere did not achieve the desired results. In one respect, the policies to combat drugs and guns have had a similar impact: the majority of those punished have been low-income, poorly educated black men. In another respect, however, they have had a similar *lack of* impact: they have failed to prevent marijuana use, and they have failed to protect the community from gun violence.

In fairness to the black gun control advocates, they had sought a much broader package than they achieved. Both Fauntroy and Conyers hoped that D.C. would be in the vanguard of a national gun control movement. Similarly, Mayor Jackson insisted that gun restrictions were part of a larger, determined effort to attack racial disparities in health, employment, and education.[124] In retrospect, we can see that Fauntroy, Conyers, and Jackson were wildly optimistic.

Conyers's gun control proposal never made it out of his own subcommittee (he lost by an embarrassing 6–1), and in the years since, Congress has never come close to passing the sort of national gun law he sought.[125] As for addressing root causes, such efforts had become an object of ridicule by 1975, a symbol of the hopeless naïveté of 1960s liberalism. Lyndon Johnson had defended Great Society programs as anticrime efforts and said that the way to stop riots was to "get at the causes." According to Johnson, "the answer is jobs. The answer is education. The answer is health."[126] To which Alabama governor George Wallace had a ready retort, attacking liberals who rationalized crime by claiming that "the killer didn't get any watermelon to eat when he was 10 years old."[127] Nixon sided with Wallace, though with greater sophistication. Poverty and unemployment did not cause crime, Nixon said; rather, crime resulted from "insufficient curbs on the appetites or impulses that naturally impel individuals towards criminal activities."[128] While many blacks embraced an all-of-the-above strategy that combined increasing criminal penalties with attacking inequality, conservatives often framed the choice as either-or. As Nixon argued, the solution to the crime problem is "not quadrupling funds for 'any governmental war on poverty' but convicting more criminals."[129] Conservatives won. By the 1980s, national gun control was a distant dream, and there was little enthusiasm for attacking poverty and racism in the way Jackson and others had called for.[130]

The net result: Prohibiting gun possession in majority-black communities like D.C., while failing to curb the vibrant national gun market or to address crime's root causes, has led to the worst of all possible worlds. Guns—and gun violence—saturate our inner cities, while the people who go to prison for possessing guns are overwhelmingly black and brown.

# 3

# REPRESENTATIVES OF THEIR RACE
## The Rise of African American Police, 1948–78

On September 7, 1976, more than sixty law enforcement executives—representing twenty-four states, fifty-five major cities, and approximately ten million black Americans—gathered at the Twin Bridges Marriott Hotel outside Washington, D.C., for a conference on reducing crime in low-income urban areas.[1] The topic itself was unremarkable; discussions of crime were a staple of the era.[2] But something else about this meeting *was* special: all the principal attendees were black. It was the first-ever national summit of black police executives.[3]

D.C.'s assistant police chief, Burtell Jefferson, had worked as hard as anyone to make this gathering possible. Jefferson was the highest-ranking black officer in the District's Metropolitan Police Department (MPD). In two years, he would be named chief and would assume command of a force that was well on its way to becoming the nation's first majority-black urban police department. Jefferson was a modest man; with a thin mustache, close-cropped hair, and Bible at hand, he reminded some of a church elder.[4] But on this day, he—and his rising generation of fellow black police leaders—would allow themselves a sense of accomplishment.

For most of American history, police departments had been almost entirely white. This was no accident. Police officers, after all, can take your liberty, or even your life. Putting such awesome power in black hands seemed preposterous to most whites, who believed that a primary police function was to control blacks. None of this was lost on black Americans. James Baldwin spoke for many when he wrote, in 1960, that the white policeman walks through the ghetto like "an occupying soldier in a bitterly hostile country."[5]

In light of this history, a room full of black police leaders was an undeniably powerful symbol. But a question loomed over the gathering: Now that policing's long-established color line had been breached, what would happen to criminal justice policy? How would black chiefs—and black officers—be different from their white predecessors? A symbolic victory had been won, yes, but the practical consequences of that victory were far from clear.

As far back as the 1860s, black Americans had been calling for the hiring of black police officers. This was an essential, if forgotten, part of our nation's civil rights struggle.[6] But while these demands were consistent, the rationales were not. Some advocates claimed that blacks would make better crime fighters: they would win black citizens' trust more easily, could more effectively cultivate informants in black communities, and, above all, would be more motivated to protect black lives. This final consideration was especially significant to those who had suffered the consequences of white indifference to crime, vice, and public disorder in black communities. Others said that black officers would be less abusive and disrespectful than their white counterparts: unencumbered by racism, they'd be less likely to harass innocent blacks or use excessive force during stops or arrests; instead of treating all blacks as suspects, they would be able to distinguish decent folks from the criminal element. Still other advocates focused on economics: police jobs were good jobs, with decent pay and even better benefits, and blacks should get their fair share of the pie. Finally, some argued that investing blacks with the power of a badge and gun would send a vital message to Americans on both sides of the color line, overturning a tradition of white resistance to the very idea of black authority.

In retrospect, it's not hard to see how these rationales might conflict in practice. To take the most obvious example (and the one that would eventually present itself most forcefully), the desire for more vigorous policing might prove incompatible with the goal of less police harassment. But for a century, no one recognized the potential for such conflicts. As long as the hiring of black officers remained a distant dream, there was no way to test any theory about the changes they would bring to law enforcement. By 1976, however, America's cities had appointed enough black police executives to fill a symposium and had hired thousands of additional blacks in rank-and-file positions. As a result, the question of what difference black police would, or could, make was suddenly urgent. With heroin and firearms swamping black America, crime on the march, and concerns about police abuse undiminished, the new black police officers faced extraordinary pressure to have a transformative impact.

The emergence of black police leaders in the 1970s did more than present new questions. It also signified the arrival of new voices to answer them. For decades, civil rights leaders, preachers, and the black press had made the case for hiring black police officers. They had made bold claims about what these officers would do once they achieved significant representation on the force. But of course, these advocates were not police officers themselves, and had no intention of joining the police.

Meanwhile, far from public view, Burtell Jefferson and his colleagues had long battled intense on-the-job discrimination in Jim Crow police departments. For twenty, thirty, even forty years, they had endured untold indignities and overcome impossible odds. Now they were at or near the top of a profession that was finally preparing to allow them—at least some of them—to assume leadership positions. Few people had bothered to ask these black officers what they would do if they were in charge. Now the nation—especially its cities with large black populations—would find out.

In 1948, Burtell Jefferson was a young man who needed a job. Born in D.C. in 1925 and educated in the city's segregated school system, he had graduated from Armstrong Technical High School six years earlier. Founded in 1902, Armstrong reflected the philosophy of Booker T. Washington, who in a speech at its dedication declared, "All forms of labor, whether with the head or with the hand, are honorable."[7] Though Armstrong offered college prep classes, it couldn't compete on that score with D.C.'s legendary Paul Laurence Dunbar High School. Dunbar was probably the most prestigious black high school in the nation under Jim Crow, and the undisputed school of choice for the city's black elite.[8] In contrast, Armstrong built its reputation on vocational training, sending its graduates into careers such as shoe repair, painting, and dressmaking.[9]

Armstrong didn't prepare students to be police officers. Considering the history of race and policing, that is hardly surprising. Many of the first police forces in the South were founded as slave patrols, explicitly charged with catching, beating, and returning runaway slaves.[10] After the Civil War, slave patrols ended—at least officially. The job of controlling and repressing blacks continued under a new division of labor: the police would enforce Jim Crow vagrancy laws and nighttime curfews, and the dirtier assignments, including lynching, cross burning, and night riding, were left to vigilante groups such as the Ku Klux Klan.[11] Still, the Klan and the police often worked together, their rosters commonly consisting of the same people. Some sheriffs not-so-secretly traded their badges for robes at sundown.[12] To blacks, the continuities between these forms of repression were obvious. As one black man in North Carolina recalled decades after slavery had ended, slave patrols had been "jes' like policemen, only worser."[13]

During Reconstruction, when blacks gained the right to vote and hold office, they also joined southern police forces for the first time.[14] But, as with much of the progress made during Reconstruction, the victory was short-lived. The very thought of black officers was both infuriating and terrifying to a society that demanded black subservience and feared retaliation for the violence of slavery. When city leaders in Raleigh, North Carolina, hired four black officers in 1868, the *Daily Sentinel* responded with headlines proclaiming "The Mongrel Regime!! Negro Police!!" Readers were warned that "this is the beginning of the end."[15] Whites in Jackson and Meridian, Mississippi, rioted when newly appointed black officers tried to do their jobs.[16] Perhaps it was Mississippi congressman Ethelbert Barksdale who best summed up the prevailing southern view: the existence of black officers would imply domination over whites, "and the white man is not used to being dominated by the colored race."[17]

When forces hostile to Reconstruction took over state governments and began instituting Jim Crow segregation, black officers provided an early target. As the historian W. Marvin Dulaney concludes, "[B]y 1910, African Americans had literally disappeared from southern police forces."[18] By that time, although 47.5 percent of the nation's black population lived in South Carolina, Georgia, Louisiana, Mississippi, or Alabama, there was not a single black officer in those states.[19] The situation was barely better in border and northern states, where the vanishingly few black officers lived a second-class existence.[20]

> 105,000 Negro Citizens Rate at Least 1 Negro Police.
>
> —Protester, Atlanta, Georgia, 1946

Blacks wanted the right to serve as police officers just as badly as white supremacists wanted to deny it to them. Throughout the first half of the twentieth century, national civil rights groups surveyed police departments in an attempt to document the number of black officers and to show that cities that *had* hired black officers were happy with the results.[21] Local civil rights advocates used this information to push for change in city after city.

In Atlanta, for example, civil rights groups, religious leaders, and the city's largest black paper, the *Atlanta Daily World*, joined forces in a decade-long campaign to bring about the hiring of black officers. Atlanta's wasn't the only such campaign, but perhaps because the city had a large black middle class (rivaling D.C.'s in size), the fight for black officers in Georgia's capital won exuberant coverage from the nation's black press. Atlanta advocates based their case on the theory that black police officers would fight crime more effectively. "Why does the high murder rate among Negroes in Atlanta continue unabated?" asked the Commission on Interracial Cooperation (CIC), a group that brought together southern white liberals and conservative blacks, some of whom were associated with Booker T. Washington's Tuskegee Institute.[22] After hosting a series of gatherings in 1936 that included some of Atlanta's most prominent blacks, the CIC issued a report blaming elevated black crime, in part, on the "laissez-faire attitudes" of white police and white jurors in cases "where Negroes kill Negroes."[23] In such cases, the report said, "murderers have been known to get off with two and three years, and in some cases with six months." White police were not only indifferent to black suffering; they were also "abusive in word and manner" toward black citizens. This caused a vicious cycle: black citizens often refused to cooperate with police, which stymied police investigations, halfhearted to begin with, leaving blacks yet more vulnerable. This description of the problem— dispiritingly similar, in many respects, to accounts of the dysfunctional relationship between police departments and black communities today—led the group to call for hiring black police.[24]

Registering the concerns of Atlanta's black elite, the CIC also argued that black officers would be capable of distinguishing among classes and types of blacks—a skill that white officers conspicuously lacked. Atlanta was home to many upstanding black citizens, but white officers either couldn't or wouldn't appreciate the difference. "Some white officers have no regard for the social standing of colored men or women," the CIC complained. "They use the same language to them [that is, to those of higher standing] as they do in the presence of gamblers and known harlots." Colored police, by contrast, would recognize social distinctions. Just as important, they "would have more respect for their women," and this treatment would have a reciprocal effect, with black officers receiving "more respect from the race."[25]

The case for black police expanded as the Atlanta movement gained strength. In November 1937, the city's branch of the NAACP circulated a pamphlet titled *Wanted: Negro Police for Negro Districts in Atlanta*. Describing black neighborhoods as overrun by crime, lacking adequate public housing and recreational facilities, and resentful of the police, the pamphlet offered three reasons to hire black police officers: they could "interpret Negro problems and Negro people," they would be more effective in enforcing the law without violence, and they would inspire community members to view the police more positively.[26]

By 1947, the *Daily World* was calling the lack of black police the city's top civil rights issue.[27] The Reverend Martin Luther King, Sr., was among the leaders of the campaign to change the city's policy. On September 20, 1947, King urged a crowd at Morehouse College's Sale Hall Chapel to continue the fight. With his son, then a Morehouse senior, almost certainly in attendance, King said that only persistent pressure would remedy the injustice of having a community of 100,000 blacks without a single black police officer to represent them. He eschewed waiting, just as his son would fifteen years later in "Letter from Birmingham Jail." As the *Daily World* noted, King "exhorted the young people to organize and work toward this end, saying that nothing comes through waiting."[28]

Two months after King's speech, with pressure mounting, the Atlanta City Council had no choice but to confront the issue. At a meeting in November 1947—which the *Daily World* called "a heated, rip roaring session that lasted three hours"—King told the council that "the time and the hour" for Negro police had come. As he had done at Morehouse, he argued that the city's black community deserved to be represented on the police force: "Taxation without representation is not right." Other speakers, including the editor of the *Daily World*, C. A. Scott, returned to the CIC's argument from 1936 and said that black police would reduce crime.[29]

Picketing outside the Georgia State Capitol building, demanding police integration, Atlanta, Georgia, 1946 (*Atlanta Journal-Constitution* Photographic Archives, Special Collections and Archives, Georgia State University Library)

The resistance from segregationists was fierce. Supporters of Herman Talmadge, Georgia's notoriously racist former governor, came out against hiring black officers, as did members of the Ku Klux Klan.[30] Echoing Congressman Barksdale's rhetoric from sixty years before, Georgia's Commissioner of Agriculture, Tom Linder, declared that "one race must dominate the other."[31] Former Atlanta mayor Walter A. Sims argued that hiring black officers was pointless, since whites would never obey blacks: "If a white man saw a red traffic signal and a Negro policeman nearby, he would just run the red light."[32]

Two weeks later, on December 1, 1947, the city council met again, this time with a resolution on the table that would require Atlanta's police department to hire eight black officers. More than a thousand whites crowded the chamber to oppose the measure.[33] But despite their vehement protestations, the campaign led by Scott and King finally succeeded: the council voted 10–7 in favor of the resolution.[34] The *Daily World* hailed its passage with the headline "The Long Awaited Dream Comes True."[35]

And yet, the new black officers would be far from equal. The resolution stipulated that they were to be hired on a trial basis, that they would work out of a separate precinct (the basement of the local YMCA), that they would patrol only in black neighborhoods, and that they would not be permitted to exercise police powers over whites.[36] If a black officer witnessed a white person committing a crime, he could detain the offender, but for an arrest, he'd have to call his supervisor and request that a white officer come to the scene.[37]

These restrictions were not atypical. All over the country, black officers were routinely and systematically humiliated in order to remind them of their second-class status and to reassure whites that the racial order remained fundamentally intact. In Savannah, for example, black officers were not allowed to wear their uniforms to or from work. In Montgomery, Alabama, they had to go around to the back door of the police station to pick up and turn in their equipment each day. Segregation was most thorough in Miami, which, until 1962, operated two completely distinct criminal justice systems, one for whites and one for blacks. The latter system had black officers, a black-only police station, and a black judge and bailiff.[38]

Despite the restrictions, Atlanta's black community rejoiced. The new officers were crowned the "Atlanta Eight" and became instant celebrities. Even before they were sworn in, crowds of black Atlantans gathered to see them in training. Hundreds more, including King, crammed into Greater Mt. Calvary Baptist Church to welcome them to active duty. Crowds spilled into the church's basement, annex, and balcony, and finally onto the streets outside. The list of speakers was long—"from the flower bedecked rostrum, speaker after speaker, both Negro and white, delivered stirring remarks in glorification of the city's hiring of Negro officers."[39] When Mayor William Hartsfield spoke, he told the officers that they carried a special burden. "You are more than just policemen," he said. "You are going out as the first representatives of your race in Atlanta. Your success is my success and the success of the City Council, the Chief, your race and the city at large." Invoking the Georgia native Jackie Robinson, who had broken baseball's color line the previous season,

Welcome ceremony for Atlanta's first eight black police officers, Atlanta, Georgia, April 30, 1948 (*Atlanta Journal-Constitution* Photographic Archives, Special Collections and Archives, Georgia State University Library)

Hartsfield urged the Atlanta Eight to "Do the kind of job that Jackie did in Brooklyn."[40]

But what about the officers themselves? What did *they* think of the moment? What were their plans for policing? Nobody knew. Save for a brief response by one of the men on the group's behalf (according to the *Daily World*, he "praised his superiors for their manner of cooperation"), the Atlanta Eight were silent.[41]

As America's black news outlets trumpeted the arrival of the Atlanta Eight, Burtell Jefferson weighed his career options. After graduating from Armstrong, he had entered the Army, serving in the Philippines and New Guinea in World War II. Honorably discharged, he had returned to D.C. and enrolled in Howard University's School of Engineering. But even after receiving some limited benefits from the GI Bill, he had found it difficult to make ends meet, and he left school after less than two years.[42]

The prospects for a black man in D.C. were bleak, and Jefferson knew it. A year earlier, in 1948, President Truman had established a commission to investigate the state of race relations in the nation's capital. The commission's report was damning:

If [a Negro] stops in Washington . . . with very few exceptions, he is refused service at downtown restaurants, he may not attend a downtown movie or play, and he has to go into the poorer section of the city to find a night's lodging. The Negro who decides to settle in the District must often find a home in an overcrowded, substandard area. He must often take a job below the level of his ability. He must send his children to the inferior public schools set aside for Negroes and entrust his family's health to medical agencies which give inferior service. In addition, he must endure the countless daily humiliations that the system of segregation imposes upon the one-third of Washington that is Negro.[43]

No facet of African American life was exempt from the stranglehold of racism. The city even held separate children's marbles competitions, crowning one white and one "colored" champion. In marbles, as was the rule with Jim Crow, separate was never equal: when the city selected its representative for national competitions, only the white champion was considered.[44]

The social effects of segregation were devastating, but the policy's most enduring impact was economic, as generations of black citizens were trapped on the bottom rungs of the occupational ladder.[45] Every sector of the economy was implicated, not just racist employers. For example, the unions that controlled many of the best trade jobs, including those representing brickmakers and electrical workers, either excluded blacks outright or kept them in segregated locals that received inferior assignments.[46] So impenetrable were the walls excluding blacks from skilled-labor jobs that even the tiniest cracks were cause for celebration. In the 1950s, for example, when three black high school graduates—*just three*—were accepted into apprenticeship training programs, an announcement was made at their commencement, eliciting joyful cheers from an audience of six hundred parents.[47] In October 1958, the *Afro* trumpeted another "break-through": The D.C. government was undertaking a new construction project and had hired, among dozens of contractors, a single black electrician.[48]

The federal government was an equally strict enforcer of segregation. One of the worst offenders was the State Department, which promoted American-brand democracy abroad while restricting blacks in the nation's capital to job categories such as chauffeur, messenger, and janitor.[49] Even when blacks gained a toehold in entry-level positions, a caste mentality dominated. One white official recalled how hard it was to integrate the department's typing pool:

> After a great deal of effort, the typing pool finally agreed to take a couple [black typists]. Two or three days later, I asked the pool supervisor how things were coming, and she replied that she had solved the problem completely, that everything was going beautifully. I asked her what she had done, and she showed me a screen in one corner of the big room—behind which the two colored girls were sitting.[50]

And so, as Jefferson prepared to enter D.C.'s apartheid job market, he had few palatable options. As he explained, "the only fields of financial stability available to me were teaching, the United States Postal Service, and the fire and police departments." When he joined the police force, he was not making a political statement in keeping with the passionate campaign of Scott and King down in Atlanta. By his own account, he was far more concerned with making a decent living. Of the fields open to him, he felt that policing would be "the most challenging."[51]

We'll beat them at their own game.

—MPD officer Burtell Jefferson

After World War II, with the struggle to end legally mandated school segregation well under way and the United States seeking to project a positive image of democracy during the early years of the Cold War, it would no longer do to blatantly prohibit blacks from getting jobs (and promotions) in the police department of the nation's capital. But that doesn't mean the system suddenly became egalitarian. Instead, as formally discriminatory policies were erased from the MPD's books, a new system of informal, under-the-table discrimination was implemented in its place. This new system achieved nearly the same results, but through subterfuge and misdirection.

So to say that policing was a possibility for Jefferson does not mean that the job was easy to get. From the moment a black applicant arrived to take the MPD's battery of written, physical, and oral exams, the scrutiny was severe. "It was extremely difficult for Negroes to get on the force," recalled Owen Davis, another black officer from that era. "Many blacks were blocked out of contention because of an ingrown toenail, that kind of thing. What could we do about it? Not much." Davis, like Jefferson, cited limited job opportunities elsewhere as his reason for joining the force. Though he had never wanted to be a police officer, the job paid almost twice as much as his job making mailbags at the post office, and it had better retirement benefits.[52]

Once Jefferson passed the tests and completed the sixteen-week police academy training program, he was posted to the city's Ninth Precinct. The assignment did not come as a surprise. The Ninth was overwhelmingly black, and the city had an informal but rigidly enforced policy of restricting black officers to predominantly black districts.[53] Nor was this the only constraint that black officers faced. For example, as was common practice across America, the MPD limited black officers to foot patrol, barring them from driving scout cars. As Jefferson recalled, "They put cars out of service rather than have blacks drive them."[54]

White officers made up 90 percent of the MPD's force and constituted a majority even in black precincts, including the Ninth.[55] And as Jefferson soon discovered, the police force was as segregated in those black precincts as it was anywhere else in the District. Black and white officers rarely patrolled together. Some commanders were unapologetic in defending segregation—one captain prohibited integrated assignments on the theory that "colored officers are more efficient and more contented when assigned with colored, likewise a white officer when assigned with white."[56] Other commanders used a more subtle "freedom of choice" explanation. For example, the chief of detectives said that he wouldn't stop a black officer and a white officer from working together, but he wouldn't compel it, either: "it would be bad for morale to force someone to work with a partner he was not happy with."[57] This approach was even endorsed by Robert Murray, D.C.'s chief of police, who acknowledged that "integration is the law of the land" without actually making any concessions. "I'm going to obey the law," Murray said, "but I'm not going to force colored and white to work together in a scout car."[58]

Of course, "freedom of choice" was merely a euphemism for de facto segregation, as any white officer could veto an assignment that meant working with a black partner.[59] Unsurprisingly, most white officers exercised this right—and not just in D.C. In 1957, the University of Pennsylvania's William M. Kephart published a study of racial attitudes among Philadelphia's police.[60] The results were dispiriting. The vast majority of white officers supported the department's policies of de facto segregation, with three-quarters asserting that black patrolmen should be assigned exclusively to black neighborhoods.[61] White people, they believed, would object to having black officers in their communities; 60 percent said that they themselves would object to riding in a car with a black partner. Why? The most common objection, Kephart found, was the "so-called body odor of the Negro." "The Negro has sweat glands that give off a choking odor," one officer said. "One time I was assigned with a Negro," recalled another. "I immediately told my sergeant to take me off and put me on sick list." A third told researchers, "Yes, in my estimation they are savages. They have an offensive odor that forty baths a day will not remove. I am also a firm believer in white supremacy."[62]

This endemic racial prejudice, confirmed by similar studies in Boston and Chicago as well as in D.C., affected more than the pairing of officers.[63] In D.C. and elsewhere, promotions were based on rankings, and rankings, in turn, were based on a test score and a "suitability for promotion" rating.[64] (The relative weights of these two determinants varied by city; in D.C., the test counted for 40 percent and the suitability rating for 60 percent.)[65] An officer's suitability rating was assigned by his or her supervisor, presenting an almost unlimited opportunity for both conscious and unconscious bias.[66] And so black patrol officers found themselves stuck: no matter how well they did on the written test, their suitability ratings disqualified them from promotion. These officers weren't naïve; everyone saw the practice for what it was. As the *Afro* put it, "There's a sneaking suspicion that the promotion system of the Metropolitan Police Department was devised by either the devil or Sen. Jim Eastland of Mississippi."[67] But there wasn't much the officers could do.

People respond to oppression in various ways, and one way is to surrender. After Owen Davis made the switch from post office employee to member of D.C.'s finest, it was impossible for him not to notice the inequities plaguing the force. "One effect all this outright discrimination had was it destroyed initiative," he recalled. "Blacks tended not to spend too much time on the [promotion] exams. What the hell. It was too much effort, for no reason."[68] Officers who didn't study would predictably receive lower test scores, and these scores, in turn, provided fodder to those who claimed that the lack of promotions had more to do with black officers' inadequacy than with white supervisors' discrimination. Cue Chief Murray: "[Blacks] won't study and they can't pass the written examinations."[69]

Burtell Jefferson himself was almost a casualty of the MPD's promotion process. In the late 1950s, after taking the test and putting in for advancement, he waited nervously for the promotion list to be posted. He had prepared for the test with his close friend Tilmon O'Bryant. In addition to studying hard, both men had compiled sterling achievement records. They were cautiously hopeful. But the list, when it was finally posted, contained neither of their names. Jefferson was despondent; O'Bryant was furious. "Not only were we not included," O'Bryant remembered, "but some pretty poor white choices got promoted ahead of us, and without even taking the police exams."

Over coffee, the two men talked out their options. They considered quitting the force but ultimately decided against it—the white flag, they felt, was exactly what the racists wanted. So even though surrender would have been understandable, the pair adopted a different strategy. They resolved, in O'Bryant's words, to "destroy the myth that it's no use for a black man to try." As they saw it, their only shot was to outperform whites on the objective measure—the written test for promotion—by a wide enough margin to compensate for low suitability ratings. "We'll figure out every possible question," Jefferson said. "We'll beat them at their own game."[70]

In 1958, Jefferson and O'Bryant started a covert class for black MPD officers seeking promotion. Thirteen officers signed up, in addition to the two in charge. The group met at Jefferson's home two nights a week. At the first meeting, Jefferson laid down the rules. Attendance was mandatory—miss more than two classes and you were expelled—and alcohol was prohibited. After six months of study, Jefferson passed the test with a high enough score to secure a promotion. So did O'Bryant and ten of their thirteen classmates.[71]

The segregationists didn't go quietly. They couldn't block the promotions, but they could try to stop this new black self-help strategy, news of which had gotten out. When the newly promoted Jefferson and O'Bryant decided to continue the classes, some white supervisors began changing days off and switching around tours of duty to make it all but impossible for black candidates to participate. Other white officers created their own study guides and kept them from blacks.[72] But the men persevered: by 1966, *The Washington Post*'s William Raspberry would write: "[M]ost of the Negro officers with rank are products of the O'Bryant-Jefferson 'school.'"[73] For Jefferson, the success vindicated his belief that even in a racist system, blacks could overcome; it just took hard work and self-sacrifice. As he put it, "Blacks *must* assume the attitude that 'you might beat me on the rating, but I'll beat you in the books.'"[74]

> Our police department is the most dangerous spot in the District.
> —Eugene Davidson, D.C. NAACP

Out in the community, D.C.'s black citizens faced a far more dangerous form of police discrimination: excessive violence. Though this kind of abuse was a perennial concern, it assumed greater urgency in 1956, when two black men were killed by the police in separate incidents. One victim, Harrison F. Finley, was a World War II veteran and the father of two young children. He was shot to death in front of his own parents while being arrested on charges of "resisting arrest" and "disorderly conduct." (The former was suspiciously common in cases where the police shot or beat someone; the latter was described by the *Afro* as "a catch-all charge that covers practically everything from talking loud to necking."[75]) The second man, Nelson Marshall, was a Safeway truck driver with five children, shot to death during an arrest for a traffic violation. The officer who killed Marshall was brought to trial but summarily acquitted by an all-white jury (in a city that was almost 50 percent black). Citing these deaths, along with a surge of police brutality complaints from black citizens citywide, the leader of the NAACP's D.C. branch, Eugene Davidson, asserted that "our police department is the most dangerous spot in the District."[76]

Davidson accused Chief Murray of perpetrating two injustices: the MPD discriminated against its black officers, and it routinely used excessive force against the city's black citizens.[77] Though these grievances might appear distinct, Davidson's NAACP branch linked them, arguing that promoting black officers would reduce police brutality. This strategy—claiming that a change in the racial composition of the police force would change something about police behavior—had been employed by advocates in Atlanta a decade earlier when they contended that hiring black officers would help fight crime by offsetting the prevailing apathy among white officers.

Davidson maintained that the shooting deaths of Finley and Marshall were part of a pattern of police misconduct. In 1957, he submitted a scathing report (he called it an exposé) to the D.C. Board of Commissioners and the police chief, recounting stories of appalling abuse. The report also included affidavits from outraged citizens and officers, as well as copies of unanswered complaints the NAACP had already sent to Chief Murray and the board. In one affidavit, a black woman named Blanche Price said she went out one night to a club in Northwest D.C. The owner refused to let her in because a police officer had told the owner that Price had a police record. When Price went in anyway, the officer attempted to drag her out and, while doing so, hit her over the head with his nightstick. When Price fell on the sidewalk, the officer repeatedly beat and kicked her.[78] Later, when she tried to lodge a complaint, the police attempted to intimidate her into silence.[79] Another affidavit came from a retired black policeman who was stopped for a traffic violation. The officer who pulled him over opened the driver's-side door, hit the man in the face, and pulled him

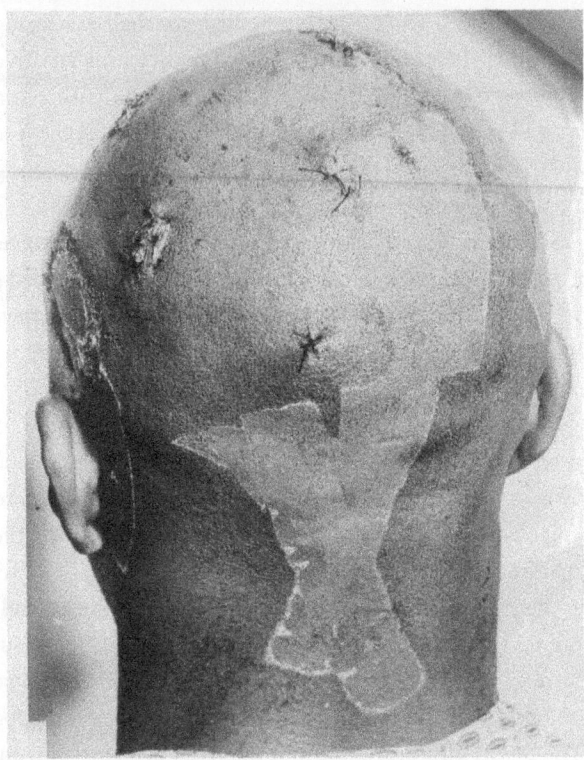

out onto the sidewalk, where he beat him with his fists before arresting him.[80] A black man named Isaac Williams, Jr., submitted documents to show that he was severely beaten about the head by several officers after they had handcuffed him outside his house. In addition to excerpts from his testimony, a photograph was attached to the report.[81]

Alongside the physical violence, black citizens were consistently subjected to verbal disrespect from the very people whose job it was to serve them. (Though less newsworthy than physical violence, this was, and remains, the most common complaint against the police.) As in Atlanta—where, in the 1930s, blacks objected that white officers had "no regard for the social standing of colored men or women"—D.C.'s middle-class blacks did not take kindly to verbal slights.[82] Some complained that white officers had a "plantation system attitude" and couldn't stomach the sight of blacks doing better than they were.[83] One black attorney recalled, "The other day some friends and I were driving in the area of 16th and K Sts. NW. When we stopped for the light, a white policeman told his companion, 'Just look at them spooks in that Cadillac. I can't even afford one.'"[84] In addition to complaining that they were singled out for mistreatment by resentful white officers, middle-class blacks also objected to being implicated in more general antiblack attitudes. As the *Afro* argued, "[S]o long as the color of a person's skin becomes a factor in the enforcement of the law no colored person, *regardless of his station in life*, is free from possible abuse."[85]

After a hearing, however, the Board of Commissioners exonerated Chief Murray, clearing his department of all allegations of brutality against black citizens and workplace discrimination against black officers.[86] Davidson had lost his case. The NAACP had expected this outcome[87]—the Board of Commissioners was not a group the city's blacks relied on to dispense justice. The commissioners were, after all, beholden to Congress, many of whose members shared the views of Theodore Bilbo, the Mississippi senator who in 1948 had boasted that he chaired the congressional committee overseeing D.C. because it allowed him to "keep Washington a segregated city."[88] Bilbo's comment lent force to complaints like those from Sterling Tucker, the Urban League president and future D.C. Council chair, who said, "We have the anomalous situation where America's only predominantly Negro city is ruled by enemies of the Negro. It's almost as if the United Nations had sent the South Africans to run the Congo."[89]

Under such hostile conditions, there was no shame in losing. As the *Afro* summed up the situation, "The NAACP has no apologies to make for its honest efforts to protect the interests of the defenseless who turn to them for guidance and relief. When you lose in a good clean fight, the only question left is: 'When do we fight again?'"[90]

The answer: Very soon.

Stick to police work and leave the race relations business to the experts.

—*The Washington Afro-American*

In the summer of 1963, hundreds of thousands of civil rights activists planned to join the March on Washington for Jobs and Freedom, which many predicted would be the biggest demonstration in the District's history. The freedom movement was sweeping the country, exposing racial discrimination in all corners of American life, and the nation's police departments were increasingly coming under scrutiny. One 1959 study revealed that 83 percent of southern departments restricted black officers to segregated districts, and that in most cities, black officers could not arrest whites.[91] In 1961, a U.S. Civil Rights Commission report found that 31 percent of the nation's police departments restricted the ability of black officers to arrest a white person suspected of a felony. Most of these departments required their black officers to hold suspects until a white policeman arrived to make the actual arrest; in a few cases, black officers were prohibited even from doing that. And across the country, their authority to make misdemeanor arrests was even more limited.[92]

Meanwhile, the abuse black citizens faced from the police was unrelenting. Brutality was on especially vivid display in the South, where scenes of cigar-chomping sheriffs attacking civil rights protesters with water hoses and dogs became regular fodder for the nightly news. In the early 1960s, civil rights groups charged that police corruption and abuse were rampant throughout the country: the police still routinely arrested suspects without warrants and held them with little or no cause. When asked, many blacks conceded that they felt powerless to respond. In 1966, a nationwide study validated their fear, finding that police officers were almost never convicted or punished in the aftermath of abuse allegations.[93]

Against this backdrop, the March on Washington presented a perfect opportunity for civil rights activists to press the case for more black police. Throughout the spring and summer of 1963, the *Afro* ran headlines such as "D.C. Needs More Colored Cops in Top Jobs to Fight Crime, Says Lawson" and "Crisis in the D.C. Police Dept.: One Reason Crime Is Rising."[94] Chuck Stone, a civil rights journalist and *Afro* editor, argued that discriminatory employment practices fueled crime by undermining black support for law enforcement. "The unvarnished truth about the District Police Department," he wrote, "is that it is saturated with more white policemen full of racial antipathy than many Deep South cities." The vast majority of white officers were "intellectually, emotionally and ancestrally incapable of treating colored people equally or with respect." Effective crime control depended on mutual respect and cooperation between officers and citizens, Stone wrote. But the District police, as constituted, would never earn black people's respect, since they were unwilling or unable to bestow it.[95]

As the day of the march approached, even the city's historically conservative black business organization, the D.C. Chamber of Commerce, joined the call for the promotion of a black officer to the rank of captain.[96] The chamber's president, Jesse Dedmon, Jr., met with Chief Murray and advised him that having a black captain in the MPD would "give the country and the world a better image of the police department in the Capital of the democracies of the world." Dedmon added that "it is important to our youth for them to know that it is possible for Negroes to achieve the higher echelons of the police department."

Dissent came from an unlikely source: Tilmon O'Bryant, the black officer—now lieutenant—who had co-organized those covert classes for black officers. In a statement to the press, O'Bryant expressed his gratitude for the activists' attention and support, and acknowledged that, were their campaign to achieve its goal, he would very likely stand to benefit. Nevertheless, he opposed the effort, objecting to the activists' overtly racial appeal for the promotion of black officers. O'Bryant still believed in the importance of police integration, but in what amounted to an early critique of affirmative action, he warned that any attempt to integrate police departments must "reject favoritism." The *Afro* pushed back, arguing that "it would have been better

for all concerned had Lieut. O'Bryant remained silent on the issue."
The *Afro* concluded, "Our advice to Lieut. O'Bryant is to stick to police work and leave the race relations business to the experts."[97]

The dispute between the *Afro* and O'Bryant probably made little
difference. Chief Murray was never going to be pressured into promoting a black officer to the rank of captain. He was an obstinate man,
and his racial views—to put it delicately—resisted evolution. That same
year, upon learning that a white commander had integrated his precinct's squad cars, Murray called him in for counseling.[98]

But the *Afro*-O'Bryant disagreement was significant as an early sign
of emerging challenges. For decades, civil rights activists and black
officers had seemed to have a rock-solid alliance predicated on mutual
interest. The activists who fought to integrate American policing typically believed that police work was central to the "race relations business," and they saw their effort in support of black police as an integral
part of their broader struggle for racial equality. But now the *Afro* was
implying that "police work" and "the race relations business" were
separate domains.

The problem ran deeper than intellectual incoherence. There was
also the matter of the paper's condescension toward O'Bryant and, by
extension, toward black officers generally. Previously, black police officers had been irrefutable heroes in the black community, held up by
activists as pioneers and role models. (Recall the celebration of the Atlanta Eight.) Indeed, for fifty years, the outside game had fit hand in
glove with the inside one. Pressure from civil rights activists—Martin
Luther King, Sr., the NAACP's Eugene Davidson, the *Afro*'s Chuck
Stone—had complemented the striving of insiders like Burtell Jefferson and Tilmon O'Bryant. But differences in strategy had suddenly
appeared, and the *Afro*'s response was to treat O'Bryant less as a dis-
senting colleague than as a delinquent subordinate. The paper's political goals may have been diametrically opposed to those of white
supremacists, but its tone was eerily similar: O'Bryant needed to
shut up and stay in his place.

The condescension was rooted in class. Those who fought for the hiring of black police occupied one stratum of black society; those who actually became officers occupied another. Eugene Davidson, for example, graduated from Harvard College and Howard University School of Law; Chuck Stone had a degree from Wesleyan.[99] By contrast, Burtell Jefferson's highest degree was his diploma from Armstrong Technical High School, and Tilmon O'Bryant had dropped out of Armstrong in the ninth grade.[100] Of course, education is not the only marker of social class, but in black America it's an especially important one. This was nowhere truer than in D.C., where the sizable black middle class (and smaller black upper middle class) had long drawn distinctions that were invisible to whites but clear to blacks. "It was a segregated city among blacks," said Calvin Rolark, who started *The Washington Informer*, which would become the city's second-most widely read black newspaper. "Lighter-skinned blacks didn't associate with the darker blacks, and the Howard University blacks didn't associate with anyone."[101] So when the *Afro* told O'Bryant to be mindful of his station and leave race relations "to the experts," black readers couldn't miss the message.

> Black policemen do not shoot black jay walkers.
>
> —*Afro-American* columnist John Lewis

On October 8, 1968, Elijah Bennett was walking near the intersection of Fourteenth and U Streets, in the heart of black D.C., when he was shot by MPD officer David Roberts. Not much is known about the interaction beyond the following: Bennett was a black man, Roberts a white one; Bennett was jaywalking; Roberts shouted for him to get out of the street; a dispute ensued; Roberts fired his pistol, and Bennett was killed.[102]

Bennett's death (like the deaths of Harrison Finley, Nelson Marshall, and, almost half a century later, Michael Brown and Eric Garner) provoked outrage and raised broad questions about the relationship between metropolitan police forces and the black citizens they were theoretically supposed to protect. For *Afro* columnist John Lewis (no relation to the civil rights leader), the outrage sprang from the fact that Bennett's offense was jaywalking: few infractions are more trivial than walking in the street when you should be in a crosswalk. As Lewis saw it, the altercation was emblematic of a deep systemic failure. To understand how an unarmed black jaywalker could end up dead, he argued, it was essential to see that white officers treated black neighborhoods as the "wild west." As a result of this mentality, the white cop believed that he "must always 'get his man and bring him back alive or dead,' regardless of the magnitude of the alleged crime." On top of that, Lewis wrote, white officers had a macho mentality that made them ashamed to call for backup, even as a strategy for de-escalating tensions and resolving the conflict with less-than-deadly force. Lewis's solution? Change the racial composition of the police force. A killing like this "would not have occurred," he wrote, "if the Washington police force was not permitted to patrol the so-called ghetto streets like a foreign occupation army and leave the city to go back to their snow white suburban homes." Black cops would make a difference, Lewis concluded, because "[b]lack policemen do not shoot black jay walkers."[103]

Lewis's piece was published in 1968, at the height of the civil rights revolution, and one part of this revolution was the spread of campaigns for the hiring of black police. In the past, such campaigns had largely taken the form of prolonged efforts waged by the black elite, but now a new pattern had emerged. Across the country, ordinary black civilians were actively protesting their treatment at the hands of the police. These protests often turned violent, and when the unrest ended, the demand for more black police was often at the top of the black community's reform agenda. In Harlem in 1964, for example, a white New York Police Department (NYPD) lieutenant shot and killed James Powell, a fifteen-year-old black boy, exacerbating the long-simmering animosity between the majority-black community and the majority-white police force that patrolled it. For six consecutive nights, the neighborhood was seized with violent protests. Harlem's congressional representative, Adam Clayton Powell, Jr., provided Mayor Robert F. Wagner, Jr., with a list of demands that included the immediate assignment of a black police captain to Harlem.[104] The demand wasn't new, but the unrest forced the city's hand. On August 14, 1964, Lloyd Sealy became Harlem's first black precinct captain.[105]

The next year it was Watts, a majority-black neighborhood in Los Angeles, that erupted in riots. A white California Highway Patrol officer stopped a black man for reckless driving. The suspect survived the encounter, but there were allegations of excessive force during the arrest. Word of the incident spread through the neighborhood, and soon Watts was in flames. The death and destruction were horrific: 34 dead, more than 1,000 injured, almost 4,000 arrested, and $40 million in property damage.[106]

As in Harlem, long-suppressed issues were forced to the surface—and once again, police racism loomed large. Watts was two-thirds black, yet its police precinct had only seven black officers on its 205-person force.[107] And those black officers, like their counterparts everywhere else, faced rampant workplace discrimination.[108] Los Angeles's leading black newspaper, the *Sentinel*, assumed the same position as D.C.'s *Afro* and Harlem's *Amsterdam News*: its pages became a bullhorn for change. The paper described black citizens' "bitter resentment" of the police and claimed that this resentment was at the heart of the recent violence. It was 1965, the *Sentinel* pointed out, yet the Los Angeles Police Department (LAPD) did not have a single black captain.[109]

In the riots' aftermath, the calls for more black officers grew in both number and volume. NAACP executive secretary Roy Wilkins cited "police problems" as a major cause of what had happened in Watts; he "urged more Negro policemen on the force, an expanded public relations program and more promotions of Negro officers."[110] At a particularly well-attended Los Angeles Police Commission meeting in 1966, everyone seemed to have an opinion about the reforms that were needed. The Ministers Council of Watts proposed increasing the number of integrated patrol cars and installing a black captain in

Watts; the 82nd Street Improvement Club suggested abolishing the oral test for new recruits on the grounds that it discriminated against black applicants; and the Commission on Human Relations called for racial integration of the LAPD's top echelons.[111]

By the late 1960s, black citizens were not the only ones pushing for more black officers: white officials at the highest levels of government had joined the fight. The most prominent call for black officers came from President Lyndon Johnson's Commission on Law Enforcement and Administration of Justice, chaired by Attorney General Nicholas Katzenbach.[112] In *The Challenge of Crime in a Free Society*, the commission concluded that "the relationship between the police and the community is so personal that every section of the community has a right to expect that its aspirations and problems, its hopes and fears, are fully reflected in its police."[113] One or two token black officers was not enough: "If there is not a substantial percentage of Negro officers among the policemen in a Negro neighborhood, many residents will reach the conclusion that the neighborhood is being policed, not for the purpose of maintaining law and order, but for the purpose of maintaining the ghetto's status quo."[114]

In 1968, the Kerner Commission—known formally as the National Advisory Commission on Civil Disorders and convened to address the riots and violence devastating American cities—would reach the same conclusion. The racial disparities in police departments were stark and undeniable: in the twenty-eight departments that provided data, blacks made up just 6 percent of the workforce, even though the cities were, on average, 24 percent black.[115] The commission approvingly cited the testimony of Patrick V. Murphy, the reform-minded police leader who had recently been appointed D.C.'s director of public safety. "One of the serious problems facing the police in the nation today," Murphy said, "is the lack of adequate representation of Negroes in police departments. I think the police have not recruited enough Negroes in the past and are not recruiting enough of them today."[116]

Black nationalists, who typically had little good to say about the Johnson administration, seconded the Katzenbach and Kerner com-

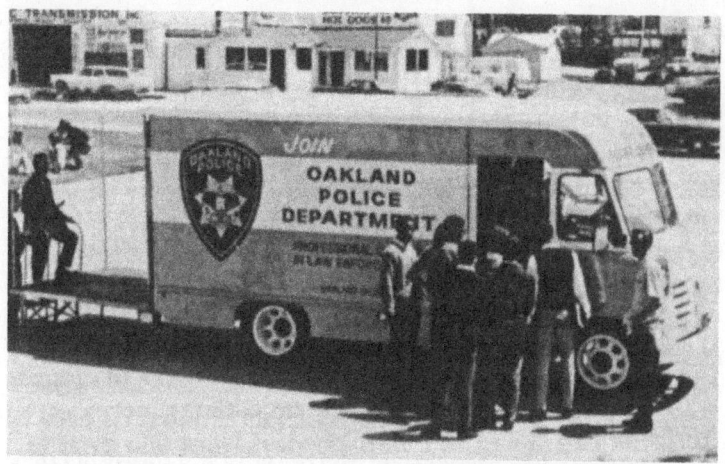

Mobile Recruiting Station, Oakland, California, 1967 (President's Commission on Law Enforcement and Administration of Justice, *The Challenge of Crime in a Free Society*, 1967)

missions' calls for more black officers. D.C.'s Black United Front (BUF), whose leadership included not only Stokely Carmichael but also future city council members Doug Moore and Sterling Tucker, developed a police reform platform that demanded the "immediate prohibition of all-white police patrols in the Black community."[117] Other planks called on the city to "cease all promotions in the Police Department and up-grade present Black policemen" and "fire Police Chief John Layton immediately and replace him with a Black man."[118] The BUF believed that the black community should be policed exclusively by black offi-cers; white officers, they wrote, "should be assigned downtown direct-ing traffic and helping old ladies to cross the street."[119]

Marion Barry, the future mayor of D.C., joined the effort. Barry's disdain for the MPD was well known—as he said at a news conference in 1966, back when he was an organizer for the D.C. chapter of SNCC, "The people in this city are tired of Gestapo cops who break into their homes illegally and arrest them on flimsy charges."[120] Barry believed that only black control of the police would change how the department treated D.C.'s black citizens. In 1969, he became even more determined: when a confrontation with a police officer over a parking ticket turned physical, Barry was hospitalized. After spending part of the night in the hospital and the rest of it in jail, he emerged to find a crowd of three hundred citizens who had gathered to protest his arrest. With dried blood on his shirt and a bandage on his head, Barry told the crowd: "This shows me that the black people need to control the nation's capital police department. The police are like mad dogs."[121]

So it came as no surprise that when D.C. began a major police recruiting campaign on black radio stations, Barry became its public voice. He took to the airwaves, offering $50 to anyone who referred a candidate to the force (provided that the candidate passed the MPD's entrance exams).[122] The campaign paid off: in 1976, a survey of D.C.'s black police found that 30 percent of the officers had heard about the job from the radio.[123]

Barry's on-air appeals were part of a national trend. In Michigan, Bill Cosby recorded ads and visited the state numerous times to recruit black officers (Detroit, at the time, was 45 percent black, with a police force that was only 12 percent black).[124] In Philadelphia, billboards urged residents to "cop in, don't cop out," and to "join [Police Commissioner Frank] Rizzo's team."[125] Recruitment efforts reached all the way to Vietnam, where the U.S. Navy's in-house newspaper ran ads featuring Bunker Bunny, a bikini-clad model. "Hey big fella," she beckoned, "bet you didn't know that gals like me are big on the fuzz, did you? Well, it's true. We all dig those handsome brutes in blue who sport the shiny silver badges in big cities like Washington, D.C."[126]

I'm not their soul brother or friend, I'm a policeman.

—Officer, Prince George's County, Maryland

The warning signs came early, but few paid attention. As the recruitment effort took root, evidence emerged that black officers might have a more limited impact than many had hoped. The most im-

Police Captain Tilmon O'Bryant hangs a recruiting poster announcing
police examinations to be given in predominantly black neighborhoods.
(D.C. Public Library)

portant reason for the disappointment was this: blacks who joined
police departments had a far more complicated set of attitudes, motivations, and incentives than those pushing for black police had assumed.
The case for black police had always been premised on the unques-
tioned assumption of racial solidarity between black citizens and
black officers. Whether it was Rev. King declaring that black police
would "represent" the race or *Afro* columnist John Lewis asserting that
"black policemen do not shoot black jay walkers," advocates had supposed that black officers would, at the very least, *identify* with the populations they policed.

But what if King and Lewis were wrong?

Unfortunately, there was reason to think they just might have been.
In San Diego and Philadelphia, for example, black citizens were hostile

to black officers, contending that those officers were as harsh as or harsher than white ones.[127] Researchers who had ridden with both black and white officers corroborated that belief, concluding that the black officers were just as physically abusive as their white counterparts.[128] Even in the Katzenbach commission's *The Challenge of Crime in a Free Society*, the clarion call for more black police was accompanied by a detailed report noting that "in some places, low-income Negroes prefer white policemen because of the severe conduct of Negro officers."[129]

It turned out that a surprising number of black officers simply didn't like other black people—at least not the poor blacks they tended to police. In 1966, the University of Michigan's Donald Black and Albert Reiss led a team of researchers who rode or walked for weeks with black and white officers in Boston, Chicago, and Washington, D.C. What they found was disturbing: though black officers were not *as* prejudiced as white ones, a significant minority of black officers still expressed antiblack attitudes. The researchers classified 28 percent of the black officers working in black precincts as "highly prejudiced" or "prejudiced."[130] Many of these black officers sounded like Klansmen. One told the researchers, "I'm talking to you as a Negro, and I'm telling you these people are savages. And they're real dirty. We were never rich, but my mother kept us and our home clean." Another said, "There have always been jobs for Negroes, but the f—— people are too stupid to go out and get an education. They all want the easy way out."[131]

Of course, most black officers didn't share those views. But even those who saw themselves as pro-black (or at least not as antiblack) engaged in aggressive tactics against black citizens whom they saw as a threat to law and order. In part, their conduct reflected class divisions within the black community. When some blacks (usually middle class) demanded action against others (usually poor), many "pro-black" officers responded with special enthusiasm. This is what James D. Bannon and G. Marie Wilt found in 1973, when they studied black officers in Detroit. Bannon and Wilt wanted to know how blacks on the force compared themselves to their white colleagues. Without exception, the black officers believed they had better rapport with black citizens and did a better job in black neighborhoods than white officers did. They cared more about black communities; in particular, they were more concerned about protecting black neighborhoods from crime, violence, drugs, and disorder. So while they were less likely than whites to use excessive force (at least according to their reports to the researchers), these officers freely admitted to being markedly more aggressive about responding to such low-level infractions as drunkenness and loitering.[132]

Other research indicated that a form of black pride was at the heart of aggressive policing. In Kephart's 1957 study of Philadelphia's police force, black officers indicated that they were embarrassed by black offenders. When asked, "Do you ever get discouraged at the large amount of Negro crime?" one officer responded:

> I feel it personally. I was coming home in the streetcar the other day—I was in street clothes. Across the aisle a colored man and a white man were sitting together. The colored man was drunk—he was pushing all over the white man, knocking his packages off his lap—just wouldn't stop. Finally, I couldn't stand it any longer. Everybody was watching. I felt it was a reflection on me—know what I mean?[133]

A black NYPD officer expressed a similar sentiment to researcher Nicholas Alex as he described his interaction with a young black suspect:

> I wanted to give this kid a lesson in civil rights. I take him into the precinct and take my gun off and tell him that I will beat the living hell out of him. He starts to cry and tells me that he doesn't fight his race. I tell him that doesn't he know that he is killing his race by doing things like that.[134]

A few black officers rejected the notion that race was at all relevant to the performance of their duties. As an officer in the D.C. suburb of Prince George's County, Maryland, said, "Sometimes we'll be cruising down a street, and a group of black teenagers will yell, 'Hey, soul brother!' So I get out and explain that I'm not their soul brother or their friend, I'm a policeman."[135]

The notion that black officers would represent the race, or treat black citizens differently, ran into another problem as well. For many black officers, as early as the 1960s, the question of being pro-black or antiblack was beside the point. They were not joining the force with dreams of becoming a warrior for (or against) the race. They were signing up because they needed a job.[136]

When Nicholas Alex interviewed hundreds of black NYPD officers in 1964 and 1965, they couldn't have been clearer about their motivations. Police work was a good job—stable, secure, with good benefits— and most blacks chose it for that reason. One black officer told Alex, "I was broke. I can't honestly recall any grandiose dreams of being a big fellow in blue." Another said, "I looked around for the highest paying nonprofessional civil service job available. I took the test for the police, fire, sanitation and correction. I passed all the tests, and the police was the first I was called for."[137]

These explanations would have been familiar to officers like Burtell Jefferson, Tilmon O'Bryant, and Owen Davis, who had faced a Jim Crow job market. There were fewer employment barriers for blacks by the late 1960s and 1970s, but they had hardly disappeared. The stability of a police job was especially appealing to blacks trying to navigate an uncertain and often discriminatory private-sector job market. As one officer told Alex, "I couldn't take the layoffs. I had a wife and a baby to support." The officer pointed out that policing came with another perk—the chance to rise in the force. "The police job is the best job I ever had in terms of much more money," he said, "and much more opportunity for advancement." Another said, "You can plan on your income because it's steady. Prior to this job . . . I had nine or ten small jobs. They would lay you off. You went from one job to another. Small jobs and not very steady."[138]

Not only did police work look good by comparison with the rest of the job market; for most officers, it was a step up from what their parents had achieved. As Eugene Beard found when he studied the backgrounds of black D.C. officers in the early 1970s, most black officers were both better educated and better paid than their parents. The most common father's occupation listed by the black officers was unskilled laborer.[139]

There is nothing wrong with seeing policing as a source of stable employment or upward mobility. But the fact that so many blacks joined the force for these reasons undermined the theory that integration would change police practice. After all, most new black officers saw policing as a job, not as another front in the civil rights movement. Expecting them to change how police fought crime was like expecting black firefighters to change how the fire department fought fire. At the same time, the limited job market for black officers made it less likely that they would do what many reformers hoped they would: buck the famously powerful police culture. The few who tried paid a high price.[140] Finally, although police work paid decently, it didn't make the officers rich, and maintaining wages and benefits was a constant political struggle. These realities would influence which battles black police—and their unions—took up in the 1980s and beyond. Even those black officers inclined to use their political capital to fight police brutality would often find themselves in the minority. Most of their colleagues—black or white—wanted to fight for wages, benefits, and an equal shot at promotions.

Burtell Jefferson was sworn in as chief on January 13, 1978. The exceedingly brief ceremony—only five minutes—was in keeping with Jefferson's understated persona, but it offered little opportunity to reflect on the day's significance: D.C.'s first black mayor handing the reins of law enforcement to its first black police chief. Indeed, Mayor Walter Washington never mentioned race during the ceremony.[141] Perhaps he thought that the symbolism was too self-evident and powerful for words.[142]

Jefferson had struggled for three decades against unfair hiring and promotion practices, and his most impressive accomplishment as a young officer was the study class that led to his own promotion. Jefferson never forgot his up-by-bootstraps history, not even as chief, and he was determined to remedy the decades of discrimination as best he could. As he put it later, "I hoped to provide growth opportunities previously denied to African Americans and other minorities to make them ready to replace me as chief or capable of becoming chiefs in other departments."[143]

Since black officers already constituted the majority of new recruits by the time he took over in 1978, Jefferson tackled the promotion process, the last barrier to black advancement. His stance was exceedingly popular among the MPD's black officers, a majority of whom listed career advancement as their top concern in a 1974 survey.[144] Nearly every officer who responded to the survey had identified the small number of black supervisors as a major problem. Even though the department had begun recruiting more black officers, two-thirds of the respondents to the 1974 survey said they trusted few or no whites on the force, and even greater majorities claimed they faced discrimination in work assignments and promotions.[145]

Luckily, Jefferson had the benefit of a favorable political environment. Many black police leaders had faced tremendous obstacles in bringing about the hiring and promotion of a nontrivial number of black officers; Jefferson, on the other hand, was able to work with a black mayor and a majority-black city council that unanimously endorsed affirmative action.[146] The former SNCC activist and gun control advocate John Wilson was especially tireless, using council oversight hearings to demand that the department move faster to close racial disparities in the supervisory ranks.[147]

And so Jefferson succeeded. Isaac Fulwood, who became D.C.'s police chief in 1989 and later served as head of the U.S. Parole Commission, called Jefferson "the all time affirmative action person." He "broke it wide open," said Fulwood, who credited Jefferson for his own success: "I stood upon Jefferson's shoulders. He blessed me with opportunities that were previously denied to us." Fulwood was not alone: more than twenty senior black police leaders, including chiefs in Atlanta, D.C., New Orleans, Charlotte, and Maryland's Prince George's County, can trace their careers back to Burtell Jefferson.[148]

But that's where the celebration ends.

Throughout the twentieth century, America's metropolitan police forces were collectively the targets of two distinct campaigns for racial equality: those that sought to end discrimination *within* police forces, and those that sought to end brutality and discrimination *by* police against the black community. Ultimately, in practice, these goals were often unrelated. While Jefferson proudly grabbed the baton from the previous two generations of activists who had campaigned for equality within the ranks of the MPD, and even as he fulfilled those activists' wildest dreams on that day in 1978 when he became chief, he assumed a harsh stance when it came to responding to crime in poor urban areas. Unfortunately, this part of Jefferson's agenda would cause great damage to the black community.

During an interview for a profile celebrating his swearing-in ceremony, Jefferson told an ominous story. Once, as a child, he'd been hanging around near a group of other black boys, and all of them got picked up by a white police officer. The other kids had been shooting dice, but Jefferson had merely been playing with a football. Still, the officer took him home to his parents.

What did Jefferson make of the incident almost fifty years later? He could have wondered why the officer had picked up an innocent kid in the first place. He could have asked whether policing looked the same in white neighborhoods. These would not have been revolutionary questions; they'd been on the table for more than a century. As far back as 1887, *The Washington Bee* had complained that prejudiced white policemen "take a great delight in arresting every little colored boy they see on the street, who may be doing something not at all offensive, and allow the white boys to do what they please."[149]

But no: the moral Jefferson drew from this story was *not* that the white officer had been wrong to pick him up, but that he, the football-tossing black boy, had deserved it. "I've always been taught," he said, "that if you yourself are not actually engaged in some wrong-doing, if you're with a crowd you're just as guilty."[150]

Any doubts about where Jefferson stood on matters of criminal punishment would be put to rest shortly thereafter, when he was faced with a decision about whether to support mandatory minimum sentences for drug and gun offenses. This debate, the subject of chapter 4, would divide the city and ultimately be resolved by voters in a citywide ballot initiative in 1981. But Jefferson was not conflicted: he was a staunch supporter of the legislation to toughen criminal penalties. In a letter to the city council, he said that mandatory minimum penalties for drug selling would "serve as a deterrent and weapon against drug sellers in the battle to rid this city of illicit drugs."[151]

In his support for mandatory minimums, Jefferson was acting in line with what most black cops wanted. In 1970, the National Council of Police Societies, the largest and oldest national organization of black police officers, urged its members to "move against pushers and others who sell" drugs.[152] D.C.'s rank-and-file officers supported tougher sentencing in general; in a 1976 survey, they reported lenient sentencing by judges as their top concern.[153]

Two years before Jefferson's historic promotion, at the conference of black law enforcement officials, the attendees abruptly voted to dispense with the rest of their agenda and dedicate their time to chartering a brand-new organization: the National Organization of Black Police Executives (NOBLE).[154] The move was evidence of the progress they had made: there were now enough black police executives to warrant the creation of a formal group.

For their founding document, NOBLE's members produced a list of policy recommendations for fighting crime. To be fair, the executives joined many of America's other black leaders in calling for root-cause solutions to crime, including socioeconomic reform and a health-care overhaul. But they also demanded "a nationwide war on drugs" and—yes—"minimum mandatory sentencing."[155]

In one respect, the century-long fight for police integration had succeeded. Its victory brought a prominent new set of voices to American criminal justice policy: those of the nation's dozens of black police chiefs. But many of these voices would propel, not constrain, an emerging tough-on-crime movement.

# PART II

## Consequences

# 4

# "LOCKING UP THUGS IS NOT VINDICTIVE"
## Sentencing, 1981–82

"How long have you been a lawyer?" Tasha Willis's question, posed at our first meeting, was a fair one, even if I was not eager to answer it. Ms. Willis had been assigned to me in 1996, the day after I advanced to Felony II Low, a docket consisting mostly of drug-selling and gun possession cases. My promotion was hardly dazzling: lawyers at the D.C. Public Defender Service (PDS) rose automatically, on a fixed calendar. Our first year was in juvenile court, our second was in adult misdemeanors, and then we moved to lower-level felony cases like Ms. Willis's. So when I answered her question—"I've been practicing for two years now"—her face fell. I could see that my limited experience was of little comfort.[1]

But no matter her doubts, Ms. Willis was stuck with me. As with all our clients, she was unable to afford a "paid lawyer," the term our clients invariably used to refer to private counsel. When this label was used, the word "paid" was often drawn out, in part unconsciously, owing to southern influences on D.C. speech, but also in part deliberately, to emphasize the grandeur of any lawyer who could demand a fee. We public defenders, by contrast, had a rather less glamorous reputation. Movies and television shows portrayed us as overworked, inefficient, and, worst of all, resigned, freely provided by the government yet woefully unable to help. But PDS had been established in the 1960s to serve as a national model of indigent defense, and my colleagues and I refused to fit the media stereotype: we cared down to our toes about the inequities of the criminal justice system. We were prepared to devote our days, nights, and weekends to our clients. If anything, we used our low status as motivation. "The best representation money can't buy," we'd say around the office, joking only in tone.

Ms. Willis didn't know any of this, and her low expectations gave me the opportunity to surprise. "Our clients have always gotten the worst of everything," a senior lawyer had told my cohort of ten new lawyers during training two years earlier. "Bad teachers. Dismissive social workers. Crap housing. No jobs or shitty jobs." We were in the PDS conference room that day, a dilapidated space in the bowels of a mostly abandoned courthouse. (When my mom visited our office, she surveyed the peeling paint, frayed carpets, and walls covered with left-leaning posters and said, "I love it. Reminds me of SNCC.") Our trainer continued, "And now you come along. Of course they will assume the worst!" There were murmurs of assent throughout the room. "But they deserve better. They deserve what society has *never* offered, not one single time. And your job is to give them that, to give them what any of us would want if we had a loved one facing trial— your job is to give them *the best*." Yes, yes, yes, I thought, joining my classmates in pounding our desks in agreement.

The speech worked: I left training ready to run through walls for my clients. But when I visited Ms. Willis in her basement apartment a few months after I took her case, it seemed as if hard work wouldn't be enough. She had been arrested after an undercover officer, approaching her on the corner of Seventh and T Streets, had purchased $10 worth of heroin with a specially marked bill. After leaving the corner, the officer identified Ms. Willis to a uniformed colleague, who made the arrest and brought her to jail. The prosecution's evidence was certainly damning—when the police searched Ms. Willis, they found the marked bill. She knew she needed a good lawyer, and I couldn't help but feel discouraged by her initial disappointment at my novice status. But the thing that really got me down—that made me fear my best would not be good enough—was the sentence Ms. Willis now faced.

When I started working as a public defender, in the fall of 1994, I would occasionally ask friends, family members, or even people I had just met at a party to guess how much prison time a person might serve for a particular crime. "What should the maximum sentence be," I would begin, "for selling a small amount of a hard drug, like heroin or cocaine?" Most answers fell somewhere between probation and a few months in jail; even my strictest respondents advocated a year of incarceration, two at the most. In each case, after receiving an answer, I would motion upward with my thumb, again and again, until the number strained, broke, and moved far beyond the limits of reason. For a first-time offender, D.C. law stipulated a maximum of thirty years in prison. For someone with a prior conviction—someone like Ms. Willis, who, five years before, had been caught selling $20 worth of heroin—a guilty verdict could mean up to sixty years behind bars.[2] Whomever I was speaking to would invariably be shocked—but then, after an uncomfortable silence, someone would introduce a more upbeat topic. To those I cornered at parties, D.C.'s sentencing system may have been appalling, but it was still just a thought experiment, not a tangible reality.

With Ms. Willis, however, there was nothing abstract about our talk. She was in her mid-forties, so the sixty-year maximum sentence for selling a $10 bag of heroin would amount to life in prison. We were sitting in her kitchen, where she was making beef stew. I accepted her offer of a bowl, and it was delicious, but I didn't eat enough to satisfy her. "Attorney Forman, you need to eat; no woman is going to want a skinny man." I had known this was coming. Ms. Willis was only about fifteen years older than I was, but she invariably had motherly advice to offer.

We laughed for a bit about my food choices—she was appalled to learn that I thought rice and beans plus salad constituted dinner—but before long we had to turn to a graver topic. I had come to explain the government's offer: if Ms. Willis pleaded guilty to an attempted heroin distribution charge, the prosecutor would cap allocution at five years (i.e., the prosecutor would recommend that the judge impose no more than a five-year sentence with the possibility of parole). Though judges were not bound by these suggestions, the judge assigned to our case was known to go along with the government's recommendations.

Ms. Willis wanted to know whether I thought this was a good deal. I said yes, because a trial would be risky, and if we lost, the consequences would be severe. Of course, not even D.C.'s harshest judge would assign the full sixty years for a case like this—but still, every so often a judge did go ballistic on some poor soul. Ten- and fifteen-year sentences were rare, but not unheard of, in low-level drug cases involving repeat offenders.

When I was done with my spiel, Ms. Willis sat quietly, looking not at me but at the white wall behind me. It was a longer silence than I was comfortable with. But just as I was about to ask her if she understood or if she had questions, she leaned forward and looked me square in the eye and said, "I don't want *that* plea offer. I want a better one." I started to respond that this was the best deal I could get, but Ms. Willis shook her head quickly, almost as if she knew what I was going to say before it came out of my mouth. "Tell the prosecutor, or the judge, or whoever," she continued, "that I don't need to go to jail." Her voice was firm and free of doubt. "Attorney Forman, tell them I can't leave my mom for five years. Tell them I need a drug program." Ms. Willis didn't lower her eyes when she was done speaking. It was clear that she wasn't *asking* me to do anything. She was telling me. As I listened to her, I couldn't help but think that in a different world, she would have made an excellent attorney herself.

But I doubted her speech would work as well in the prosecutor's office as it did in her kitchen. It's not that I thought she was wrong— according to her court records and personal statements, she was most definitely an addict. The problem was that I had already told all this to the prosecutor. Her name was Bernice Lester, and she was one of the good ones, a friendly African American woman who had been in her job only slightly longer than I had been in mine. Nine months earlier, in a different case, Bernice had used her discretion to permit one of my clients to avoid prison and enter a diversion program.

This time, in her office just a few blocks from PDS, Bernice had listened to my pitch as I described Ms. Willis's pathway to addiction. Ms. Willis had worked for the post office before suffering a serious back injury when she tried to lift a package meant for two to carry. No matter how much pain medicine she took, it never seemed enough, and over time she became hooked on pills and, eventually, heroin. She lost her job and fell deeper and deeper into her addiction.

As I was finishing my appeal, Bernice looked through the stack of case folders on her desk, found the one marked *United States v. Tasha Willis*, and promptly shook her head. "No," she said, skimming the first page in the file, "I just can't. My office won't do it—she's got priors and already had two chances at drug programs. Programs don't work for her."

This answer—that drug programs "don't work" for a defendant— was a common one among prosecutors, and it always infuriated me. Anybody who has ever been addicted, loved somebody with an addiction, or studied addiction knows that many people relapse multiple times before getting clean for a sustained period.[3] "So what?" I demanded, leaning forward, my voice sounding angrier than I had intended. Bernice just looked at me, her smile fading fast. It would have been a good time to hit the wrap-it-up button. But I pressed ahead, my voice filled with righteous indignation. "How come with drug programs, we act as if one or two chances is all you should get? How come we don't treat prison the same way?"

After all, I pointed out, Ms. Willis had already served one mandatory prison sentence, with no treatment, and had gone back to using and small-time selling as soon as she got out. And yet, I said, our system never treated the failure of prison as a reason not to try more prison.

Bernice was unmoved. "There are already long waiting lists for the few programs around," she told me, "and they should go to people who haven't had a chance before." So that was it. No drug treatment program for Tasha Willis. Five years in prison was the best Bernice could, or would, do. Her last words couldn't have been clearer: "Tell your client to take the deal or we go to trial."

The severe penalty that Tasha Willis faced was the result of decisions that D.C. had made fifteen years before, when city politicians and voters dramatically toughened criminal sentencing in the District. Two prominent figures had campaigned for this policy change: John Ray, a lawyer who had recently been elected to the city council, and Burtell Jefferson, who had just stepped down from his position as police chief. Their goals were to increase the maximum sentences for selling drugs and to implement mandatory minimum sentences for certain drug and gun crimes. Their efforts helped establish a national precedent for punitive sentencing, and at the same time served as an example of America's failure to consider alternative responses to the ravages of drug addiction.

Ray and Jefferson launched their campaign at a time when almost everyone agreed that D.C.'s drug laws needed updating. Since 1938, offenders in D.C. had faced a one-year maximum sentence for drug crimes, with a ten-year maximum for a second offense.[4] The law did not distinguish between substances—heroin, cocaine, and marijuana were all treated equally—nor did it distinguish between possession and sale.

By the late 1970s and early 1980s, pressure was growing to do something to make these laws tougher. Despite the city council's 1975 decisions to keep marijuana criminalized and to prohibit gun possession, drugs and crime had continued to decimate the city—especially its poor and working-class black neighborhoods. The complaints seemed to come from everywhere, but nowhere more vociferously than the neighborhoods of Shaw, U Street, and Columbia Heights. These once-vibrant communities had been devastated by the riots following the assassination of Martin Luther King, Jr., in 1968. Most businesses never reopened, and in the 1970s, many residents began to denounce what a coalition from the Fourteenth Street neighborhood called the "open and notorious" drug markets flourishing in public spaces.[5] Council member John Wilson, who had led the fight for gun control five years earlier, complained that at the corner of Tenth and O Streets, "droves of drug dealers, sometimes numbering fifty to one hundred, can be regularly seen stopping cars and passersby."[6] About a mile north, narrow one-way Chapin Street was home to passels of young dealers flagging down cars and soliciting pedestrians with impunity. According to one resident, the block had become "the McDonald's of the marijuana business."[7]

It is hard to overstate just how dire the situation was, or just how widespread the outrage. Children were often invoked as the drug trade's victims. "I try to keep my kids in the back of the house," complained one Chapin Street resident, "so they don't see the kids selling pot in the front."[8] Gloria Cole, an antidrug activist in Southeast D.C., worried that these dealers would lure children into the trade. "I've told the youngsters a million times not to go up there," she said, referring to a neighborhood drug trafficking hot spot, but "they go anyway because it's something different to see. It's like an all-night parade."[9] When the D.C. Board of Education member Frank Smith visited Cleveland Elementary School, in the heart of Shaw, he had to brave a throng of drug buyers and sellers before he could go inside. "There were so many young men between the ages of 18 and 32 in the one block around the school that I was frankly frightened to enter the building," he recounted.[10]

D.C. residents were forced to take matters into their own hands. In Capitol View, an African American community in the far eastern part of the city, residents adopted a variety of protective measures, from the mundane to the exotic. One concerned citizen reported keeping a pet fox to ward off intruders. Another resident had, in his own words, "brought home from overseas a wild bird that will attack a human."[11]

However bizarre these improvised strategies may appear in retrospect, their adaptive breadth reveals just how scared and vulnerable people felt. The angriest residents went on offense. Tony Hillary, chairman of the Advisory Neighborhood Commission in Adams Morgan, was a librarian by day and leader of a "citizens patrol group" by night.[12] Hillary and his fellow vigilantes took to the streets, determined to combat heroin dealing as well as the burglaries, assaults, and rapes that the drug trade spawned.[13] He carried a loaded handgun during these patrols, in open defiance of D.C.'s gun ban. He viewed his group as securing the kind of safety that the city's police force had failed to provide. "The police say, 'Close your eyes and the neighborhood will change,'" Hillary declared. "Well, I can't close my eyes. It's time we took retaliatory measures."[14] When asked about his intentions, he warned, "We're going to shoot to kill."[15]

Although Hillary took his dissatisfaction with law enforcement to the extreme, his dim view of the criminal justice system was far from unique. Complaints fell roughly into two camps. First, people lambasted what they viewed as lackadaisical street-level enforcement by the police. Often, these complaints were racially inflected, as when the Shaw activist Ibrahim Mumin argued that overt street dealing "wouldn't be tolerated in Georgetown and other [predominantly white] communities."[16] In a letter to the city council, another Shaw resident called the continued drug presence on Fourteenth Street "prejudicial and shameful." Drug deals "are made in the presence

Librarian and anticrime activist Tony Hillary, standing by his front door at 1422 Harvard Street, NW
(*The Washington Post*)

of policemen," the author wrote. "There is no congregation of this sort in predominantly white areas of the city."[17] The *Afro-American* editorial board joined the chorus. "Some lawmen may be sharing in the narcotics profits," they wrote, "or are looking the wrong way because it is too much trouble to do their jobs." Fearing that "the hard won gains of the civil rights movement are being flushed down the drain by the persistent prevalence of narcotics in our communities," D.C.'s leading black paper called the unchecked drug market "[a] new kind of slavery."[18]

The court system was the second target of complaints. Some of the objections to excessive leniency focused on the release of suspects after their arrest and before trial. In February 1979, for example, when Burtell Jefferson addressed the D.C. Federation of Civic Associations, a collection of neighborhood organizations in historically black neighborhoods, the group was in the midst of a campaign urging judges and prosecutors to keep more people in jail while awaiting trial.[19] "Too often," the *Afro* wrote, "breaking the law has meant nothing to would-be criminals because they felt they would be 'back on the street' within a few hours after an arrest."[20] Others complained about the short prison sentences—or probation with no prison time—imposed after conviction. Still others focused on a parole system that released people too early and too easily. While distinct, these three concerns were variations on a theme: revolving door justice.

Today, with so much attention paid to the severity of our criminal justice system, it is difficult to imagine a time when prison doors were seen as anything but locked. But in the mid- to late 1970s, the phrase "revolving door justice" became a commonplace. The term was especially popular with conservative politicians and publications: *U.S. News & World Report* ran a 1976 cover story titled " 'Revolving Door' Justice: Why Criminals Go Free," focusing especially on D.C. courts. But the three words gained currency across the political spectrum.[21] In 1975, for example, Ted Kennedy, the liberal senator from Massachusetts, published an op-ed in *The New York Times* arguing that " 'revolving door' justice convinces the criminal that his chances of actually being

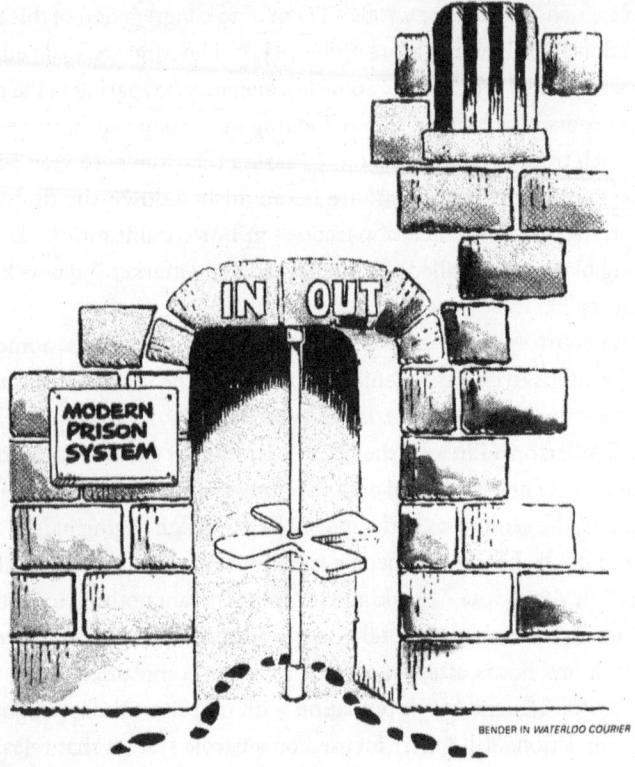

(*U.S. News & World Report*, May 10, 1976)

caught, tried, convicted and jailed are too slim to be taken seriously." As a result, Kennedy continued, "Our existing criminal justice system is no deterrent at all to violent crime in our society."[22]

To many African American observers, the revolving door was discriminatory: it spun fastest for the criminals who victimized blacks. "The poor and the uninformed are easy to prey upon, and the courts don't give a damn about the victims," wrote Carl Rowan, one of the nation's most prominent African American columnists, in a piece titled "Locking Up Thugs Is Not Vindictive." The courts, indifferent to the plight of black victims, "let the perpetrators of unconscionable violence go free to terrorize minority communities again and again."[23]

In the spring of 1981, David Clarke, chair of the Judiciary Committee of the D.C. Council, submitted a proposal for strengthening the District's sentencing guidelines for drug offenses. His solutions largely mirrored those that had been adopted by the federal government and many states: he wanted to separate drugs into classes and distinguish between possession and sale, generally reducing penalties for the former but increasing them for the latter. Clarke, who had fought so hard for marijuana decriminalization a few years earlier, was no drug warrior. But he was a politician, and he knew that the mood in the city, and trends in the nation, were all pushing toward longer sentences. So in place of the one-year maximums that had been the law since 1938, Clarke proposed a maximum penalty of ten years for the sale of heroin and five years for the sale of cocaine (he kept the one-year maximum for marijuana).

This wasn't enough for Burtell Jefferson; the police chief supported raising the ceiling for drug sentences higher than Clarke had proposed, and he wanted to raise the floor, too. The appeal of mandatory minimums to police officers is not difficult to understand when we consider the judicial system from their vantage point. Where lawyers and judges see due process, many officers see a series of incoherent, permissive decisions that conspire to undo the hard, often dangerous work that produced an arrest in the first place. A prosecutor might drop a case because of a legal technicality; a judge might release a defendant on bail, and that defendant might immediately resume dealing drugs on the same corner where he was arrested; a jury might find reasonable doubt, even when presented with strong evidence; and for the rare defendant who does get convicted, a judge might opt for probation, which, no matter how onerous the conditions, invariably reads to the arresting officer as a slap on the wrist. "Our hands are tied by the criminal justice system," complained MPD

"Open-Door Policy".

(*U.S. News & World Report*, May 10, 1976)

lieutenant Kenneth Brown. "How do you think we feel when we arrest a joker today and he's back on the street tomorrow?"[24] Mandatory minimums might not be a panacea, but from the police officer's perspective, they were a valid and necessary response to rising crime.

No matter how strongly Jefferson believed in mandatory minimums, however, he could not vote on council legislation. Luckily, he met somebody who could: John Ray, an ambitious thirty-seven-year-old council member who had run for mayor once and was considering another shot. The two men were natural allies: both valued reserve over flash and hard work over talk.

Raised by his grandmother in rural Georgia, in a two-bedroom house that had to accommodate fifteen family members, Ray woke up daily at six a.m. to work the cotton and tobacco fields and tap pine trees for turpentine. He never met his father, and his mother had been forced to move to Florida in search of work. But Ray flourished. In 1961, he graduated from Herctoma High School; of the thirty-five students who had been in his first-grade class, he was the only one to graduate on time, and he did so as both class president and valedictorian. In an earlier era—even just a decade or two earlier—being smart and disciplined would not have been enough to overcome the grinding racism of rural Georgia. But Ray had been born just as the Jim Crow regime was beginning to crack. Ray joined the Air Force after graduation; from there, he made his way to D.C., where he attended George Washington University for both college and law school. (While earning his law degree, he spent a summer working for former Supreme Court Justice Abe Fortas, who later hosted Ray's wedding at his home, even playing the violin during the ceremony.) Before long, Ray began collecting the marks of success in law: a clerkship with Judge Spottswood W. Robinson III on the U.S. Court of Appeals, a stint as legal counsel for Senator Ted Kennedy, and a position as attorney adviser in the Department of Justice's Office of Legal Counsel. In 1978, he entered electoral politics, securing an at-large position on the city council (and unseating, in the process, none other than Doug Moore, the black nationalist anti-marijuana crusader and gun rights advocate).[25]

Ray had not campaigned on an anticrime platform, but in 1981, when he reviewed Clarke's proposed reforms, he found them too weak to solve the city's crime problem. Ray wanted to raise the statutory maximums even higher: whereas Clarke had proposed a maximum of ten years for selling heroin, five years for cocaine, and one year for marijuana, Ray argued for fifteen for heroin, ten for cocaine, and three for marijuana.[26]

But raising the maximums was not enough, Ray believed, because judges would still have the leeway to hand out probation. Like Jefferson, Ray wanted to freeze the revolving door, and throughout the spring of 1981 he offered a series of amendments to do just that. At the heart of Ray's plan were longer maximum sentences *and* mandatory minimum sentences for gun and drug offenses: five years' mandatory time for committing a crime with a gun, four years for selling heroin, and two years for selling cocaine. Much like Doug Moore, whose arguments against marijuana decriminalization were rooted in a race-conscious defense of the black community, John Ray advocated mandatory minimums in the language of racial and class justice. "Black crimes against blacks get very low sentences," Ray noted, citing NAACP and Urban League research in his critique of the existing system. "Black crimes against whites get very big sentences, and low-status whites get longer sentences than higher-status whites." These disparities existed in drug cases, too, Ray said. The rich drug defendant escapes unscathed, "while the poor lad on the street is put away in Lorton [D.C.'s prison]."[27]

When Ray spoke to civic and church groups, he was met with nodding heads and murmured assent. But apart from Jefferson, the city's leaders remained skeptical of mandatory minimum sentencing. On March 12 and 13, the council held hearings on the proposals from Clarke and Ray, and the tough-on-crime legislator was met by a phalanx of opposing witnesses. Edward Hailes, the president of the local NAACP chapter, stressed that despite the group's outrage over crime (the chapter had recently launched a "War on Crime" after the brutal slaying of one of its members), the NAACP nonetheless viewed mandatory minimums as too blunt a response. Ray's solution was "a club," Hailes argued, and he recommended that the council instead "use a scalpel—a scalpel of justice to cut crime out of the community."[28] The Washington Urban League's president, Jerome Page, told council members that harsher punishments would not solve D.C.'s crime problem; he urged the council to focus instead on root causes. Criticizing proposals for "stiffer penalties, longer sentences, and more incarceration," Page said that these "all seem to discount the importance of community-based crime prevention efforts, and the conditions of poverty that are so much a part of the crime problem."[29] Even those tasked with public safety, such as the Corporation Counsel for D.C., the Department of Corrections, and the Board of Parole, also urged the council to reject mandatory minimums, citing the likely strain on the District's already overextended correctional resources.

But of all the witnesses who testified against Ray's bill, the most unlikely, and potentially consequential, was Charles Ruff. As U.S. Attorney for the District of Columbia,[30] Ruff (who would go on to serve as

White House counsel under President Bill Clinton) argued that mandatory sentences would clog the system and impose unjust penalties on defendants who deserved leniency. "Picture the case of your mother or sister who is charged with an offense," Ruff said to the council. "Don't you want the prosecutor to have the discretion to say your sister is a special person, and hers is a one-time offense?"[31] The rhetorical question infuriated Ray, who, in response, called it "hogwash." For Ray, prosecutorial discretion was the cause of injustice, not the solution to it. Too often, he said, those with means or connections got a break, while "those who are poor, those who are black, are the ones who end up with the tough sentences." Ruff, in turn, forcefully rejected Ray's claim: "I think there is no evidence—none—that there is any discrimination in sentencing between the black man and the white man."[32]

This remarkable standoff does not fit our standard narrative about the politics of punishment. Here, in 1981, and three years *before* the federal government would pass its own set of mandatory minimums, we find John Ray, a black politician born under Jim Crow, demanding mandatory sentences on the grounds that they would be fairer to blacks—and facing stern opposition from a white federal prosecutor. Ruff's opposition—and the fact that the Department of Justice allowed him to testify against the proposal—highlights the extent to which Ray and Jefferson were at the forefront of a revolution in American criminal justice.[33]

Ray and Jefferson expected mandatory minimum sentences to be a tough sell, and they were right. On May 19, when the council passed new drug legislation, it overwhelmingly rejected the proposal for mandatory minimums.[34]

Nonetheless, the two men had achieved something important. While the opposition had homed in on their mandatory minimum proposals, they had quietly won something just as significant. The legislation contained the higher *maximum* sentences that Ray and Jefferson had called for—not the ones in Clarke's original proposal. Now, for example, a first-time offender charged with selling heroin would face a fifteen-year maximum, no matter the amount of the sale.

Moreover, although the council had rejected their calls for mandatory minimums, Ray and Jefferson believed that D.C.'s residents might reach a different conclusion—and the initiative process, which allowed citizens to vote directly on a ballot measure, would give them a chance to find out. The fight was far from over.

Ray and Jefferson had counterparts in cities across the country; many of the earliest crusaders for tougher drug laws were African Americans. In New York City, as we have seen, a coalition of Harlem activists demanded an increased police presence and stiffer penalties from the courts.[35] While heroin was the object of community outrage in New York, in Los Angeles it was phencyclidine, more commonly known as angel dust or PCP. The drug, which had first arrived in Los Angeles in the mid-1960s, exploded in popularity over the next decades. In 1979, the LAPD made 3,905 PCP-related arrests—sixteen times the number it had made just four year earlier.[36] The crisis was covered extensively by the city's leading black newspaper, the *Los Angeles Sentinel*.

California State Assemblywoman Maxine Waters, a black woman representing the 48th District, took the lead in the fight against PCP.[37] Waters, formerly a partner in a public relations firm, had been elected to the California State Assembly in 1976.[38] Her district, which included a portion of South Central Los Angeles, was among those hit hardest by PCP, and she was a regular presence at anti-PCP community rallies. "Waters Attacks PCP," ran a *Sentinel* headline in March 1978; the article quotes her as saying, "We must take a hard-line approach to those convicted of selling and manufacturing this deadly chemical." That spring, she introduced a bill to increase the maximum penalties for the manufacture or sale of PCP—with "manufacture" including the possession of certain chemical precursors—from two to four years to three to five years.[39] Her proposal received overwhelming support and became law in April 1978.[40]

But Waters's bill did little to ease the crisis. Because the PCP trade was so lucrative—an initial investment of $1,000 could result in profits

Attend Anti-PCP Rally Sunday, Oct. 12

(*Los Angeles Sentinel*, October 9, 1980)

of up to $25,000 for a local dealer—PCP seemed unstoppable. Especially in the projects of South Central L.A., PCP continued its march. In the fall of 1979, the *Sentinel* somberly declared, "L.A. Becomes PCP Capital of the World."[41]

As use of the drug escalated, so did the *Sentinel*'s response: the paper moved from journalism to activism. In September 1980, the editors published "An Open Letter to PCP Dealers & Other Dogs!" on the front page. Rejecting the notion that drug dealing was a nonviolent crime, they declared:

> [Y]ou are guilty of murder, rape, theft, robbery, matricide, patricide, fratricide, and every other crime committed by any human being under the influence of PCP . . . [Y]ou will have to stand before a tribunal for your crimes. It will not be a court of law. There will be no prosecutor or defense attorney. And there will be no official sentencing date, nor will there be a probation department report. The community has already judged you guilty and the only thing left is for the sentence to be carried out.

No punishment was too harsh: PCP dealers, according to the *Sentinel*'s editors, deserved to be "tarred and feathered, burned at the stake, castrated, and any other horrendous thing which can be imagined."[42] The letter was signed "The Los Angeles Sentinel and the rest of the Black Community."

Castration, of course, was not a viable option—but mandatory minimum sentences were legally possible, and the *Sentinel*'s writers strongly endorsed them. In the eyes of the columnist Ed Davis, for example, Assemblywoman Waters's bill wasn't tough enough. In a 1980 column headlined "Pushers: The Grandfathers of PCP Crimes," Davis advocated a twenty-five-year mandatory sentence for selling the drug. "This Grandfather crime brings about the myriad of acts of violence in the Black community," he wrote: "man beating wife, mother killing child, son attacking father, self-defense shootings, PCP user driving automobile into buildings and other acts of aggression."[43] Davis's argument—that drug dealers were directly responsible for the collateral damage in their communities—was a familiar and resonant one in black neighborhoods across the country, and it goes a long way toward explaining why so many blacks were in favor of harsher drug punishments.

Alongside its calls for tougher laws, the *Sentinel* also urged community action. In an editorial headlined "*Sentinel* Declares World War III on PCP,"[44] the paper's executive editor, James H. Cleaver, wrote that the PCP epidemic "represented the worst invasion since Hitler marched into Poland." No longer content with simply documenting and denouncing the havoc wrought by PCP, he urged the black community to rally at open-air drug markets, which he said operated with grotesque impunity across the city. "The areas where PCP is constantly sold will have to be literally closed down," Cleaver wrote. His message to the city's black residents was unequivocal: "If you are not a part of the solution then YOU are a part of the problem."

Between 1980 and 1982, black Los Angelenos heeded the call, gathering by the hundreds—sometimes even by the thousands—to hear clergymen, musicians, and politicians rail against the scourge of PCP. One of the rally regulars was Johnnie Cochran, the county's first black assistant district attorney. Cochran, who would later became famous for his defense of O. J. Simpson, called PCP a "brain altering and brain destroying" drug. Its purveyors, he declared, "should be dealt with swiftly, surely and in those instances where facts warrant it—harshly."[45]

For Cochran, the PCP epidemic was part of a broader crisis in black communities: crime, and the tendency he saw among blacks to excuse it. That so much of this crime was perpetrated by blacks upon other blacks only made matters worse. In Houston, Brooklyn, and other cities, black newspapers reporting on rising homicide rates isolated the problem as one of "Black on Black crime." The most prominent use of the term came from the national magazine *Ebony*, which devoted its 1979 annual special issue to the topic. In his publisher's note, John H. Johnson wrote that although "this is an issue we wish we didn't have to publish," the magazine had no choice because "Black on Black crime has reached a critical level that threatens our existence as a people."[46]

In 1980, after the National Bar Association (the nation's leading organization of black lawyers) devoted its annual conference to the ques-

A JOHNSON PUBLICATION

# EBONY

**AUGUST 1979 $1.25**
**SPECIAL ISSUE**

# BLACK ON BLACK CRIME

### THE CAUSES
### THE CONSEQUENCES
### THE CURES

tion of black-on-black crime, Johnnie Cochran urged other blacks not to be "apologists for the crime in our communities."[47] Getting tough, he believed, required two changes: judges must hand out longer sentences, up to and including the maximum, and legislators must stiffen the available penalties.[48]

In January 1982, John Ray launched a bid for the mayor's office, challenging the incumbent, Marion Barry. Though this campaign never gained momentum, shortly thereafter he announced another one—a ballot measure for mandatory sentences—that would. The provisions of Ray's ballot measure, which would be voted on in September, were similar to those in his original proposal. For individuals convicted of committing a violent crime while armed with a gun, the mandatory minimum would be five years in prison for a first offense and ten years for all subsequent offenses. For individuals convicted of selling drugs, the minimum would vary according to the substance: four years for heroin, two years for cocaine, and one year for marijuana (but in the case of marijuana, only if the person had sold very large amounts).[49] The ballot initiative, known as Initiative 9, contained an exemption for addicts. It allowed judges to waive the mandatory minimums for addicts who sold to support their habit, as long as it was the person's first conviction for selling drugs. Under D.C. law, an initiative required fourteen thousand signatures to appear on the ballot; Ray and his supporters collected more than twenty-four thousand.[50] The majority of these signatures, they claimed, came from Wards 5, 6, and 7—areas that included many of the city's black middle- and working-class neighborhoods."[51]

Ray still had his ally Burtell Jefferson. The police chief had retired in 1981 and a year later assumed the leadership of Citizens for Safer Streets, a group supporting Ray's proposal. Beyond Jefferson, however, a broad coalition rose up in resistance. From elected officials such as Marion Barry and Walter Fauntroy, the D.C. delegate to Congress, to race-conscious civic organizations such as the NAACP, the Urban League, and the National Conference of Black Lawyers, to progressive groups such as the National Lawyers Guild, the local branch of the American Federation of Government Employees, the Gay Activists Alliance, the National Moratorium on Prison Construction, the League of Women Voters, and the ACLU, the civic and legal elite was united in opposition.[52] Even Charles Ruff, who had stepped down from his role as U.S. Attorney in October 1981, continued to voice his opposition, publishing an article in *The District Lawyer* raising doubts about the initiative.[53] Stanley Harris, whom President Reagan had appointed as Ruff's replacement, added his own criticism, saying that while the U.S. Attorney's offices supported mandatory sentencing "in appropriate and carefully defined circumstances," Initiative 9 "is not crafted in such a way as to meet our concerns."[54] If Initiative 9 was a recapitulation of Ray's original proposal, its detractors' arguments were a restatement of earlier objections: mandatory minimums, they claimed, would create a massive backlog in the courts, eliminate judicial discretion, overcrowd jails, and, most important, fail to reduce crime rates.

That spring and summer, the two sides engaged in a protracted duel, making their cases with pamphlets, speeches, radio appearances, and visits to neighborhood forums.[55] Ray's and Jefferson's message was exceedingly simple: Crime is out of hand, so we must get tough. In addition to stopping the "revolving door," Ray argued, mandatory minimums would deter crime by sending the message that drugs and guns would no longer be tolerated.[56] "Most of our citizens believe punishment does deter crime," Ray said two weeks before the vote, recognizing the intuitive appeal of this logic. They were "responding to what they view as a reasonable approach."[57]

Opponents of Initiative 9 struggled to make their case equally compelling. Though their ranks included many high-profile figures, theirs was an uphill battle. Unlike an open-ended legislative session, a ballot initiative entailed an up-or-down vote, meaning that Initiative 9's opponents could not present an alternative to Ray's proposal: their only option was to point out the bill's flaws. And their uninspiring slogans—

which included the near rhyme "Thumbs down on Nine. It won't stop crime"—offered little hope to besieged communities.[58]

Indeed, in the months following the passage of D.C.'s 1981 antidrug bill (the one that passed without Ray's proposed mandatory minimums), the situation had not improved. In August 1981, three months after that bill's passage, Juan Williams, then a writer for *The Washington Post*, published an op-ed titled "Heroin in My Neighborhood." The piece described the open-air drug market on Seventh and S Streets—a corner not far from where my client Tasha Willis would be arrested for selling heroin almost fifteen years later. "By 6:00 pm the crowd of about 300 is swarming: swollen, scarred junkies waiting for dealers; minor-league drug dealers waiting for a drop from a bigger dealer, 'the candy man'; and the part-time junkies, driving by, looking for a dealer they recognize so they can start their weekend of wasting away a little early." Williams, who lived nearby, had witnessed increasingly radical measures to clear the block. Since users and dealers often stashed their supplies under car tires, the police had adopted the strategy of opening fire hydrants and flooding the gutters to wash away drugs and syringes. The strategy was quickly abandoned because it evoked memories of policing during the civil rights movement, when southern officers blasted demonstrators with water hoses. But Williams criticized the MPD's decision to terminate the floods. "With that crowd, that blight, in your neighborhood, near your wife and child, you lose all concern for appearances," he wrote. His top priority, by a wide margin, was making the neighborhood safe: "If water gushing down the streets will stop the drug deals and make the small-time thieves, punks and crazies go elsewhere, then turn on the hydrant, chief."[59]

Ray capitalized on the collective anger of citizens like Williams, shrewdly taking his campaign to the middle of known drug markets. In the spring of 1982, for example, as the campaign was heating up, Ray traveled to one of the city's most notorious open-air markets, at 14th and W Streets, for a press conference announcing the release of a position paper on crime.[60] There, in plain view of some crowd members, a drug dealer completed a transaction.[61] By venturing into these areas, Ray dramatized the fight over public space that had been lost to the drug trade.

Another impromptu moment from that same press conference allowed Ray to powerfully defuse one of the primary objections to Initiative 9. In the middle of the event, a man in sunglasses began heckling Ray. "Selling drugs, selling socks, selling dogs. Man has got to feed his family!" he shouted. "Why don't y'all get them some jobs?" But Ray was ready for this root-cause argument, retorting that the drug dealer was effectively poisoning his "black brothers and sisters." The notion of the drug dealer as race traitor, established in the 1970s by black nationalists like Hassan Jeru-Ahmed, was an especially visceral one, particularly for poor and working-class blacks who bore daily witness to the devastation of addiction. So when the heckler called this rebuttal "irrelevant," suggesting that Ray's privilege kept him from understanding the plight of the black poor, Ray seized the opportunity to deploy his own biography. "Let me say that my grandmother, grandfather went through life and had a very hard time," he said, reminding the man—and the listening crowd—that he had grown up "dipping turpentine" in the backwoods of Georgia. "We went through a depression and they didn't sell drugs to their sisters and brothers, didn't sell drugs to young people," Ray said. "I don't care who you are, there is no excuse for selling drugs."[62]

In the weeks leading up to the vote, the political battle intensified. Ray and Jefferson heightened their visibility, campaigning for their initiative by walking from one murder scene to another, thereby making a political spectacle not only of the city's crime problem but also of their committed response. As election day approached, the campaign for mandatory minimums looked to be gaining steam—a poll conducted two weeks before the vote suggested that 71 percent of registered voters favored the measure—and Ray and Jefferson got more good news when the National Rifle Association lent its last-minute support. The NRA dispatched its members across the city to distribute fifty thousand pamphlets encouraging citizens to "Vote Prison Time for Violent Crime."[63]

On September 14, 1982, a warm, late-summer D.C. day, voters went to the polls. It was a blowout. Initiative 9 prevailed in all eight of the city's wards, from the affluent Ward 3, home to the majority of D.C.'s whites (67 percent in favor), to Ward 5, a set of mostly black, mixed-income neighborhoods (75 percent), to Ward 8, the low-income, overwhelmingly black area east of the Anacostia River (75 percent). Overall, the proposal passed with a dominating 73 percent of the vote.[64]

Mandatory minimums also won approval across economic classes. The city's eight wards are further subdivided into voting precincts containing just a few thousand voters each. Initiative 9 was favored by voters in 136 of the city's 137 precincts, receiving its highest vote margins in some of the city's poorest pockets and those hardest hit by the drug traffic. In fact, the only precinct in which the initiative failed to win a majority of votes was in the Palisades, a wealthy, mostly white neighborhood bordering Georgetown and the Potomac River.[65]

When the vote was reported, Jefferson expressed hope that the victory "was a message to those persons committing crimes that they can expect swift and certain punishment."[66] But in the years to follow, despite the sponsors' hopes, D.C. crime would only get worse. After an initial dip in the vote's immediate aftermath, the homicide rate would explode later in the decade. As for drugs, prices remained stable and overdose fatalities continued to rise, climbing from 41 in 1979 to 155 in 1985.[67]

But if the initiative left the city's drug market unaltered, it succeeded wildly in reshaping the application of criminal justice. In the two years following Initiative 9's passage, as the system absorbed the law's incentives, drug prosecutions skyrocketed nearly 300 percent, from 838 in 1982 to 2,277 in 1984.[68] Other changes were equally profound. In 1980, for example, only 3 percent of drug arrests were for sales, while 97 percent were for possession. Over the next four years, however, sales arrests increased by a factor of fifteen, to 45 percent, leaving only 55 percent for possession.[69]

At first blush, these numbers might suggest that police were arresting a different group of people—sellers, not users. In fact, the same people were being arrested, but now prosecutors were charging them with the more serious offense. Before Initiative 9, the maximum penalty for possession had been the same as the maximum penalties for sale and for possession with intent to distribute (PWID). Under that system, prosecutors had no incentive to take a case that was on the borderline between possession and possession with the intent to distribute and charge PWID. But now, under the new system, someone convicted of PWID faced up to fifteen years in prison, with a minimum sentence of two or even four years, depending on the drug. As a result, prosecutors began charging defendants with PWID indiscriminately, even in cases when an arrestee had only $50 to $100 worth of drugs on her person (i.e., the amount a heavy user could consume in a day or two). The new guidelines also changed the average defendant's strategy: the prospect of a fifteen-year sentence dramatically increased the pressure to plead guilty and take a deal. Even the police force modified its tactics, increasingly conducting buy-bust operations like the one that, almost fifteen years later, would catch Tasha Willis.

From the perspective of a present-day observer, the black community's overwhelming support for Initiative 9 may appear astonishing. Mandatory minimums have come to epitomize everything that is wrong with America's criminal justice system and with the tough-on-crime course we have charted over the last forty years. Their racial impact, first recognized by the United States Sentencing Commission in 1991, is now thoroughly documented.[70] Attorney General Eric Holder cited mandatory minimums explicitly in his 2013 declaration, "Too many Americans go to too many prisons for far too long, and for no truly good law enforcement reason."[71]

And yet, when we take a historical perspective, the passage of Initiative 9 is easier to understand. The term "nonviolent drug offense," ubiquitous today, was virtually unheard of in 1981. In the years leading up to Initiative 9, the link between drugs and violence had been so tightly drawn that many saw the two as interchangeable. The editors of the *Los Angeles Sentinel*, for example, promoted the widely held view that drug dealers were directly responsible for what their products did to customers and, by extension, for what those customers did to others. Ray implicitly relied on this view when he cited the crimes of D.C.'s addicts—who, by his estimate, annually stole property worth more than $300 million—as a reason to toughen penalties against distributors.[72] Jefferson had done the same in 1980 when he pointed to the mounting violence between groups seeking to control the city's drug markets.[73] Other commentators, such as the *Post*'s Juan Williams, saw the drug trade's occupation of public space as a form of violence in itself. In many cases, regardless of their specific rationale for making the drugs–violence connection, writers portrayed drug distribution as a violent crime: "It is just plain stupid to let someone on probation continue to roam free," wrote Carl Rowan in 1976, "if he is accused anew of crimes like murder, rape, robbery, felonious assault, [or] narcotics peddling."[74] So when Ray and Jefferson decided to combine, in a single ballot question, mandatory minimums for drug selling *and* for possession of a gun during a crime, they did so based on the common assumption of equivalence between drugs and violence. What many today see as two separate (if interrelated) issues, they insisted were one.

Ray's exchange with the heckler also reveals a key feature of the strategy that he and Jefferson adopted in their campaign for Initiative 9. The back-and-forth ended with Ray's emphatic assertion, "There is no excuse for selling drugs." But Initiative 9 was not asking voters whether they believed drug dealing was excusable; it was asking them to endorse mandatory prison terms. Ray and Jefferson succeeded by erasing the space between excuse and mandatory punishment, and by convincing voters to do the same. Ray's response to the heckler effectively framed the crowd's political choice: If they believed that taking over sidewalks to sell drugs to other black people was inexcusable, then mandatory minimums were the sensible answer. Once the issue was defined in those terms, the punitive response was hard to resist.

Opponents of Initiative 9, by contrast, failed to appreciate the exigencies of the moment. In his testimony against Ray's proposal, for example, the Urban League's Jerome Page had said, "Crime has always been a fact of life in our poorest neighborhoods," and he predicted that it would remain a fact of life until the city addressed crime's root causes: "poverty, discrimination, and lack of opportunity."[75] Most black voters agreed with Page on the importance of these battles—but poverty and discrimination weren't going away anytime soon.[76] In the meantime, a Board of Education member had publicly voiced his fears about entering an elementary school, an armed librarian was leading neighborhood patrols against drug dealers, and council members were deluged with pleas for relief from city residents afraid to walk in their own neighborhoods.

Ray and Jefferson knew that even in the most economically isolated pockets of black America, most people do not sell drugs or commit acts of criminal violence. So while Ray's response to his heckler—"-There is no excuse for selling drugs"—may have fit into an established pattern of middle-class blacks chastising poor blacks for their moral failings, his argument also appealed to working-class and poor blacks.[77] Even neighborhoods portrayed by the media as "drug-infested" are always much more than just that: they are crowded, also, with mothers trying to avoid dealers while walking their children to school, small-business owners struggling to keep their stoops clear and their stores open, grandparents wondering what happened to the neighborhood they grew up in, pastors working to keep their congregants safe.[78] These people were as indignant as anyone else about crime and public drug markets—perhaps even more so. They and their families were under immediate threat. Ray and Jefferson offered an answer, and in times of crisis, even a bad answer beats no answer at all.

All of which begs the question: What *would* the best answer have been? The drug trade—in particular the city's open-air drug markets—had produced a state of emergency, and there was no doubt that addiction was driving crime. But this didn't mean that addiction had to be labeled a criminal justice issue. What if, instead, D.C.'s leaders had called it a public health disaster?

In 1977, the city's Narcotics Treatment Administration (NTA) was equipped to treat just one-tenth of the addicts who needed help: 1,250 beds in a city with an estimated twelve thousand addicts.[79] And yet, as the drug crisis deepened, the city mostly ignored the question of treatment. In the wake of Initiative 9, the number of beds remained frozen at a fraction of what was needed, and the programs designed to rehabilitate addicts—programs that were few and far between—were underfunded and of low quality. What if Ray and Jefferson had proposed a massive increase in treatment beds, as opposed to prison cells? What if they had worked to eliminate the waiting lists at all clinics and treatment facilities? What if the addict exception to mandatory minimums hadn't been limited to a person's first offense, but instead had recognized that many addicts would need multiple chances before getting clean? What if they had pressed for pre- and posttrial diversion programs so that judges could use the threat of prison to compel recalcitrant repeat offenders into treatment? What if police officers had been trained not to arrest addicts, but to refer them directly to treatment? None of this is impossible to imagine: several of these ideas had already been implemented in other cities, and several more have since been tested and proven effective.

The fact that no such proposals were made speaks volumes about the ways in which we as a society categorize drug use. In the debate over mandatory minimums, Ray and Jefferson treated D.C.'s drug epidemic as a law enforcement problem, while their opponents cast it as a symptom of poverty. But nobody approached it as a public health issue. In 1978, for example, Arthur Carter, the publisher of the *Afro*, wrote to David Clarke to complain about the used syringes in the alley behind the *Afro*'s building and about the "constant congregation of persons" at Twelfth and U Streets, near the paper's front door. Clarke forwarded the letter to Jefferson, requesting that patrol officers give special attention to that corner.[80] In response, Jefferson assured Clarke that the MPD would handle the problem, writing, "Aggressive investigation and enforcement action shall continue by the Drug Enforcement Unit, and uniformed patrols of the Third District will provide high visibility patrol to deter illegal activities."[81] Carter may have been a more prominent figure than most, but the contents of his letter— and Clarke's response—were thoroughly typical: council members and their staffs received hundreds of such letters during the late 1970s and early 1980s, and even the most ardent opponents of mandatory minimums, including Clarke, would invariably respond by turning to the police department. (Jefferson would often reply to the council members, offering his assurances and occasionally even reporting the number of arrests and seizures the department had made.) By contrast, I have not found a single instance of a council member forwarding a letter to the head of the Narcotics Treatment Administration. The choice of which agency to call on might seem inconsequential, but the policy consensus it reflected and reinforced was of great import. When an urgent problem required a short-term solution, law enforcement was regarded as the only answer.

When we ask ourselves how America became the world's greatest jailer, it is natural to focus on bright, shiny objects: national campaigns, federal legislation, executive orders from the Oval Office. But we should train our eyes, also, on more mundane decisions and directives, many of which took place on the local level. Which agency director did a public official enlist in response to citizen complaints about used syringes in back alleys? Such small choices, made daily, over time, in every corner of our nation, are the bricks that built our prison nation.

Ms. Willis rejected the plea offer. After trying and failing to secure a better one, I was left to prepare for trial. The situation seemed hopeless; I began walking from office to office, peddling my paperwork to senior lawyers, hoping they would find something I had missed. But no matter whom I buttonholed, from our trial chief to our training director, each conversation ended with some version of "Tell me again—what was that plea offer?"

On the morning of the trial, Ms. Willis and I sat outside the court-room. Ms. Willis did not look well. I couldn't be sure, and I didn't know if anyone else would notice, but she appeared to be sleepy. Maybe she was just tired; maybe the stress of a looming court date had been keeping her awake at night. But nodding off was a sign of heroin use, and I certainly didn't want her doing it in front of the judge. I brought up the plea offer one last time. As lethargic as she was, Ms. Willis stayed firm. She had not changed her mind.

The courtroom, when we finally entered, was brimming with de-fense lawyers and prosecutors who shuttled in and out negotiating last-minute pleas. The courtroom clerk called case after case, her voice flat and uninterested. Shortly after eleven a.m., after we had waited two hours, I heard her call Ms. Willis's name. When we got to the defense table, the judge launched into the standard, all-but-scripted routine. The first step was establishing that all parties were present. After opening the case file, he turned to the prosecutor, Bernice Lester, and asked, "Is the government ready for trial?"

Unless an important witness had failed to appear or the prosecutor had suddenly noticed a glaring problem, the answer was typically yes. Sometimes prosecutors would reply, "Ready call," which in court-house lingo meant "We are ready in concept, and our witnesses are standing by the phone; we just need to call them over." Defense lawyers hated "ready call": we were convinced that the prosecution used it when they weren't really ready but hoped to buy extra time to find a witness. It was a good strategy, if a manipulative one: in the face of this final bit of pressure, many of my clients caved.

But this time, I heard Bernice Lester say, "No, Your Honor." She said nothing more. The government wasn't ready.

I inhaled sharply. "Your Honor," I said, operating by sheer reflex, "we move to dismiss for want of prosecution." The judge granted the motion—the standard response when the prosecution offered no extenuating reason for being unprepared—and I immediately grabbed Ms. Willis's elbow. I wanted to escort her out of the courtroom before our luck was somehow revoked. Ms. Willis moved slowly—a little too slowly, I thought—and I tried to help her along without revealing how desperate I was to escape. But I was just being paranoid: the clerk, the judge, and the prosecutor had already moved on. Before we made it to the door, another defendant was making his way to the counsel table, lawyer at his side. Nobody in the courtroom was thinking about Ms. Willis.

She was eager to go home, and I had another case to attend to in a courtroom down the hall. But there was time for a goodbye hug, and for Ms. Willis to remind me that she'd been right about the plea offer. She claimed she'd had a sense that the police weren't going to show up. "Knew all along," she said. I smiled, but I didn't say the truth: we had no way of knowing why the case was dismissed. On that day, for whatever reason—a missed deadline, a lost folder, a police officer who overslept—Ms. Willis had won the dismissal lottery.

As she turned to leave, she looked at me one last time. "Don't worry about me, Mr. Forman," she said, reading my mind. "I'm going to get the help I need." I really do think she believed those words. But I didn't. Finding a treatment bed within the criminal justice system was hard enough; finding an affordable option outside the system was next to impossible. Poor people languished on waiting lists for years.

No: Ms. Willis would not get the treatment she needed. As I watched her walk down the hall and out of the building, I knew that what little D.C. had to offer her—what little America had to offer her—was back in that courtroom. And it was police and prison, not help.

# 5

## "THE WORST THING TO HIT US SINCE SLAVERY"
### Crack and the Advent of Warrior Policing, 1988–92

When I said goodbye to Tasha Willis in the hallway of the court-house, I knew she would return to the Shaw neighborhood near Seventh and T Streets, NW. I didn't expect to end up there myself. But a few years later, that's exactly what happened; in the spring of 2000, I was working on the second floor of the Maya Angelou Public Charter School at the corner of Ninth and T, just two blocks from the corner where Ms. Willis had been arrested.

The Maya Angelou School was the brainchild of David Domenici, a Stanford Law School graduate with an understated manner and a relentless work ethic. Mutual friends introduced us in 1995, when I was in my second year at the Public Defender Service (PDS) and David was an attorney at Wilmer, Cutler and Pickering (now WilmerHale), a prominent D.C. corporate law firm. David didn't really belong in a big firm; his true passion was education. In the fall of 1995, we met at a coffee shop near the courthouse, and he told me about his dream: launching a program that would offer a high-quality education, on-site counseling, and paid employment to court-involved teens. David knew that many of my clients were juveniles, and he wanted to know whether such a program would appeal to them.

I was sold on his idea immediately. What David was describing was just what my clients had been telling me they wanted: a good school and a chance to make money. I began to imagine the impact his idea could have on young people caught up—or at risk of being caught up—in the criminal justice system. Most of my clients had struggled in school or dropped out altogether before they were arrested. If a program like the one David was describing had existed, I thought, they might never have become my clients in the first place. At PDS, my colleagues and I sometimes joked about how great it would be if crime dropped so low that we had to find other jobs. We knew this would never happen. But a program that reached troubled kids early, providing them with effective teachers and tutors, professional counseling, and paying jobs, seemed like a step in the right direction.

In the spring of 1997, David quit his job to start the program, and I was granted a year's leave of absence from PDS to help. By that fall, we had hired a few teachers and cobbled together enough money from foundations and well-heeled lawyers to make our payroll for a month or two. We had also persuaded twenty students, all from the court system, to take a chance on our unproven program, which we named after the poet Maya Angelou.

We faced all the challenges you would expect. Our students were overwhelmingly from low-income families, and most were sixteen or seventeen years old but performing at a fifth- or sixth-grade level. Our first application included a math problem: "You have $10.00. You order three slices of pizza. Each slice costs $1.75. How much change do you have after you pay for the three slices?" Of the first twenty students to enroll, about ten missed this question. Many of their transcripts looked like a bomb had been dropped on them. But David was undeterred; when reviewing applications, he used to say, "All F's and one D—our perfect student." Even though he smiled when he said it, he wasn't joking—he was reminding the rest of us that these were precisely the students we were here to serve.

Academic struggles were just the beginning. Many of our students had experienced trauma—they had lost parents, friends, and siblings to violence, addiction, and prison. Some had endured physical or emotional abuse. Many suffered from depression but had never received treatment. We had a full-time counselor on staff from the day we opened, and even in a school with only twenty students, her office was never empty.

As hard as it was to deal with those issues, at least we had anticipated them. But we were blindsided by an entirely different obstacle: the police. Our students complained constantly about how the police treated them. They told us they were routinely subjected to verbal abuse, stopped and searched for drugs or weapons, or even punched, choked, or shoved. Most of them felt at risk whenever an officer approached.

In the spring of 2000, the staff of the Maya Angelou Public Charter School witnessed the abuse firsthand. Not long after we moved into our building on Ninth and T, the police began raiding our corner. About once a week that entire spring, a team of officers would descend on our block, throw students against the wall, and search them for weapons or drugs. I had learned the concepts of "stop-and-frisk" and "search and seizure" in law school, and as a lawyer, I had filed hundreds of motions alleging that the police lacked "reasonable articulable suspicion" or "probable cause," the legal standards for conducting searches of this kind. But the searches on our corner defied those standards: if the police had a rationale for choosing their targets among the assembled teenagers, I couldn't see it. Nor was I prepared for the force and violence that can accompany these police actions—especially when they take place in poor black communities where police are accustomed to having their way. When the police rushed onto our corner, our students were forced to "assume the position," with their legs spread, faces against the wall or squad car, and hands behind their heads. Then they were searched, with the officers feeling every inch of their bodies, turning backpacks and pockets inside out, leaving the sidewalks strewn with notebooks, broken pencils, lipstick, and combs. Not once, over the course of about ten searches, did the police recover anything illegal.

Usually the searches ended there, with shaken nerves and a messy street. But every so often the situation would escalate, especially if a student resisted or, even worse, ran. In the scariest incident during my time there, a police officer chased a seventeen-year-old student into the school, wrestled him to the ground, and, in front of dozens of terrified students and teachers, drew his gun. On another occasion, a tenth grader was taking a break between classes and standing, legally, on the corner in front of our building. When he refused a police officer's request to move from the corner, the officer grabbed and handcuffed him. By the time a school official intervened, our student was already being placed in the police van. Luckily, our staff member was able to persuade the officer not to go through with the arrest.

All our students were black, as were most of the police officers; one staff member suggested, only half-jokingly, that this illegal and unprovoked harassment was a form of black-on-black crime. For our students, shared racial identity did little to make the encounters less humiliating. Those of us on staff did our best to assist our students once the police had sped off. We would offer kind words, tell our students they hadn't done anything wrong, and help pick up their possessions off the street. Their privacy and dignity, however, could not be so easily restored.

Unfortunately, the abuses that our students endured were part of a larger pattern. For decades, D.C. and the nation had been consumed by a drug war whose major fronts were the sidewalks and street corners of America's poorest neighborhoods. And the police, accordingly, had been trained to act like warriors. As Seth Stoughton, a police officer turned law professor, explains, "Under this warrior worldview, officers are locked in intermittent and unpredictable combat with unknown but highly lethal enemies."[1]

It didn't matter that our students weren't selling drugs, that they were simply taking a break between Algebra and American History, standing around in the aimless way of teenagers everywhere. As young people in a high-crime community, they were automatically viewed as potential enemies. This fact points to one of the most destructive aspects of modern policing. Although officers recognize some segments of the community—the shopkeepers, the pastors, the elderly grandmothers—as law-abiding citizens, they regard most neighborhood residents, and young people in particular, with generalized suspicion. Unable to distinguish between a student on break and a drug dealer working the corner, the police treat them both as menaces to public safety.[2]

In this way, the warrior model inverts the presumption of innocence. In the ghetto, you are not presumed innocent until proven otherwise. Rather, you are presumed guilty, or at least suspicious, and you must spend an extraordinary amount of energy—through careful attention to dress, behavior, and speech—to mark yourself as innocent. All with no guarantee that these efforts will work. The War on Drugs exacts a similar toll on the presumption of innocence. Once that spring, following yet another unprovoked search, one of our more assertive students shouted that the police had yet again failed to find anything. In response, a departing officer yelled back, "Not *this* time." The officer's response reveals how devastating it is to lose the presumption of innocence: no amount of good behavior is enough to reclaim it. Even proof of innocence is dismissed by a system incapable of questioning the assumptions that led it to mark you as guilty.

The overt hostility that such officers displayed toward our students—the constant targeting, the rough treatment, the refusal to grant them autonomy of their bodies—has deep historical roots. In *The Condemnation of Blackness: Race, Crime, and the Making of Modern Urban America*, Khalil Gibran Muhammad shows how the stereotype of black criminality has been invoked for centuries to justify all manner of discriminatory treatment.[3] Indeed, warrior policing would have looked familiar to James Baldwin, whose 1960 essay "Fifth

Avenue, Uptown: A Letter from Harlem" stands as a classic indictment of ghetto policing. The function of an urban police force, Baldwin wrote, was "to keep the black man corralled up here, in his place," and, to that end, "the only way to police a ghetto is to be oppressive."[4]

But the harsh treatment our students experienced also had more proximate causes. Warrior policing as we now know it emerged in the late 1980s, when a terrifying new drug—crack cocaine—invaded America's ghettos.

In the magnitude of the threat it posed to black America, the crack epidemic exceeded even the heroin crisis of the 1960s. This drug was seen as so damaging because it created so many addicts so quickly, and because its damage couldn't be contained: not just the addict, but his or her children, family, friends, and neighbors went down as well. Crack also spawned violent drug markets the likes of which American cities had never seen. In their fight for territory, heavily armed gangs turned urban neighborhoods into killing fields. Concerns about drug-related violence weren't new—Hassan Jeru-Ahmed had articulated them during the heroin epidemic in D.C., and John Ray and Burtell Jefferson had done the same while promoting Initiative 9—but the unprecedented carnage of the crack years seemed to put the point beyond doubt: the drug war was not just about drugs. It could be—indeed, *must* be—understood as a fight against violent crime.

The menace crack presented in turn provoked a set of responses that have helped produce the harsh and bloated criminal justice system we have today. Most of all, the fight against crack helped to enshrine the notion that police must be warriors, aggressive and armored, working ghetto corners as an army might patrol enemy territory. At the same time, aggressive policing was part of a larger set of legal and policy changes that included mandatory minimums, longer prison sentences, and the seizing of assets of drug dealers and users. In addition, elected officials, police chiefs, journalists, and everyday citizens increasingly heaped shame and scorn upon lawbreakers. This hostile, unforgiving mind-set wasn't born in the crack era, but it was then that it became entrenched, influencing even to this day how we think about drugs, violence, and punishment.

> I won't take it from the Klan with a rope; I won't take it from a neighbor with dope.
>
> —Rev. Jesse Jackson[5]

Broad swaths of black America were struggling in the mid-1980s, hit hard by massive job losses as American corporations moved factories overseas, as middle-class families fled to the suburbs, and as rapacious lenders offered predatory mortgages to black buyers, stripping many families of what little wealth they had managed to accumulate.

Government policy wasn't helping. During the 1970s, many black leaders had adopted an all-of-the-above approach to fighting crime. While supporting tough-on-crime measures, they also called for federal investment in longer-term, root-cause solutions such as welfare, education, and job training programs. Some, most notably Representative John Conyers, proposed a Marshall Plan for the inner cities, asking the federal government to rebuild America's ghettos just as George Marshall had helped rebuild Europe in the wake of World War II. By the end of the decade, however, these efforts had come to naught. Instead of an all-of-the-above response to drugs, violence, and disorder, black America had gotten only one of the above: punitive crime measures.

Prospects for disadvantaged communities became even bleaker in 1980, when Ronald Reagan won the presidency. One of Reagan's signature achievements as California's governor had been kicking "cheaters" off the welfare rolls; now, as president, he was determined to reduce federal spending on social programs.[6] During his first year in office, Congress did just that, passing legislation that changed the formulas governing eligibility and payouts for certain means-tested entitlements.[7] These changes led to a roughly 2 percent increase in the poverty rate, the brunt of which was borne by African Americans.[8] The federal cuts, in tandem with the Reagan administration's hostility toward affirmative action and other civil rights measures, led black leaders to strike increasingly pessimistic tones by the mid-1980s. "In the best of worlds we would be reporting that the Black condition has shown marked improvement over the past decade," said John Jacob, president of the Urban League, in 1985. "But the facts argue otherwise. In virtually every area of life that counts, Black people made strong progress in the 1960s, peaked in the '70s and have been sliding back ever since."[9]

And then came crack. Its introduction into America's poorest communities was, as journalists Harry Jaffe and Tom Sherwood recall, like "throwing a match into a bucket of gasoline."[10] An adulterated version of powder cocaine, crack is created by mixing cocaine with water and baking soda over heat. But unlike powder cocaine, which is typically sniffed, a rock of crack is easily smoked, which allows the fumes to enter the bloodstream more quickly and deliver a more intense high.[11] This distinguishing feature made crack more appealing—and more addictive.[12] In 1984, 15 percent of D.C.'s arrestees tested positive for cocaine; by 1987, that figure had quadrupled, to 60 percent, with virtually every user having ingested the drug as crack.[13]

One way to understand the fear crack induced in black America is to consider the analogies it provoked. At the height of the epidemic, black political and civic leaders often compared crack to the greatest evils that African Americans had ever suffered. In March 1988, the president of the NAACP chapter in Prince George's County, Maryland, called the drug "the worst thing to hit us since slavery."[14] Two months later, Rev. Jesse Jackson equated drug dealers with Klansmen. "No one has the right to kill our children," he declared. "I won't take it from the Klan with a rope; I won't take it from a neighbor with dope."[15] "This is perhaps the most serious threat we have faced since the end of slavery," announced the *Los Angeles Sentinel*, that city's leading black newspaper, in an alarm bell of an editorial. "And unless we face up to it and do something about it, we are doomed as a community."[16]

What is wrong with us as a people?
—Assistant Police Chief Isaac "Ike" Fulwood

When Michael Saunders was found, still breathing, with a gunshot wound to his head, he was sprawled on the corner of First and N Streets with sixty packets of crack in his coat and a pistol in his jeans. He had been shot in the jaw, and the bullet had pierced his skull. He was rushed to the hospital, but it was too late: the nineteen-year-old died two hours later, at four in the morning on January 1, 1988.[17] At year's end, Isaac Fulwood, then the Metropolitan Police Department's assistant chief, would look back on 1988 and call it "Washington's Year of Shame." Saunders was the year's first victim—but many more soon followed.[18]

Two days after Saunders's death, Osahon Sandy Emovon, twenty-seven, was found in a parked car in Southeast Washington with multiple gunshot wounds to the head.[19] That same afternoon, half a mile away, several men forced themselves into thirty-year-old Gwendolyn Scott's apartment, where they began shooting, killing Scott and seriously wounding a companion.[20] On January 6, just before midnight, a man was killed by gunfire and another two were wounded while standing in a grassy area in Southwest D.C.[21] The next day, a man leaped from his car in Southwest and, armed with a machine gun, started firing at a group of friends, killing Thomas Arnold, forty.[22] On January 10, hours after Curtis Briscoe got into a heated argument with three men, he was found shot to death in a courtyard in Northwest. That same day, nineteen-year-old Ricardo Washington was shot fatally in the back outside a Southeast apartment complex.[23]

The next day, January 11, John Clem was stabbed to death during a fight in Northwest. On January 15, Clifford Jackson was found on the front steps of an apartment complex, shot to death. One day later, Bernard Smith, thirty-nine, and Joseph Williams, twenty-one, were both found dead; Smith had been left to die on the sidewalk after sustaining a gunshot wound to the chest. On January 19, Beverly Anita Thompson, twenty-five, was found in an abandoned, burning apartment in Northeast; she had been raped, beaten, and strangled to death. Thompson was survived by her eighteen-month-old son, Steven.[24] On January 20, at two in the morning, a gunman fired into the East Side Night Club, seriously injuring James Ward, twenty-four, and killing George Pringle, twenty, a father of three.[25] Later that day, Richard Cole, thirty-five, was found stabbed to death in a basement in Northwest, and on the other side of the city, Horace Pinnock, thirty-four, was shot dead in his third-floor apartment.[26] On January 26, a pedestrian alerted the police to an abandoned car in a creek in Northeast; when the police opened the trunk, they found the body of Ralph Bailey, Jr., twenty-three, stabbed, shot, and badly burned.[27] On January 27, a masked gunman walked into Gregg's Barbershop in Northwest and, with customers looking on in horror, unloaded several bullets into William Lee Goins before calmly exiting the building.[28] On January 31, Fred Parris, forty-three, an elementary school science teacher, was walking up the stairs to his apartment when two men approached him from behind and demanded money; one of the thieves shot Parris in the back, killing him, and the men fled empty-handed.[29] That same day, Reginald Small, fifteen, an eighth grader at Frederick Douglass Junior High School, was shot and killed near his home in Southeast.[30] His was the thirty-seventh and final murder of what had become the deadliest month in D.C. history.[31]

D.C. was midway through a seven-year stretch in which its homicide rate tripled, eventually earning the city the ignominious title America's Murder Capital. Ike Fulwood, the assistant police chief, took the violence personally. "I've been to the scene of these crimes," he wrote, "and seen a 17-year-old kid lying there with his head blown open and his brains lying out on the sidewalk and said to myself: 'What is wrong with us as a people?'"[32] It was a question that many of the city's black residents were asking.

D.C.'s spiking murder rate served notice that addiction, as terrible as it was, was far from the worst consequence of crack. Not all these deaths were related to the crack trade, but many were—either di-

rectly, as a result of turf wars or deals gone south, or indirectly, cata-
lyzed by violent highs, destructive lows, or the sheer desperation of
securing the next fix. "I'd rather be in a crack market than be, say, held
at gunpoint, or have boiling oil poured on me," writes the criminologist David Kennedy, who worked in some of America's hardest-hit
neighborhoods. "Short of that, things don't get much worse."[33]

The crack markets also brought a rush of guns into the city. Despite D.C.'s 1975 law outlawing gun possession and Initiative 9's mandatory minimums for crimes committed while armed, D.C. could do
little to stop the weapons from pouring in from Virginia or Maryland.
"Guns are a constant," noted Mike Tidwell, who worked as a counselor at a D.C. halfway house during the crack years. "They are in the
pants, on the sofa, under the car seat. They are part of the scenery, an
accepted accoutrement of life."[34] People had begun using guns to re-
solve more than drug disputes: even the pettiest of arguments—over
a girl, clothes, or just a hard look at the wrong person—could lead to
guns being drawn.

And the guns were far more powerful. Even now, thirty years
later, many D.C. residents can recall the arrival of this new weaponry
in their neighborhoods. For example, Albert Herring, who would
later serve as Assistant United States Attorney for D.C., lived in Southwest in the mid-1980s. He had long been familiar with the sound of
traditional gunfire, but one day he heard something different outside
his apartment window. "I didn't really know what to make of it at
the time," he told me. "It didn't sound like firecrackers, but it was the
same sort of rapid *pa-pa-pa-pa-pa-pa-pa-pa-pa-pa* sound."[35] The guns
Herring knew—revolvers—did not sound like that. When he learned
that the police had recovered Uzi shell casings from a nearby park, he
understood what he'd heard.

As the death toll mounted, the victims remained concentrated in
D.C.'s poor black neighborhoods. In 1989, D.C. was 30 percent white,
but nine out of every ten homicide victims were black. The Department of Justice would later estimate that in the mid-1990s, a black

American male faced a 1-in-35 chance of being murdered over his lifetime—a risk that was eight times higher than a white man's, whose chances were 1 in 251.[36]

The city's extreme residential segregation meant that while some parts of the city resembled war zones, large areas remained unaffected. In 1991, for example, Ward 3, the leafy, manicured D.C. neighborhood that houses the city's upper middle class (and attracts many of its tourists), saw only three homicides.[37] The economically barren and almost entirely black Ward 8, by contrast, had a homicide rate that was thirty times higher.[38] And while being black and poor were risk factors, so was age: of the 483 murders D.C. witnessed in 1990, half of the victims were African Americans under the age of twenty-five.[39]

While murders quite rightly received the most coverage, the ranks of the maimed and wounded were growing, too. For every person killed by a bullet, there were at least three others—by some estimates, more than four—who survived.[40] By the late 1980s, big-city hospitals had begun to resemble military trauma units; one Vietnam veteran with experience in both places compared the emergency room of D.C. General to a Navy battle aid station. In 1990, when the United States launched the first Gulf War, the military sent surgeons to train in big-city hospitals, where they could prepare, mentally and physically, for the horrors of the front lines.[41]

Not all the damage was so visible. As a generation of black children grew up seeing friends shot over matters as serious as a drug debt—or as trivial as staring too long at the wrong person—the resulting trauma was as real as the physical harm. Children exposed to violence are less likely to attend school (and more likely to be disruptive when they do go to class). They are also more likely to carry weapons and to require less provocation before using them. Underlying these behaviors is usually a profound sense of hopelessness: Why sacrifice for a tomorrow that may never come?[42]

In neighborhoods wracked by violence, young people must devote immense psychological resources to their day-to-day survival. I would learn this lesson from the students at Maya Angelou. Once, a student named Bobby asked for more time to finish a writing assignment for a criminal justice class I was teaching. Our school days were long, he pointed out, and he hadn't had enough time in the evening to get it done. I started picking apart his day, trying to point out times when he could have at least been thinking about the project. I told him that I composed arguments and essays in my head as I was walking or driving to work. Bobby should use his travel time in the same way, I suggested. Bobby, with a half smile (I think he might have been trying to stop himself from laughing at me), said, "Look, James, I'm just trying to *get* here, and I'm sorry, but I'm not trying to get jumped looking like a fool walking down the street daydreaming about your work." The teacher in me never stopped pressing Bobby and the other students about turning in their assignments on time. But I did gain a deeper appreciation for how living amidst violence constrained not just their bodies, but their minds.[43]

The toll of violence may manifest most acutely in children, but it is paid by the entire community. Exposure to violence breeds chronic anxiety, tension, and hypervigilance.[44] Since violent neighborhoods are also more likely to be poor ones, these ills have myriad causes—but fear of violence is surely one. Then there are the more subtle effects, both psychological and economic: the office assistant who declines to work extra hours (and make much-needed money) because she doesn't want to walk home alone at night; the would-be student who forgoes evening classes and never gets her GED; the higher prices charged at local convenience stores by shopkeepers passing along the cost of alarm systems, window bars, and floodlights.

A proper accounting of crack's impact on black America allows us to see why many, seeking to convey the damage wrought, compared it to slavery and other dismal chapters of American history. David Kennedy is right to look back at those years and say that when "crack blew through America's poor black neighborhoods," it was as if "the Four Horsemen of the Apocalypse had traded their steeds for super-charged bulldozers."[45] But alongside the damage from crack itself lies

another set of harms—the damage caused by the criminal justice
system's increasingly harsh response to the epidemic.

> We're going to fight drugs and crime until the drug dealer's teeth
> rattle.
>
> —Atlanta mayor Maynard Jackson[46]

The federal role in the War on Drugs escalated in the age of crack.[47]
In 1984, 1986, and 1988, Congress lengthened sentences and established ever-stiffer mandatory minimums.[48] The process was often as
hurried as the outcomes were draconian. Instead of holding public
hearings and soliciting expert testimony on proposed legislation,
members of Congress engaged in a bipartisan bidding war to raise the
penalties ever higher.[49] "The way these sentences were arrived at—it
was like an auction house," explains Eric Sterling, who was then assistant counsel to the House Judiciary Subcommittee on Crime. "It
was this frenzied, panicked atmosphere—I'll see your five years and
I'll raise you five years. It was the craziest political poker game."[50]

The most notorious outcome of this poker game was the hundred-
to-one cocaine-to-crack ratio. Under this policy, someone selling a
small amount of crack would incur the same severe mandatory minimum sentence as someone selling one hundred times as much cocaine. This distinction was based on racialized fear, not science. As
the legal scholar David Sklansky documented more than twenty years
ago, the most prominent motivation in the congressional debate over
crack was the fear that "a black drug, sold by black men" was making
its way out of the ghetto and into white communities.[51] Because the
hundred-to-one ratio had so little to justify it, and because African
Americans were more likely to be involved in the crack trade, the
law's harsher treatment of crack defendants became one of the most
grotesque examples of racial discrimination in the criminal justice
system.[52]

Although the federal government played a critical role in the drug
war, its actions are only part of the story. The nation's urban centers

exercised their own power—especially when it came to policing. And African Americans, often underrepresented in federal and state government, featured prominently in many municipal governments. By 1990, for example, there were 130 black police chiefs nationwide, including the top cops in D.C., New York, Philadelphia, Baltimore, Detroit, Chicago, and Houston.[53] There were also more than three hundred African American mayors, including those in D.C., New York, Los Angeles, Philadelphia, Detroit, Baltimore, Atlanta, and Oakland.[54] The words and deeds of these black law enforcement officials and politicians, so often overlooked in histories of the War on Drugs, are crucial to explaining why and how the war developed as it did in American cities.

As we have seen, the crack trade and the violence it generated stirred fear and outrage among residents of inner-city neighborhoods. Public officials echoed these sentiments and reinforced them. D.C.'s Mayor Marion Barry, nine years before his own arrest for crack possession, called drug dealers "the scourge of the earth."[55] Barry was also fond of the phrase "gun thugs and drug thugs," invoking it to explain why the police needed more powerful weapons ("so they can protect themselves against these gun thugs and drug thugs") and to dismiss concerns about jail overcrowding ("let me just say that we will find space to put those drug thugs and gun thugs who get convicted of carrying guns and selling drugs").[56] After one shooting, Barry told a reporter that he wanted the police to go after murderers and "hunt them down like mad dogs."[57]

In Atlanta, Mayor Maynard Jackson matched Barry's anger, pledging to make "the drug dealer's teeth rattle."[58] If a drug or gun sale resulted in a death, Jackson said, the seller deserved to "roast" or "fry." In 1989 he proposed a program to seize the assets of drug dealers—the program was known by the name "Kick Their Assets."[59] Jackson's point of view was widely shared among Atlanta's black leadership. In 1990, when the majority-black city council began searching for a new police chief, council president Marvin Arrington said they were looking for "an ass kicker." Arrington and his colleagues soon settled on

Eldrin Bell, who, according to *The Atlanta Journal-Constitution*, was known to fill cells "faster than corrections officials can draw up new prison plans." Upon his appointment, Bell declared war on drug dealers: "Unless we arrest them, incarcerate them and spit them back out with only their underwear," he declared, "they've beat the system."[60]

Some African American politicians embraced the war metaphor in describing the fight against drugs and crime. During the 1988 presidential campaign, Rev. Jesse Jackson dismissed his rivals by saying, "I welcome Mr. Bush and Mr. Dukakis as lieutenants, but I am the general in this war to fight drugs."[61] And Jackson wasn't the only African American politician making this claim; Charles Rangel, Harlem's long-serving congressional representative, touted his drug warrior credentials in a 1989 *Ebony* story titled "Charles Rangel: The Front-Line General in the War on Drugs."[62]

If wars require generals, then those generals need armies. During the crack years, some African Americans went beyond metaphor and requested that actual troops be sent to ghetto streets. In 1988, in response to D.C.'s exploding homicide rate, council member Nadine Winter asked President Reagan to declare a state of emergency and to deploy the National Guard.[63] Others seconded Winter's request, including council member H. R. Crawford. "We owe those people who live scared some immediate relief," he said. "We don't need more summits, more meetings, more discussion. If this is really war, let's declare war."[64]

Maybe it was just talk. After all, the list of topics for which rhetoric is unmatched by action is long and varied, and includes global warming, income inequality, and poverty. But in the case of crack, the bellicose talk was matched by deeds.

As inner-city drug sellers increased their firepower, the police responded in kind. Through the late 1980s—and even, in some cities, into the early 1990s—America's police officers carried revolvers. Earlier in the century, some observers had hoped that one day even those would become unnecessary. Walter Fauntroy, who as D.C.'s delegate to Congress had helped lead the 1975 push for stricter gun control, once predicted, "As handguns disappear from the national scene, this nation and this city may approach an era of domestic tranquillity which will allow us to implement a system similar to that now existing in many European countries, where even the police do not carry guns except in emergency situations."[65] But instead of moving in the direction of tranquillity, police officers began seeing themselves outgunned by teenagers. In response, the police armored up, starting with 9mm semiautomatic weapons. In February 1988, Mayor Barry and Police Chief Maurice T. Turner, Jr., displayed these new weapons at a press event, with Barry himself shooting at a target and marveling at the speed with which the guns could fire.[66] No longer would an officer find himself pinned down, struggling to reload his revolver, while a drug dealer, equipped with a large-capacity magazine, poured semiautomatic gunfire into the door of the cruiser.[67]

The new weaponry did not go unused. In many American cities, the police adopted military-inspired "operations" to battle drugs and violence, with such names as Operation Hammer (Los Angeles), Operation TNT (New York), Operation Invincible (Memphis), and Operation Clean Sweep (Chicago).[68] D.C.'s main antidrug initiative—also called Operation Clean Sweep—granted hundreds of officers vast powers, including the prerogative to clear corners, establish roadblocks, make undercover purchases, seize cars, and condemn apartments.

Operation Clean Sweep was conceived of and spearheaded by Assistant Chief Fulwood, who had joined the MPD in 1964. A burly man with an imposing demeanor and a can-do attitude, Fulwood had acquired an aggressive, gung-ho reputation on the streets as a young officer. At the same time, he prided himself on developing relationships with neighborhood residents, and his success in a community relations post caught the attention of Burtell Jefferson, who was on his way to becoming D.C.'s first black police chief. Fulwood and Jefferson were both firmly rooted in the African American tradition of overcoming racism through individual effort, and Fulwood remembered Jefferson's advice about how to rise in the face of the police department's internal racism. "Things are not always going to be like this," Jefferson told him. "You guys have to study. If you don't study, you can't use race as a crutch." Fulwood followed Jefferson's example, passing the department's various promotional exams, and once Jefferson was named police chief, he helped Fulwood ascend rapidly through the ranks.[69]

Fulwood carried out Operation Clean Sweep with the full support of the city's top leadership. In 1986, a few months before the operation was launched, Fulwood's boss, Chief Maurice Turner, said about drug dealers, "We're going to arrest every one of those [s.o.b.s] that we can get."[70] Fifteen months later, standing in the sweltering swamp that is Washington, D.C., in August, Mayor Barry heralded the new strategy by saying, "If you think it's hot today, we're going to make it hotter on drug dealers and pushers who are destroying the minds of our young people."[71]

Just as important, Fulwood had buy-in from the police force itself— a force that, by the time of Clean Sweep, was more than 50 percent black. Propelled by Jefferson's efforts, the percentage of black officers had been increasing steadily since the 1970s, making D.C. the first large American city with a majority-black police department. And that department delivered on Barry's promise. Clean Sweep lasted only a couple of years, but it produced an unprecedented number of drug arrests and, perhaps more significantly, ushered in a new era of policing, one that would endure long after the decline of the open-air drug markets to which the operation had initially responded.

Fulwood, however, never matched Barry's rhetorical posturing (few could), and the vigor with which he attacked drug trafficking and gun violence in the city was shadowed by ambivalence. When asked what he thought about the fact that D.C. had come to lead the nation in drug arrests, Fulwood sounded almost apologetic. "It shows that we are very proficient at arresting drug dealers and users," he said. "But those arrest figures are a sad commentary on the situation in the

District. I would take more pride in less arrests if that meant the problem had been abated." He also admitted that the police themselves were relatively powerless to solve the city's drug problem: "We have to do a heck of a lot more in terms of education and treatment."[72] But Fulwood didn't run a school system or drug treatment center; he commanded a police force.[73]

Fulwood's conflicting emotions may have had a personal source. In the late 1960s, just as he was beginning his career in law enforcement, his brother Teddy was entering a lifetime of addiction. Teddy fell victim to heroin and spent much of the 1970s and 1980s moving between jail, prison, and various attempts at rehab. His addiction had a destructive impact on Ike Fulwood and the entire family—sometimes directly, as when Teddy stole hundreds of dollars' worth of tools from their father to buy drugs. For Ike, the implications were clear: libertarians were wrong to claim that a drug user should be left alone because he "ain't causing no harm but to himself." As he saw it, "If you live in one of these neighborhoods, it is more than that. The community is facing peril because of their conduct."[74]

But just as Fulwood knew that addiction could fuel crime and ravage a family, he also knew the pain that incarceration could exact. When he became the city's third consecutive African American police chief in 1989, his entire family was present at the swearing-in ceremony—all except Teddy, who, courtesy of his brother's police force, was in D.C. Jail awaiting trial on crack charges.

Whatever Fulwood's personal views, there was nothing half-hearted about Operation Clean Sweep. Its specialized units included "jump-out" squads: teams of officers, typically in unmarked vehicles, who would roll onto corners known for drug dealing and jump out of their cars. Anyone standing on the corner was fair game; not surprisingly, most tried to flee when the jump-outs descended. Lenese Herbert, a former D.C. prosecutor, described the process: As the police swarm in, "the swiftest go free. The slowest are subject to, at a minimum, verbal questioning and physical searches."[75]

Clean Sweep also helped entrench the specialized units—antidrug, antigun, and antigang—that would proliferate in the 1990s and that still operate today. Under Fulwood, the Rapid Deployment Unit (RDU), which focused on drugs and guns, was the most prominent. The RDU consisted mostly of young officers lauded by their commander for being "super-aggressive." As one RDU recruit explained, he had joined the force because he craved excitement. "I came here to be a police officer, not to get fat," he said. "I'm not a public relations kind of guy."[76]

This officer wasn't alone in his preference for action—and in not caring about the public image it conveyed. After observing RDU officers for *The Washington Post*, the journalists Michael York and Pierre Thomas noted, "They seem to thrive on humbling some suspects, sometimes even humiliating the rowdy ones."[77] In the early 1990s, the sociologist William Chambliss spent time riding with the RDU and reached a similar conclusion:

> The RDU patrols the ghetto continuously looking for cars with young black men in them. They are especially attentive to newer-model cars . . . based on the belief that they are the favorite cars of drug dealers. During our observations, however, the RDU officers came to the conclusion that drug dealers were leaving their fancy cars at home to avoid vehicular stops. It thus became commonplace for RDU officers to stop any car with young black men in it.[78]

One RDU officer was candid about the unit's tactics. "This is the jungle," he said. "We rewrite the Constitution every day down here."[79] This same officer believed that constant stops would teach dealers to leave their contraband at home.[80] "If we pull everyone over they will eventually learn that we aren't playing games anymore," he said. "We are real serious about getting the crap off the street."[81]

The RDU and its warrior policing had support from both public officials and many residents. Ward 7 council member H. R. Crawford complimented the RDU for forcing criminals "to run for cover." Responding to concerns over rough treatment, Crawford said, "In a war . . . we must give up some rights in order to recapture the streets."[82] When members of the Frederick Douglass Community Improvement Council wrote David Clarke to request more police, they specifically asked for more jump-out squads.[83]

But the aggressiveness came at an appalling human—and, eventually, financial—cost. A seventy-three-year-old retired postal worker was beaten after officers mistook him for a suspect; the man ended up with a broken arm. A fifty-six-year-old woman was beaten with a nightstick after challenging officers involved in an altercation with two of her children; another woman was cursed at, hit, and maced outside the restaurant where she worked. Much like Staten Island's Eric Garner, a thirty-one-year-old deaf man named Frankie Murphy stopped breathing while an MPD officer held him in a choke hold; he died in police custody. After a dangerous ride in a police wagon—not unlike the one suffered by Freddie Gray in Baltimore—a twenty-eight-year-old former U.S. Marine named James Cox won two separate lawsuits against the police. As a result of such incidents, D.C. paid out about $1 million a year to victims of police misconduct during the early 1990s.[84] Yet the abuses continued.

At the same time, a culture of impunity flourished with regard to less violent, but more common, police intrusions into the daily lives of black citizens. Swearing and yelling, making belittling remarks, issuing illegitimate orders, conducting random and unwarranted searches, demanding that suspects "get against the wall"—these behaviors rarely led to lawsuits or newspaper coverage. But for residents of the city's poorest neighborhoods, especially young people, this treatment became part of the social contract, a tax paid in exchange for the right to move in public spaces. Police mistreatment, that is, became part of growing up.

Short of filing suit, it was virtually impossible for citizens to obtain redress for police abuse. D.C.'s Civilian Complaint Review Board, the mechanism by which the MPD could supposedly be held account- able for its actions, was hopelessly inadequate—under-resourced, overburdened, and generally impotent. In 1993, U.S. District Court Judge Joyce H. Green concluded, "The District of Columbia made a conscious choice to close its eyes and cover its ears to the clamor of the complaints of police brutality languishing before its Board."[85]

I'm for confiscating cars. Houses. Jewelry. Television sets.

—Mayor Marion Barry

These heavy-handed police tactics were accompanied by asset for- feiture, a law enforcement tool that allowed the police to seize property—including cars and homes—used in drug transactions or purchased with drug money. Asset forfeiture dates back hundreds of years in American law, but in the late 1970s and 1980s, Congress and many states expanded its scope. D.C. leaders embraced this change, adopting, in the late 1980s and early 1990s, perhaps the most robust asset forfeiture protocol in the country.[86]

Fulwood had long defended asset forfeiture, declaring in 1986, "We're going to make it expensive to come into this man's town and buy drugs." To Fulwood, the type of drug involved in a sale did not matter. Neither did the volume of the transaction or the distinction between user and seller. "If you come into the District and buy a nickel bag of marijuana, and we see you and stop you and you are the owner of the car," he warned, "we are going to seize that vehicle."[87] Mayor Barry, who as a city council member had voted in favor of marijuana decriminalization in 1975, now adopted a much more punitive posi- tion. "If you are caught with half a gram of cocaine, we will take away your car," he said. "If you are caught with one marijuana joint, we want your car."[88] But Barry's list of targets for seizure did not stop at cars. "We've got to take the profit motivation out of drugs," he said at a National Press Club event in March 1989. At another event he an- nounced, "I'm for confiscating cars. Houses. Jewelry. Television sets.

That may sound rather harsh and cruel, but if a drug dealer buys his mother a bedroom suite, or some luggage, I'm for taking the luggage and the bedroom suite at the same time."[89]

These were not idle threats. One evening, shortly after Clean Sweep's launch, a man bought $20 worth of PCP at the well-known drug market on Chapin Street, NW. After driving off in his red Cutlass Supreme, the man was ambushed by multiple squad cars. Police officers forced him onto the hood of his car, searched the vehicle, and found the two tins of drugs. The PCP dealers, it turned out, had been undercover operatives; the police promptly arrested the man and, under the new seizure law, confiscated his Cutlass. This strategy—posing as street-level drug sellers, then arresting buyers and seizing their cars—had become standard practice in late-1980s D.C. After the driver of the red Cutlass was placed in the police wagon, one of the arresting officers slammed the door, saying, "You guys just don't learn."[90]

Arrest, conviction, a possible jail or prison sentence, forfeiture of property, and a lifetime of collateral consequences—today many would conclude that this cumulative set of punishments was disproportionate to the offense of PCP possession. It appears all the more unjust—even cruel—given how few drug treatment slots were available for addicts seeking help. But that's not how it looked to many black citizens facing the horrors of the crack epidemic. "Thanks to Operation Clean Sweep we are now getting control of our streets and community," said Calvin Rolark, chairman of the MPD's Citizens Advisory Committee.[91] The *Afro* supported Clean Sweep, saying that the drug industry was "a threat to our race."[92] While lawyers fretted about certain police tactics, the paper reported that Clean Sweep brought "relief to many District residents living in neighborhoods with a high rate of drug trafficking."[93] Even the Girl Scouts were on board: Troop #1589 wrote "to honor the Ladies and Gentlemen of the 'Clean Sweep Task Force' . . . for their tireless efforts in trying to keep our community free of drugs."[94] The community in question, Ward 8, had the city's highest homicide rate.

There was not a single rock of crack anywhere in the District of Columbia that wasn't stained with the blood of some mother's child.

—Albert Herring, former Assistant United States Attorney, Washington, D.C.[95]

When I talk to my students about the drug war, what they find most incomprehensible (other than marijuana prohibition) is our exceedingly tough treatment of users and street-level dealers. After all, in theory, drug enforcement takes account of the defendant's place in the hierarchy. The proverbial kingpin is supposed to be treated as the most culpable; the kid making minor sales on the street corner is less culpable; and the individual user is the least culpable of all. But the theory doesn't always play out in practice. Small-time users and sellers are routinely sentenced to prison. Many are sent to jail while awaiting trial and may spend days, weeks, or months in a cell, away from their families, before they are able to post bond. Even those who never end up behind bars can suffer severe consequences: a months-long legal process, dragged out over multiple court dates, might require a defendant to miss work—which, in the low-wage sector, can mean losing her job. And a criminal conviction, even for something as minor as small-scale marijuana distribution, can make it more difficult (or outright impossible) to vote, land a job, find housing, or be admitted to college.

The crack years help explain why we became so punitive toward users and low-level dealers. Rampant violence associated with crack markets became a way of justifying harsh treatment all the way down the line. As Albert Herring explains,

When I think back to my days as a prosecutor in the District of Columbia, when I think back to those days where the murder rate was above 400 [a year], when I think back to the days when . . . mothers were burying their children faster than funeral homes could schedule appointments, I am quite convinced—as convinced as I am grown, black, and free—that there was not a single rock of crack anywhere in the District of Columbia that wasn't stained with the blood of some mother's child.[96]

Today, drug users and sellers have become the paradigmatic "non-violent offenders" in the national criminal justice reform conversation, but Herring's comments are a reminder of how foreign such a characterization would have seemed to many during the crack era. Sounding like most of the prosecutors I encountered in the 1990s, he argues that anybody who participated in the distribution chain "bore a moral responsibility for all the blood that had flowed in order for that network . . . to have been built, and to be as vibrant as it was."[97]

Herring's wrath was limited to sellers, but others set their sights on users as well. Reagan administration officials, recognizing that there would be no crack markets if not for consumer demand, were especially inclined to blame drug users for the markets' violence. In 1985, Ed Meese, in his first speech as U.S. Attorney General, declared at the National Press Club that even the casual user effectively subsidized "terror, torture and death."[98] The next month, testifying before Congress, the U.S. Attorney for D.C., Joseph diGenova, repeated Meese's accusation: "Drug users, whether occasional or regular, are stockholders in organized crime."[99] But drug users' most ardent enemy was Reagan's drug czar, William Bennett, who believed that users should lose their driver's licenses and face jail time. "Casual use," Bennett argued, "is no casual matter."[100]

D.C.'s Black Police Caucus, an organization of black officers, agreed with Bennett that drug users should lose their driver's licenses; in a letter to Mayor Barry, they argued that "registration/tags should be confiscated for all automobiles that are found to contain narcotics and individuals that are arrested for narcotics violations should be stripped of their driving privileges."[101] Fulwood agreed that users should face tough consequences, reasoning that "the buyers are the financiers

of the whole narcotics enterprise." Without them, he said, "drug trafficking would not exist."[102] In an editorial, the *Afro* cheered Fulwood's
remarks, saying, "Truer words were never spoken."[103]

Attacking users, some argued, would bring a measure of racial
and class fairness to the drug war. In a column titled "Go After the
Drug Buyers Too," William Raspberry characterized the average user
as "a college student, a young professional, a wage earner or a suburban sophisticate."[104] In his eyes, then, going after drug users would
shift the focus of enforcement and prosecution from blacks to whites,
and from the poor to the middle-class and wealthy. But the notion
that suburban sophisticates would end up in the back of a squad car
underestimated the ability of the privileged and powerful to navigate
their way around the drug war's harshest consequences. In D.C. and
elsewhere, those with the financial means and networks quickly
found alternative, and less risky, ways to buy drugs. Those left to
purchase (and be arrested) on street corners were demographically
indistinguishable from the sellers with whom they shared their cells:
poor, black, and, in more ways than one, trapped.

> . . . purposeless infliction of pain with no conceivable penological jus-
> tification . . .
>
> —U.S. District Court Judge June L. Green

In the first eighteen months of Clean Sweep, the MPD made forty-six
thousand arrests—one for every fourteen D.C. residents. This was
more drug arrests per capita than in any other comparable American
city.[105] Some suspects were released immediately with notices to
return to court, but many ended up spending days or weeks in D.C.
Jail, and some eventually served sentences at Lorton prison in
Virginia. These facilities had never been known for their decency
or humanity; the prisoners who endorsed Doug Moore in his initial campaign for city council in 1974 had hoped that he would do
something about the terrible conditions of their confinement. But by
the crack era, Lorton had become even more overcrowded, dangerous,

and miserable.[106] Male prisoners had it bad—squalid cells, violent assaults, negligent or outright abusive corrections officers, a broken health-care system that, according to a ruling by U.S. District Court Judge June L. Green, resulted in "purposeless infliction of pain with no conceivable penological justification."[107] But the situation faced by female prisoners was arguably even worse. For them, the litany of abuses included sexual predation. Corrections officers raped and assaulted female inmates with impunity; those who complained were placed in "protective custody," which most prisoners experienced as further punishment (the practice often included twenty-three hours a day of isolation). The physical assaults were compounded by verbal ones—upon learning that a prisoner was going to shower, one officer told her, "Well, you go ahead and do that and I'll be in there to stick my rod up in you"—and an extreme lack of privacy, as corrections officers would appear unannounced in women's dressing areas.

Judge Green, who presided over many of the inmates' lawsuits, repeatedly found that D.C. officials were "deliberately indifferent" to conditions in the city's jails, conditions that effectively amounted to a humanitarian crisis. But instead of addressing the problems, the city government remained determined to prosecute and incarcerate more people, despite the fact that overcrowding was a leading cause of the hellish conditions. Before Clean Sweep was launched, Mayor Barry had rejected the idea that overcrowding should constrain law enforcement, saying, "We are not going to let any absence of jail space be any deterrent to us locking people up." And the mayor remained defiant in the face of multiple lawsuits: "Even if I have to be held in contempt of court for violating a court [order] of overcrowding, I'm prepared to do that if it means getting drug dealers and drug pushers off the streets."[108]

The city council shared Barry's antipathy toward those behind bars, even if it expressed its attitude less flamboyantly. In 1990, for example, in the middle of the overcrowding crisis, the council quietly eviscerated the D.C. Jail's budget for medical services. A year earlier, a court-appointed monitor had concluded that the city's prison was woefully understaffed—resulting, he said, in "inadequate care and unnecessary suffering." Charles Phillips, who spent twelve years in the city's prison system, reported seeing more than one fellow inmate die from treatable causes. "It's sad," he said, "but society seems to look at a guy in prison as not a guy who should receive the basic things a human being needs for survival. They seem to think of it as being part of the punishment."[109]

When Ike Fulwood designed Clean Sweep as an assistant chief in 1986, his goal had been to suppress the drug trade and reduce the violence associated with it. Once he was promoted to chief in 1989, he asserted those same priorities, asking to be judged by his ability to bring down the escalating murder rate. But on that measure he had already failed, spectacularly. Despite Clean Sweep's aggressive policing and escalating arrest numbers, the bodies continued to fall. In 1988, the year before Fulwood became chief, 372 people were murdered. Instead of declining, the toll continued to rise: 434 in 1989, 483 in 1990, and 489 in 1991.

The number of killings, and the nature of them, weighed heavily on Fulwood. He recalled tracking down one killer who had shot two people in their faces, blowing the tops of their heads off. When police found the teenage shooter a few hours later, he was at home, asleep in bed. Fulwood was appalled, asking, "What kind of kid can blow two people away and then go to sleep?"[110] Fulwood went to as many of the murder scenes as he could—a small gesture toward ensuring that these black lives weren't forgotten. At one scene he looked down at the teenage victim, shot to death in an alley, and all he could see were the boy's sneakers poking out from under the sheet police had laid over his body. They were the same style of Nikes that his own son, about the same age as the victim, wore. Another time he went to the scene of a quadruple homicide and interviewed a nine-year-old boy who casually discussed death with him. Later, Fulwood remembered thinking that he would likely arrest this boy one day. As Fulwood saw it, in D.C. during the crack years, murder had become no big deal; instead of the ultimate step, to be taken only in the most extreme circumstances, it had become a routine option "for valueless people without a soul."[111]

A city can't be well served by a despairing police chief, and Fulwood, to his credit, knew it. He resigned in 1992, admitting that he was stepping down in part because he hadn't done the one thing he had set out to do: cut the city's murder rate. At his retirement ceremony, reflecting on his twenty-eight-year career in law enforcement, he conceded the pain the city's murders had caused him. "The number one low," he recalled, "has been the record number of homicides, the record number of young black men killed needlessly."[112] And not long after retiring, he acknowledged that racial disparities contributed to his frustration. "I'm tired of seeing black children locked up every five minutes," he said. "And it's not having a significant impact."[113]

Fulwood had hoped that retiring would provide him with a respite from the violence engulfing the city. It did not. Two months after he resigned, he received the call his family had long feared. His brother Teddy, who had been released from prison the previous year, had returned to the neighborhood where the two boys had grown up—an area that, like much of the city, had become rougher. In all likelihood, Fulwood knew, he had also gone back to using, and maybe dealing, heroin.

On November 19, 1992, Teddy became the city's 401st murder victim of the year. He was shot just a few blocks from the home where he and Ike had been raised. Like so many of the murders from that era, the crime would never be solved. "Maybe it was a gambling debt," Fulwood said. "Maybe it was a drug debt. We just don't know."

How can you tell us we can be anything if they treat us like we're nothing?

—High school junior, Maya Angelou Public
Charter School, Washington, D.C.

By 2000, the crack epidemic had subsided in D.C. and nationally. Although experts do not agree on the precise reasons for the decline in crack use, most cite crack's reputation as a dangerous drug, especially among people who saw what it did to an addict's family members and neighbors. Crack-associated violence also subsided, partly because stabilized open-air markets reduced violent turf battles, lower prices reduced the incentive for sellers to steal drugs and caused others to exit the market, and the drop in the number of users meant fewer people resorting to crime to obtain money to buy crack.

But despite the drug's declining popularity, its legacy remained, in the form of combative policing practices that continued long after the termination of Operation Clean Sweep and similar campaigns. These were the practices to which students at our school were subjected on the corner of Ninth and T.

In the spring of 2000, after our students had faced a series of particularly nightmarish encounters with police, the staff met to organize a response. As terrifying and humiliating as the police raids were, we hoped to turn them into "teachable moments"—to help our students process their experiences and maybe even pressure the police to change their behavior. After holding a series of small-group discussions and schoolwide town halls, we reached out to the local precinct. Despite the department's professed commitment to community policing, getting a response was a challenge. But eventually a commander agreed to send some officers to the school for a town hall conversation with our students and teachers.

The meeting started well. The teachers explained that we recruited kids who had struggled, been arrested, or kicked out of school, but who were determined to turn their lives around. The police searches, they explained, risked undermining our delicate work. Then our students spoke up, explaining what it felt like to be stopped and searched without reason, to be made to feel powerless, deprived of dignity and privacy, degraded in public view. One student asked the officers, who were seated in folding chairs at the front of the room, how they would feel watching their own children receive this kind of treatment. When their testimony was over, the room fell silent—a rarity in our boisterous building—as we waited for the officers to respond. The air was charged with our students' anger, but also with the vulnerability that comes with dropping a tough exterior and exposing a raw wound. Watching from the side of the room, I assumed that the quiet officers, most of whom were African Americans, felt some compassion for our students. I secretly hoped they felt some shame, too.

But if they did, their response did not convey it. Only one officer ended up having the chance to speak. He was African American and looked to be in his forties, and he stood and explained, in a matter-of-fact but not unfriendly tone, that our school was located in a high-crime neighborhood. Our corner was known for drug sales, he said. Neighbors had called to complain, and the police had no choice but to actively suppress the dealing. In response to our students' vocal objections ("But we aren't selling drugs! So don't hassle us!"), the officer turned toward our staff and said, "Maybe you could have your students wear large student IDs. Something we can see. Then we will know who your kids are and we can leave them alone."

This suggestion, to put it mildly, did not go over well. Some of our students had studied slavery and knew about the antebellum laws requiring free blacks to carry papers proving their status. Others had completed a World History unit on South Africa and knew about the laws requiring nonwhite citizens to carry passbooks when they traveled. Even those students who had studied none of this history could intuit the problem with IDs: as free citizens, they deserved the presumption of innocence. The meeting degenerated into a shouting match, and the officers left quickly.

In the town hall's aftermath, several students told us that we, the school's adults, had been lying to them. We had said that if they obeyed the law and worked hard, society would give them a chance. But the police officers' behavior on the corner, topped off by their performance at the meeting, made our promises seem hollow. "We can be perfect, perfect, doing everything right, and they still treat us like dogs," one sixteen-year-old student told me. Another asked, "How can you tell us we can be anything if they treat us like we're nothing?"

I did not have good answers to these questions, and I was furious at the police for forcing our students to ask them. Many of the students had felt hopeless before enrolling in our program, and some continued to struggle. They knew people who were telling them to give up on school, to quit working so hard, even to live like an outlaw. We urged our students not to give in to those voices, but we knew full well that our proposed path was steep.

About half of our teachers and staff were African American, some from poor and working-class backgrounds. Many had their own stories of police harassment. Our curriculum was full of material on America's history of racial discrimination. We were, in effect, walking the same tightrope black parents know so well: we taught the history and persistence of American racism while simultaneously preaching the gospel of hard work and education.

Under these circumstances, it seemed to me that the police officers' conduct was more than just wrong; it was self-defeating. If their mission was to reduce crime, shouldn't they have seen us as allies and gone out of their way to encourage our students' success? I thought so. But their raids were having precisely the opposite effect: to persuade poor kids of color that society would never let them escape, that their race and class and neighborhood would forever preemptively mark them as guilty.

The officer's suggestion that our students wear IDs to avoid being harassed only made matters worse. To my mind, the very idea betrayed the hopes of an earlier generation of racial justice advocates. Back in the 1960s, when civil rights activists and black newspapers demanded the hiring of black officers to patrol black neighborhoods, they did so believing that these officers would be able to distinguish between law-abiding citizens and the criminal element. But the officers at the town hall were admitting that they couldn't make that distinction. They didn't know the community, and they certainly didn't know the Maya Angelou kids.

But that was just the beginning of what was wrong with the proposal. Suppose our students had agreed to wear IDs so the police could tell they weren't drug dealers. That wouldn't have solved the problem—because even a suspected drug dealer shouldn't be slammed against the wall or verbally abused. The officers shouldn't have treated anyone the way they were treating our students.

The police were also failing to adopt a model of law enforcement that could have reduced crime without abusive tactics. Under the approach known as community policing, the officers could have enlisted our students as allies in the project of making the neighborhood safer. Such an alliance might seem unlikely, given the prevailing distrust between black youth and the police. But because young people are at the greatest risk of neighborhood violence, they have tremendous incentives to help prevent crime and achieve justice for its victims. Treating our students as assets, not enemies, would have enhanced the officers' mission in two ways. First, it would have encouraged the students to cooperate with law enforcement by reporting crimes and assisting with investigations. Second, and even more important, it would have encouraged our students and other young people to obey the law and prepare themselves for a future in a society that had a place for them.[114]

But none of this was on offer for black kids on the corner of Ninth and T or elsewhere in the city. And as angry as I was, I knew that this wasn't entirely, or even mostly, the fault of the officers themselves. The real problem was both more profound and more tragic. The officers who rousted the Maya Angelou students sincerely wanted to protect the community from drug dealing and violence, and they were right to feel that the community desperately needed protecting. But they knew only one way to do that job—through the militaristic policing strategies forged in the violence and chaos of the crack epidemic. Whatever their individual intentions or motivations, these officers were bound by a system, and that system was the source of their orders, training, and beliefs. Their job was to make "teeth rattle," "to arrest those s.o.b.s," and to prove, in the words of Ike Fulwood, that they were the "biggest gang in town." And so they did.

In cities across America, they still do.

# 6

# WHAT WOULD MARTIN LUTHER KING, JR., SAY?
## Stop and Search, 1995

Nobody liked working "duty day," but as the name implied, it wasn't a choice. About once a month, each of us in the public defender's office set aside our cases and took a turn serving as a lawyer for the general public. Whoever walked or called in became your responsibility. If the issue involved the criminal justice system, you helped them directly. If it didn't, you referred them to another agency or service provider. The original idea behind duty day was that a lawyer should always be available if somebody had a legal emergency and needed a public defender. The classic scenario we imagined was the person who called saying, "The police are at my door with a search warrant—do I have to let them in?" Calls like that did come in now and then. One of my first murder cases began when a mother called to say that her son was at police headquarters speaking to homicide detectives. She thought he might be a suspect and wanted to know if it was a good idea for him to be talking to the police. (Answer: No, it wasn't.)

But duty day mostly involved issues that were less attention-grabbing. I once counseled a grandmother who feared that she would lose her public housing if she allowed her grandson to move in with her upon his release from prison; housing authorities were notoriously hostile to people with criminal convictions. I tried to help a man who called to say that he had been denied permission to visit his cousin in the D.C. Jail; jail officials later said that they banned him because, years earlier, he had gotten into a fistfight in the jail's waiting room. I met with a middle-aged taxicab driver from Guyana whose car had been seized by police; they had arrested an alleged prostitute in the backseat and accused the driver of using the cab to facilitate prostitution. (This case had a happy ending when friends of mine from law school who worked at a big D.C. firm agreed to take the case pro bono. They got the cab back and won money damages after proving that the police had illegally seized it.)

By far the most common duty-day requests were from people trying to get their arrest records sealed. These cases were as difficult as they were frequent. In D.C., as in most of the country, there were few legal grounds to erase an arrest from your record, even if the case was quickly dismissed and never led to a criminal conviction. But despite the long odds of success, there was at least a way for individual citizens to make the request. They needed to file a relatively simple legal motion, and our duty-day job was to tell people about the law, give them a copy of the paperwork, and show them where to fill in the blanks. These consultations normally took less than twenty minutes.

But Sandra Dozier clearly had no intention of leaving so quickly. In her early thirties, with a caramel complexion, a short-cropped Afro, and a determined manner, Ms. Dozier was telling me about the traffic stop that led to her arrest. After hearing the words "arrest" and "clear my record," I had assumed she needed the simple motion to seal. But she kept talking, barely glancing at the forms I pushed in her direction. Since I could see that she wasn't going to leave until I had heard the entire story, I took out my yellow legal pad and started taking notes.

Ms. Dozier had been driving home from her mother's house, along with her nineteen-year-old cousin, Charles, and two-year-old daughter,

Tanisha. She was on Alabama Avenue, near the intersection with Good Hope Road, in Southeast D.C., when a police car pulled up behind her with its lights flashing. After she pulled over, an officer came to her window—she couldn't remember much about him except that he had dark brown skin and was tall and polite ("a southern gentleman type," she said). Another officer came to the passenger window, where Charles was sitting—she remembered only that he was white, with a "red face," and that he didn't say much.

The brown-skinned officer asked her for her license and registration. She gave them to him, but not before she asked, "Why are y'all messing with me? I'm coming home from work." I didn't ask, but I thought I knew why she had mentioned her job. The area where Ms. Dozier lived and had been stopped suffered from chronic unemployment. My clients who worked were quick to use that fact as a form of character evidence when confronted by police or other authorities.

Without answering Ms. Dozier's question, the officer took her documents back to his police car. A few minutes later, he returned with the papers and told her that he needed to check whether the tint levels on her windows were "too high." It was a common tactic: traffic regulations in D.C. and elsewhere often limit how dark a car's windows can be. Stops for exceeding the tint limits were a police favorite. Ms. Dozier told the officer he must be mistaken; she had had the tinting done at a reputable place that knew what was permitted.

Despite her protestations, the officer said he needed to check anyway. His red-faced partner, the one who had been standing near Charles on the passenger side, brought over a small machine and fitted the edge of the car window into a groove in the machine.

While that was happening, Ms. Dozier said, the brown-skinned officer told her, "We've been having a lot of problems with shootings and guns and weapons out here. Do you have anything like that with you? In the car?" Ms. Dozier remembered thinking that the officer must be crazy—what would she be doing with anything like that? One of her brothers had been shot a few years before, and another was locked up on a gun charge, and she was determined to stay far, far away from all that. She told him, "You have the wrong person if you are looking for guns."

She said the officer nodded, that he seemed to understand where she was coming from. Then he said, "Since you don't have anything, you don't mind if we check real quick?"

I had been expecting this. I didn't know the precise words the police would use—those varied—but I knew that at some point during the encounter with Ms. Dozier, they would try to search her car.

That was, after all, the entire point of the stop. To understand what was happening to Ms. Dozier, it is crucial to distinguish between the various types of traffic stops the police conduct. Not all stops are created equal. Sometimes the police pull people over for traffic safety reasons—for speeding or running a red light, for example. More nefariously, recent reports by the Department of Justice and others have shown that police departments in Ferguson, Missouri, and elsewhere have used traffic enforcement to generate fines to fund local government.[1]

But Ms. Dozier had fallen prey to another type of traffic stop, one whose motive is neither traffic safety nor revenue enhancement. This kind of stop—an investigatory or pretext stop—uses the traffic laws to uncover more serious crime. Such stops (and subsequent searches) exploded in popularity during the 1990s as part of police efforts to target drugs and guns.

"What did you say?" I asked Ms. Dozier. She looked down—it was the first time she seemed less than assertive—and said, "I told him to go ahead." Before I became a public defender, this response would have surprised me. I remember studying the law of search and seizure in law school and wondering why anybody would consent to a search, especially if they knew that there was something illegal in their car. But studies showed that most people—90 percent or more—did eventually give consent.[2] From what I had seen, it was closer to 100 percent.

When I talked to my clients about why they allowed police to search their cars, such behavior became more comprehensible. A few said they figured the police wouldn't find what they had hidden, but most had a more basic reason: they didn't think they *could* refuse. This was Ms. Dozier's reason, though she had an extra flourish as well. As she explained, "I figured they would search if they wanted to, regardless, so I thought, if I say yes, maybe they won't even bother, since they will see I have nothing to hide."

I had heard this explanation many times before. It was quite logical, I thought—indeed, if I hadn't seen so many of these cases, I would have given consent for the same reason. But it never worked. The police still always searched—as they did with Ms. Dozier.

Soon after granting the police request, she found herself standing with Charles in front of the car and trying to console the whimpering Tanisha. The southern gentleman kept an eye on the three of them while the red-faced officer looked under the seats, in the center console, in the trunk, and, eventually, in the glove compartment. All in all, she said, the search was "on the gentle side"—she had seen police tear cars apart, and she appreciated that the red-faced officer didn't do that. He was businesslike, but not mean, and not messy.

As she had promised, there were no guns or weapons to be found. But even a gentle search was enough to find the two small baggies of marijuana (about twenty dollars' worth) in the glove compartment. When the red-faced officer emerged holding them, Ms. Dozier lost it. "I started crying, telling them I couldn't be locked up for this, that I had just started a new job, that I had to be at work in the morning, that I couldn't miss work or I'd be fired."

Now that she was crying, Tanisha started wailing, while Charles leaned over trying to comfort them both. "We were a mess. All crying and hugging on the side of Alabama Avenue, with people driving by wondering what was going on."

The officers conferred, and the southern gentleman came back in a few minutes. He had what seemed like good news. Since Ms. Dozier had no record and no outstanding warrants, he could release her from the police station with a citation to appear in court. This was much better than the alternative, in which she would be held in jail overnight and wouldn't see a judge till sometime the next day, missing work as a result.

Ms. Dozier was thrilled to learn that she'd be able to go to work the next day. A few weeks later, she got more good news: she went to court and after waiting all day was told that the marijuana possession charges had been "no papered," D.C. court lingo meaning that the prosecutor's office had decided not to bring charges.

Ms. Dozier was free to go, and she rushed quickly out of the courthouse. She had no pending charges and no criminal conviction. She was a free citizen in the eyes of the law.

So what was she doing in my office? Ms. Dozier had been a new employee at FedEx, and at the end of her probationary period, they asked her to bring them proof of a clean record. This was a routine request, but in Ms. Dozier's case, the paperwork came back showing her recent arrest for marijuana possession. And FedEx promptly fired her.

She opened a folder and put some papers on my hopelessly cluttered desk. On top was a printout I had seen many times. It was from the D.C. Superior Court Clerk's office, and it contained Ms. Dozier's criminal record. An eight-hour duty-day shift typically included three or four inquiries from frustrated citizens who had requested proof of a clean record to give their employers, only to find that the police, or the Superior Court, still had evidence of a past arrest on file. The system sometimes seemed like a lottery: I had seen cases where it missed multiple arrests for a single individual, and others in which it had captured every detail, even a minor citation like this one.

As I looked down at the printout, I couldn't help but notice how unusually "clean" Ms. Dozier's record was. I was representing people charged with serious felonies, including murder, armed robbery, and sexual assault, and it was rare for me to encounter somebody whose only criminal involvement was a single no-papered arrest for marijuana possession.

"So, can you help me?" It was Ms. Dozier's voice, and I realized that I needed to refocus. She had to get her job back.

It looked bleak. As an at-will employee on probationary status, she had almost no job protection. The law permitted employers to consider any criminal record—including mere arrests—in making hiring decisions. I told her this, and her body seemed to shrink in her chair. Nobody came to our office if they had other options, and now her lawyer of last resort was letting her down as well. Desperate to try something, I told her, "Well, I can call FedEx and see if I can talk them into giving you another chance."

Ms. Dozier liked the idea. She was organized and prepared, and she fished her supervisor's phone number out of the sheaf of papers she had with her. After what seemed like a dozen rings, I heard a deep, thick "Hello," and when I asked for Mr. Mills, he said, "The one and only."

"I'm calling on behalf of Sandra Dozier," I said, and launched into my pitch. (Since no one was eager to talk to public defenders, we had learned to jump in fast, before people had time to put us off.) I focused on the prosecutor's decision not to bring charges and explained that only the most frivolous cases got no papered. I couldn't say Ms. Dozier was innocent of possessing marijuana, because she had never suggested that the baggies weren't hers. But I went as far as I could, pointing out that an arrest wasn't a conviction, that the case had been dismissed, and that she had no pending charges. She would never need to miss work for a court hearing or probation appointment. Legally, I told him, she was a person with a clean record. She was a free citizen who deserved the chance to keep her job.

Mr. Mills was sympathetic. He said that he liked Ms. Dozier, had been rooting for her, and was very disappointed when the record check came back with an arrest. It was one of the final stages of the process before an employee moved off probationary status. He even agreed that marijuana possession was a small-time charge, saying at one point, "You're right, weed is everywhere, she just got caught with it."

I brightened at his understanding. I normally addressed audiences that ranged from indifferent to downright hostile: probation officers who doubted a client's explanation for why he had missed an appointment, prosecutors who could pick apart a rap sheet to argue that somebody was a menace to society, judges who feared public outcry if they were too lenient.

So Mr. Mills's empathy was a welcome change of pace. I was on the verge of giving Ms. Dozier a thumbs-up sign when Mr. Mills said, "But here is the thing. It isn't my decision. We have a firm policy that if you get arrested while you are on probation with us, we can't hire you."

I started to reply—I'm not sure what I was going to say, but I had to interrupt his flow—when he shut me down for good.

"Look, that's all there is to it. It's company policy. It's done. I've got to go." I murmured my thanks to him for taking my call, and we both hung up.

I didn't have to relay the details to Ms. Dozier. She could read the bad news on my face, in my tone of voice, and in the abrupt way the call had ended.

I tried to think of something positive to say, but I had nothing to offer. The call had been my last shot, and it had failed. Ms. Dozier was gathering up her things and heading for the door when I remembered that my office had recently gotten copies of flyers for an upcoming job fair hosted by the D.C. government and various employers. Maybe this would help?

As soon as I handed her the flyer, I could see it was a mistake. She glanced at it for all of two seconds, then looked up at me with a mixture of disdain and despair. "Right. Another job fair. I know about all the job fairs. For almost a year I've been going to every one I can find, standing in lines that stretch for miles. Finally, finally, I got this job. And I'd still have it, except for this." Ms. Dozier was pointing at the police form, the one that showed her arrest. Her eyes were wet. Her jaw was no longer holding firm. She turned and walked down the hall and out of the office.

"I'm sorry," I said to her back, the useless words serving as final proof of my inadequacy.

Now *I* wanted to cry. It wasn't an unusual feeling during my years as a public defender; sometimes the only thing that stopped the tears was another case or client who needed me right then. And so it was on duty day. I don't remember who came in after Ms. Dozier, but there was invariably a line of clients in the waiting room, not to mention calls to be returned.

Duty day finally came to an end, and as I set about straightening up my desk, I noticed that Ms. Dozier had accidentally left a small stack of papers. On top was her printout from the courthouse. Underneath was a letter of commendation from sometime in high school when she had been Intern of the Month during a summer job with the D.C. government. The last piece of paper was a photocopy of her diploma—she had graduated from Ballou High School in Southeast D.C., a school more often in the news for fights or disorder than for anything good.

I stared at the letter and the diploma, and I imagined that she had brought them for the same reason she had told the officer she had a job. They were her armor, her stereotype busters, her proof to the world that she was one of the good ones. I imagined her taking them with her to job fairs, to FedEx, to anyone she thought might have any power.

And I hated the futility of her effort. A just world would care that she had grown up in a neighborhood with few jobs, attended a school with a 50 percent dropout rate, lost family members to prison and violence, yet had resisted and transcended all that. A just world would label her an achiever, a striver, a person with grit. But her strength of character, her diploma, her Intern of the Month certificate—none of it mattered now. What governed her life was a single line on a Superior Court printout: "Sandra Dozier, DOB: 7/3/77, Arrest: Possession Controlled Substance (Marijuana), 2/15/00."

When Ms. Dozier was stopped, she asked the officers, "Why are y'all messing with me?" She never got an answer, and despite the officers' tint machine ritual, she was never persuaded that dark windows were

the reason she had been singled out for questioning. She was right to
have her doubts.

Ms. Dozier had become the victim of the latest pretext-stop strategy. Designed to get guns off the street, it required casting a wide
net—wide enough to capture lots of minor offenders like Sandra
Dozier with her two baggies of marijuana. Yet even this was only part
of the problem. As we shall see, this policing strategy was reserved
for the city's black neighborhoods—and its poorest. As a result, its burdens fell on residents who, like Ms. Dozier, could least afford the
consequences of an arrest.

> The people of Washington, D.C., in 1995 are in some respects no
> freer than the people of Selma, Alabama, in 1955.
>                                    —Eric H. Holder, Jr., United States Attorney for the
>                                                         District of Columbia, 1995

On January 13, 1995, a racially diverse audience of more than a thousand people crowded into the main ballroom at the Sheraton Hotel in
Arlington, Virginia, for a birthday celebration honoring the memory
of Dr. Martin Luther King, Jr. The featured speaker, Eric Holder, was
the first African American to serve as U.S. Attorney for the District of
Columbia. Holder's appointment just over a year earlier had been big
news. Though black leadership was well established at the local level
(police chief, mayor, city council), no African American had ever
served as the District's chief prosecutor, a fact that had long rankled
many blacks in the city.

As Holder took the stage, D.C. had emerged from the worst of the
crack years, but just barely. Though homicide and other violent
crimes had fallen from the record levels they reached during the epidemic, they were still extraordinarily high: D.C.'s murder rate was
almost three times what it had been in 1985, before the crack explo-
sion.[3] The risk was greatest for the city's black residents, as it was for
blacks nationally. A Department of Justice survey of criminal victimization in 1997 would find that blacks experienced violent victim-

ization at rates 50 percent higher than those for whites.⁴ Blacks
understood that they lived at greater risk: in a national survey in 1994,
58 percent of blacks said there was an area within a mile of their house
where they were afraid to walk alone at night; 45 percent of whites
said the same.⁵

Using a conceit common among King Day speakers, Holder asked
the enormous audience to imagine what Martin Luther King, Jr.,
would think about the state of black America today. According to
Holder, "Dr. King would be shocked and disheartened by the condition of his people in 1995—and I, for one, would be ashamed to reveal
to him what we have let happen to our community."⁶ Holder reminded the crowd that in the fifteen months since he had become
the city's top prosecutor, more than five hundred people had been
murdered—nearly all of them black. Those doing the killing, Holder
declared, were betraying King's legacy. "Did Martin Luther King successfully fight the likes of Bull Connor so that we could ultimately
lose the struggle for civil rights to misguided or malicious members
of our own race?"⁷

Holder's critique was part of a national trend. In the mid-1990s, it
was difficult to attend a Martin Luther King Day sermon without
hearing a minister or other speaker invoke King's memory in order to
denounce crime and violence in black America. The year before
Holder's speech at the Arlington Sheraton, Rev. Jesse Jackson had a
similar message for an interracial crowd of more than six hundred
people at Washington National Cathedral. Saying that "violence—
particularly black-on-black violence—is spiritual surrender," Jackson
pointed out that more blacks had been killed by other blacks in one
year than had been lynched throughout history.⁸

Appeals to King's memory could take a hard edge. During a visit
to Alabama's Birmingham Jail in 1995, Jackson chastised a group of
prisoners for betraying King's dream. "You are costing everybody's
freedom," Jackson said, by "taking up the money we need for day care
and Head Start." He urged them to change their ways: "You've got
dignity. You're God's child. You can rise above this if you change your

mind. I appeal to you. Your mothers appealed to you. Dr. King died for you." Jackson's tough-love approach left little room for gentleness: after seeing a female prisoner wearing a T-shirt with a picture of King on it, Jackson said, "If he's your hero, you wouldn't be in here." The woman bowed her head and cried.[9]

President Bill Clinton had his own version of the "what would Dr. King say about the black condition" talk. In November 1993, Clinton traveled to the Mason Temple Church of God in Christ, in Memphis, Tennessee, to the same pulpit from which King delivered his final sermon the night before he was assassinated. Speaking to a gathering of black ministers, Clinton wondered aloud what King would say if he were to "reappear by my side today and give us a report card on the last 25 years." On the one hand, Clinton said, King would be pleased with the increased political power of African Americans, their elevation into the top ranks of the armed forces and the government, and the growth of the black middle class. On the other hand, Clinton imagined King assailing drug abuse and gun violence in the nation's urban centers: "I did not live and die to see 13-year-old boys get automatic weapons and gun down 9-year-olds just for the kick of it. I did not live and die to see young people destroy their own lives with drugs and then build fortunes destroying the lives of others. This is not what I came here to do."[10] Citing recent crimes against black children in Baltimore and Washington, D.C., Clinton imagined King saying, "I did not fight for the right of black people to murder other black people with reckless abandonment."[11]

Although the language Holder and Clinton used was similar to that of religious and civic leaders like Jesse Jackson, Holder and Clinton had concrete power that those leaders did not. In Clinton's case, he invoked black victims in support of a variety of tough-on-crime positions, including the 1994 federal crime legislation that funded prison construction across the country.[12]

In Holder's case, he asked the King Day audience at the Arlington Sheraton to join him in a community-wide effort against gun violence. Tougher law enforcement alone wouldn't be enough, Holder said, telling the crowd that he wanted to enlist athletes and musicians in a public relations campaign to "break our young people's fascination" with guns.[13] But while Holder embraced root-cause responses to violence—in 1994 he told the D.C. radio journalist Derek McGinty that "if we want to get a handle on this problem long-term we're going to have to deal with the social conditions that breed crime"—such broader solutions were beyond Holder's direct control and would take years to show an impact.[14] Meanwhile, people were dying right now.

Reducing violence in the short term, said Holder, required getting guns out of the hands of those most likely to use them to commit crimes—primarily young black men. But the means for disarming these potential offenders were limited. D.C. already had some of the nation's toughest gun laws, and national legislation remained politically impossible. What was left?

Holder's answer was straightforward: Stop cars, search cars, seize guns. He called it Operation Ceasefire.[15]

In embracing investigatory stops, Holder was part of a movement. In a much-discussed op-ed in *The New York Times* in March 1994, the prominent criminologist James Q. Wilson had argued that police should conduct more pretext stops of pedestrians and frisk them in order to detect illegal guns. The practice would have costs, Wilson admitted: "Innocent people will be stopped. Young black and Hispanic men will probably be stopped more often than older white Anglo males or women of any race. But if we are serious about reducing drive-by shootings, fatal gang wars and lethal quarrels in public places, we must get illegal guns off the street." That same year, the New York Police Department adopted a strategy similar to the one Wilson had proposed. In *Getting Guns Off the Streets of New York*, the NYPD detailed its aggressive strategy of stopping, questioning, and frisking more citizens, especially young men of color.[16]

Holder wanted to do to drivers what Wilson and the NYPD sought to do to pedestrians. In 1995, new research from Kansas City suggested that such a plan just might work. Dubbed the "Kansas City Gun Experiment," the federally funded program aimed to increase the number of investigatory stops in a "target beat." Officers working overtime and assigned to "hot spots patrols" were instructed to identify suspicious vehicles and then use any available legal pretext to pull them over and search the drivers as well as their cars. These officers also increased the number of pedestrian stops.[17] The results, when first published, were inspiring to law enforcement: gun violence decreased by 49 percent in the target beat, and the participating officers seized significantly more guns than their counterparts did in an area of the city that didn't deploy the tactic.

As the political scientist Charles Epp and his coauthors explain, "It is hard to overstate the influence of the Kansas City Gun Experiment."[18] A program in Indianapolis attempted to replicate its findings, and both initiatives generated major national news coverage.[19] While Holder's office planned the new gun interdiction program for D.C., Holder's special counsel, Monty Wilkinson, traveled to Kansas City and Indianapolis to study their efforts firsthand.[20]

Holder proposed to train and equip teams of D.C. officers to look for vehicles they deemed suspicious, with the goal of searching them for guns whenever possible.[21] Prosecutors would then back up the police effort by vigorously pressing charges in court, making sure the cases didn't get dropped or fall through the cracks, and seeking jail time for those convicted of illegal gun possession.[22]

Pretext traffic stops were an attractive tool for Holder's purposes because D.C., like every other city, has a dizzying number of traffic regulations, and most drivers violate at least one every time they get behind the wheel. (As Attorney General Robert Jackson said in 1940, "No local police force can strictly enforce the traffic laws, or it would arrest half the driving population on any given morning.") Thus, if a car draws suspicion from the police, they can almost invariably find a way to stop it legally, especially if they follow it long enough.[23] This tactic has been deemed constitutional by the Supreme Court, despite its obvious invitation to selective enforcement and racial profiling.[24]

Holder had no such qualms. Ten days after his Martin Luther King

Day speech, he appeared as a guest of the D.C.-based radio journalist Diane Rehm in order to build public support for Operation Ceasefire. Holder told Rehm that his goal was to cut violent crime in the city by 40 percent over the next four years and that "the cornerstone of this effort" would be getting "guns out of the hands of criminals."[25] Citing the Kansas City Gun Experiment, Holder said that he wanted to train D.C. police "to do constitutional, appropriate things to confront people" and, ultimately, get their guns. When Rehm asked him to explain what he meant by "constitutional means," his response laid bare why pretextual policing was so powerful—and so problematic.

Investigatory car searches start, said Holder, with the fact that the police have broad authority to pull over any driver who violates the traffic laws. "[T]he police for instance are able to stop cars that do not have their lights on at night," he said. "The police are able to stop cars that don't have license plates." These examples were two of the more serious traffic violations. Holder didn't mention that many less serious, even petty, traffic infractions give the police just as much authority to pull over a car.[26] A broken taillight or vent window, too much tint on the windows, a rear license plate but no front one, or even too many air fresheners hanging from the rearview mirror—these are also valid bases for a traffic stop.

But the stop itself, as Holder went on to explain, is just the beginning. Once the police pull a car over for even the most minor violation, they have been given broad power by the courts, starting with the authority to "look inside of a car." Just looking could be an effective crime-fighting tool, Holder said, telling Rehm that she would "be surprised [at] the number of cases . . . where police officers are just looking in from outside and see guns that are hastily shoved under seats."[27]

What if police didn't see anything illegal? Most people who haven't been subjected to a pretext stop would assume that the encounter would end there, perhaps with the officer writing a ticket. But, Holder said, the police have another tool available to them: "techniques where they ask people to allow them to search cars." Like looking inside a car, consent searches were successful more often than Rehm's listeners might think: "Surprising again, people—even though they have guns in their cars—will consent to those searches, and guns were taken that way."[28]

What "techniques" do the police use to obtain such consent? Often, as with Ms. Dozier, just asking is good enough, especially because most people don't know that they can refuse.[29] For drivers who are more reluctant, officers are trained in how to wrangle consent, and the best are very good at it. A core tactic is to blur the distinction between commands that a driver must obey (such as providing a license and registration, or stepping out of the car) and requests that he may decline (such as giving permission to search).[30] Many people don't know the difference, and having acceded to a series of commands, they are primed to assume that the final, crucial request to search is also one they must obey. Finally, if the driver is adamant in refusing consent, there is always the fallback option: search anyway and later claim that you got consent.

Although Holder was remarkably forthright in outlining his plan, there were two aspects he failed to emphasize. First, he didn't discuss the immense volume of innocent people who would have to be stopped in order to obtain a sizable number of guns. This volume of stops is necessary because the overwhelming majority of cars the police stop and search won't contain guns. (Results vary from study to study, but most conclude that somewhere from 1 out of 20 to 1 out of 100 searches of cars will recover weapons.)[31] Although not widely shared with the general public, the fact that hit rates for firearms are so low was well known in the police academies where officers learned to conduct pretext stops. As a popular textbook explained,

> Remember, you need a lot of contacts to find the relatively few felony offenders you're most interested in. To get the volume you want, you're going to have to intensively enforce the traffic laws. You may need to call upon more trivial violations or public safety consider- ations, like having a taillight out or a cracked windshield, changing lanes without signaling, impeding traffic, following too closely,

failing to dim lights, speeding 3 to 5 mph over the limit . . . and so on.[32]

Even the Kansas City and Indianapolis studies showed how seldom guns were actually found. In Kansas City, police in the target area seized guns in only 3.57 percent of traffic stops, while in Indianapolis they found guns in less than 1 percent of traffic stops.[33]

The other aspect of Operation Ceasefire that Holder failed to mention was that, although relatively few cars will contain guns, many more will contain evidence of minor crimes such as possession of marijuana.[34] Police are sworn to enforce the law, and although it is theoretically possible to imagine a pretext-stop program in which police seize guns but ignore other minor offenses, it would be extremely difficult to execute. Among other obstacles, officers would need to be trained on which minor offenses to overlook, and few police chiefs would be eager to attend a public oversight hearing in which they were forced to explain where they got the authority to decide which laws mattered. As a result, pretext-stop regimes invariably operate as Ceasefire did. Officers may start out with a particular goal, such as seizing illegal guns, but if they uncover other illegal items, even less serious ones, they typically arrest.

But not everybody was at equal risk. In D.C., one police district was officially exempt from Operation Ceasefire: the city's Second District, which included middle- and upper-middle-class white neighborhoods such as Georgetown, Foggy Bottom, and Woodley Park. The exemption was intentional. The Second District, Holder explained, had almost no gun crime, so there was no need for pretext stops there.[35]

Holder's explanation was entirely rational. In 1993, two years before Operation Ceasefire went into effect, there were 399 homicides in Washington, D.C.[36] Only two of them were in Ward 3 (which largely covers the Second District), despite the fact that this ward contained more than 13 percent of the city's population.[37] In one respect, though, the exemption of the Second District was problematic. By concentrating pretext policing in the areas where gun crime was highest, Operation Ceasefire created unwarranted disparities in other areas, such as drug enforcement. Drivers in majority-black neighborhoods were no more likely to possess drugs than were drivers in majority-white neighborhoods, but under Holder's plan, they were more likely to be stopped, searched, and arrested. These drivers—including Ms. Dozier—were the collateral damage from Operation Ceasefire's response to gun violence.

Such discrimination, one might think, would have been sure to raise alarm bells in the city. But few seemed to care. Robert Wilkins from the Public Defender Service challenged Operation Ceasefire before the city council. Wilkins, who later would be appointed to the Court of Appeals for the D.C. Circuit, criticized the program because it relied on racial profiling and because such profiles "are frequently wrong, resulting in innocent people being targeted by the police."[38] Wilkins knew whereof he spoke, as he had successfully sued the Maryland State Police after he and his family were stopped pursuant to a racial profile in 1992.[39] The case won substantial media attention, and Wilkins told his story at the hearing. But apart from an expression of concern from a single council member, Wilkins's critique attracted minimal support, and Operation Ceasefire continued unimpeded.[40]

Why was Wilkins the lone voice? What explains the lack of opposition to the racial discrimination inherent in the structure of Operation Ceasefire?

Some of the answers are similar to those we have seen earlier. Memories of the crack years were fresh, their trauma lasting. When Holder told the audience at the Arlington Sheraton that 94 percent of black homicide victims were slain by black assailants, he was simply putting a number on a problem his audience knew well. A range of black voices—and not just from law enforcement—agreed with Holder that safety was a civil rights issue. "If we're not safe within our homes, if we're not safe within our person, then every other civil right just doesn't matter," said Wade Henderson, the head of the NAACP's

Washington office.[41] In such times, when Holder asked other blacks to help him respond to black America's "group suicide," few would say no.

That the call for pretext policing came from Eric Holder, a highly respected African American prosecutor, was also crucial. Black federal prosecutors are viewed with tremendous respect in majority-black communities. Lenese Herbert, who worked under Holder, recalls that black prosecutors, along with other black lawyers and judges, were viewed as "part of the race's success," its "shining Black princes and princesses."[42] Paul Butler, a former federal prosecutor, describes how his stature helped him win convictions from majority-black juries in D.C.:

> In my black city, I love to stand in front of the black jurors and point, like I learned in training, at the black defendant. I represent the United States of America, I boast, and I am going to present evidence that proves beyond a reasonable doubt that that guy over there is a big jerk. Then I proceed to kick a little butt myself.[43]

Holder's standing lent him similar credibility when he spoke to black audiences about Operation Ceasefire. "I'm not going to be naïve about it," he told an audience at a community meeting on upper Georgia Avenue. "The people who will be stopped will be young black males, overwhelmingly." But, as he had done in his King Day speech, Holder argued that such concerns were outweighed by the need to protect blacks from crime.[44] He took a similar tack when celebrating the first anniversary of Operation Ceasefire with officers from the city's gun squads, which had seized 768 guns and $250,000 in cash and had made 2,300 arrests. Holder acknowledged that most of the arrestees were black. But he had no regrets, he told the assembled officers, and neither should they. "Young black males are 1 percent of the nation's population but account for 18 percent of the nation's homicides," he said. "You all are saving lives, not just getting guns off the street."[45]

Holder's approach was embraced by the black police chiefs who were running departments in several major cities by the late 1990s. In response to allegations that police were engaged in racial profiling, Bernard Parks, the African American police chief in Los Angeles, said that racial disparities resulted from the choices of criminals, not police bias. "It's not the fault of the police when they stop minority males or put them in jail," said Parks. "It's the fault of the minority males for committing the crime. In my mind it is not a great revelation that if officers are looking for criminal activity, they're going to look at the kind of people who are listed on crime reports." Charles Ramsey, who became D.C.'s police chief in 1998, agreed. "Not to say that [racial profiling] doesn't happen, but it's clearly not as serious or widespread as the publicity suggests," Ramsey said. "I get so tired of hearing that 'Driving While Black' stuff. It's just used to the point where it has no meaning. I drive while black—I'm black. I sleep while black too. It's victimology."[46]

But it was more than fear of crime or the credibility of black law enforcement officials that sold Operation Ceasefire. Also critical was the fact that the program targeted guns, not drugs.

From the late 1960s through the late 1980s, much of black America had remained committed to the War on Drugs, even supporting mandatory minimum sentences. But African American public opinion began to shift, if slowly, by the early 1990s as evidence of the drug war's racial impact began to mount. In 1990, Michael Isikoff and Tracy Thompson of *The Washington Post* found that federal judges had become frustrated with mandatory minimums and the harsh treatment of offenses involving crack cocaine. Stringent antidrug laws, the reporters wrote, had given rise to a "form of robotic justice which metes out harsh penalties every day to low-level offenders—most of them poor, young and members of minority groups."[47] That same year, in a front-page story headlined "Blacks Feel Brunt of Drug War," the *Los Angeles Times* reporter Ron Harris reported that studies from both the FBI and the National Institute on Drug Abuse had found that blacks and whites used drugs at comparable rates. Yet a visitor to a courtroom or jail would conclude that most drug users were black. The only way to explain this disparity was to recognize that blacks were being unfairly targeted; or, as Harris put it, "the nation's war on drugs has in effect become a war on black people."[48]

Shifting attitudes toward the War on Drugs could also be seen among members of the Congressional Black Caucus (CBC). African American members of Congress had been evenly divided over the 1986 federal law that introduced stiff penalties for drug offenses, including the provision that punished crack offenses much more harshly than powder cocaine offenses. But as the racial effects of mandatory minimums and the crack/cocaine disparity became apparent, the CBC came together in unanimous and increasingly vocal opposition to the law.[49] At the local level, concerns about unfair drug sentencing led the D.C. Council in 1995 to roll back the mandatory minimums for drug crimes that voters had approved in 1982. (The resistance went only so far, however, as the council doubled the statutory maximums.)

While the drug war was beginning to come under attack, the D.C.-based Sentencing Project started documenting the damage that America's increasingly punitive criminal justice system was doing to black America. In 1990, the group published a report with an explosive and unprecedented finding: one in four young black men were trapped in the criminal justice system—either through probation, parole, prison, or jail. The next year, the group issued a report showing that the United States had surpassed South Africa and Russia to become the world's largest jailer (a status it retains today). Both reports were widely disseminated and discussed, especially by black commentators, with the ACLU's Nkechi Taifa, for example, comparing the double standard in American criminal justice to slavery and Jim Crow.[50]

The growing opposition to discriminatory policing and overincarceration was also reflected in editorial cartoons in black newspapers. In the 1970s and 1980s, the cartoons had emphasized rising

*(The Washington Afro-American*, March 3, 1990)

crime and lawlessness. Now, increasingly, they dramatized the costs of punitive crime policy.

But while critics were increasingly vocal in challenging the drug war, when the topic turned to guns, the opposition grew quiet. The roots of the tough-on-guns stance can be traced to the gun control debate of the 1970s, when spiraling gun violence persuaded African Americans in D.C. and elsewhere to embrace prison sentences, including mandatory minimums, for gun possession.[51] By the 1990s, with the wounds from the crack years barely healed, the tough-on-guns posture had solidified to the point that antigun tactics were almost immune to criticism.[52]

For example, even as D.C. eliminated mandatory minimum sentences for certain drug offenses in 1995, it kept those punishments for a long list of gun crimes.[53] Similarly, in Richmond, Virginia, a black federal prosecutor joined forces with a black police chief to create Project Exile, which sought to ensure that any felon arrested with a gun would be prosecuted in federal court and receive a mandatory minimum sentence.[54] In New York, Bronx district attorney Robert Johnson, the

(*Los Angeles Sentinel*, November 13, 1997)

state's first African American D.A., began referring gun possession cases to federal court in hopes of securing harsher mandatory prison terms.[55]

Against this backdrop, the lack of resistance to Operation Ceasefire is not surprising. If Holder's plan had targeted drugs, it might have faced resistance. But because the target was guns, Robert Wilkins was the only witness at the city council hearing raising questions about racial profiling.

Still, even the focus on guns didn't ensure support for Operation Ceasefire. There was one more factor, often ignored in discussions of the politics of crime and punishment in black communities: class.

(*Los Angeles Sentinel*, July 24, 1997)

They know who they can push around and who they can't.
—Resident of low-income black neighborhood in D.C.

When Holder announced Operation Ceasefire on Martin Luther King Day, he spoke before an audience that included members of D.C.'s black establishment. They came from Howard University; from Prince George's County, Maryland, the nation's wealthiest black suburb; and from the Gold Coast, the black middle- and upper-middle-class neighborhoods along Sixteenth Street. But the policing strategy Holder announced would mostly pass over those communities and instead exact its toll in places that, if anything, seemed more thoroughly depressed and permanently abandoned than they had been under Jim Crow.

The class discrimination line wasn't drawn as formally as its racial counterpart. Whereas the majority-white neighborhoods west of Rock Creek Park were officially exempt from Operation Ceasefire, most black residents of D.C., including many of its more privileged citizens, lived in police precincts that, at least on paper, were subject to the gun squads. As a result, it wasn't unheard of for the police to conduct a pretext stop on a member of the black establishment.[56] But in the main, pretext policing was concentrated in the poorest parts of D.C.

My colleagues and I at PDS were well aware that the police operated differently in the wealthier majority-black neighborhoods. When Ms. Dozier was describing how she was stopped and searched, before she even told me where she was driving, I had already started to imagine likely locations. All of them were in the city's poorest black communities. I made the assumption, in part, because that's where most of our cases came from, and also because I and many of my black colleagues lived in the city's more privileged black neighborhoods, and we could see with our own eyes that the policing styles on our streets were typically less aggressive than those our clients experienced.

My evidence was entirely anecdotal, but research by the sociologist Ronald Weitzer confirmed my impressions. In 1996 and 1997, Weitzer began studying police-citizen relations in three Washington, D.C., neighborhoods: a white middle-class neighborhood he referred to as Cloverdale, a black middle-class neighborhood he called Merrifield, and a lower-class black neighborhood he called Spartanburg. Along with his graduate students, Weitzer conducted more than 150 interviews of residents, attended police-community meetings, and observed traffic stops and other police-citizen interactions. As he had expected, the affluent white community didn't interact with police much and was generally satisfied with officers in the neighborhood. The results from the black neighborhoods were more interesting: Weitzer quickly saw the power of neighborhood class. African Americans who lived in the middle-class Merrifield neighborhood

were generally pleased with their local police and reported few instances of unjustified stops, verbal abuse, or excessive force. Those
who lived in lower-class Spartanburg, by contrast, were four to seven
times more likely than Merrifield residents to complain of unjustified
stops or abuse.[57]

These different attitudes showed up in community meetings as
well as in survey results. In Merrifield, when it came time for community members to ask questions of the officers running a meeting,
Weitzer was surprised at how often people would take the chance to
express their gratitude, saying things like, "Well, this isn't a question,
but I just want to thank you for all the hard work you do day in and
day out, and the police really never get enough credit." Spartanburg
residents were much more likely to complain about police treatment.
Weitzer recalled seeing small groups of young black men, normally
sitting in the back of the room, waiting for the chance to speak. When
their turn came, they would say, "You know, racial profiling, it happens every day, what are you gonna do about it? Me and my friends are
out there and we're being stopped for no good reason, and it doesn't
happen once, it happens repeatedly, and we're sick and tired of it."[58]

Complaints often revolved around a particular type of police action: the pretext stops that Holder thought were essential to reducing
gun violence. According to Weitzer, "Police are thought to engage in
fishing expeditions: pretextual stops ostensibly for minor traffic violations but actually intended to discover evidence of some other offense."[59]
Spartanburg residents were clear-eyed about why police could treat
them like this: they were poor and black, living in a neighborhood that
was poor and black. These facts were far more powerful than shared
racial identity with the city's black political establishment. As one
twenty-four-year-old black man from Spartanburg put it,

> Up there [Georgetown, Gold Coast—affluent white and black com-
> munities] I know they don't treat them like that. Those people got a
> lot of influence. Police could lose their jobs, you know? For us, come
> on, what can you do if you're stopped on the street? You're just a

regular Joe. You could go file a complaint or write a letter, but that's all that's going to happen. But these [affluent] people can make two or three phone calls, and there's going to be an investigation. We don't have that power. They know who they can push around and who they can't.[60]

The poor weren't the only ones to understand how class worked in D.C.'s black communities. Merrifield's black middle-class residents did, too—their neighborhood was full of doctors, lawyers, and other politically connected people, and they knew that their status influenced their interactions with law enforcement. One man told researchers that if police mistreated Merrifield residents, "citizens would be up in arms," and an officer interviewed for the study confirmed that these citizens had " 'pull' with city officials and the police hierarchy."[61] Weitzer's subjects spoke a truth I knew well. A black judge lived on my block, and two others lived close by. Even though I tangled with them in the courthouse, I had little doubt about whom I would call with a complaint about police conduct.

It is no small success that the African Americans on my block, or the residents of Merrifield, felt this way. To the generations of black middle-class D.C. residents routinely humiliated and harassed by Jim Crow policing, respectful police treatment would have seemed an impossible dream. The idea of a majority-black police department would have seemed equally miraculous. But for Ms. Dozier and the black poor trapped in Spartanburg, there was nothing to celebrate. Indeed, in one crucial respect, things had gotten worse: they were still being stopped and searched because of where they lived and the color of their skin, but now they were told that this is how Dr. King would have wanted it.

There are a lot of Sandra Doziers. In the twenty years since Holder unveiled Operation Ceasefire, its brand of pretext stops has become part of the fabric of policing in cities across America. In D.C., the journalist David Shipler rode with officers doing the same things the police were doing the night they stopped Ms. Dozier: working the city's poor black neighborhoods exclusively, pulling people over for minor traffic violations (tinted windows remain a favorite), and cajoling their way inside cars.[62] As Shipler recalls, after a night of watching the Gun Recovery Unit at work,

> [h]ardly any of the searches had been justified by probable cause or even by the lesser standard of reasonable suspicion. The [Gun Recovery Unit] had relied almost entirely on citizens' acquiescence. While officers combed through vehicles, I asked drivers who were sitting on curbs or leaning on trunks whether their permission had been requested. Some looked blank, as if they hadn't known that a policeman had to ask and that a citizen could say no.[63]

The problem is hardly limited to D.C. The New York City Police Department came under sustained political and legal attack for its reliance on stop-and-frisk, a tactic we might think of as Operation Ceasefire applied to pedestrians. Although the NYPD has dramatically reduced its use of stop-and-frisk since 2011, it continues to target drivers for minor traffic offenses. And it does so for the same reason that D.C. police adopted Operation Ceasefire: as a pretext to question drivers and, whenever possible, search their cars. In 2014, for example, the NYPD conducted just over 47,000 stop-and-frisks; in the same year, it gave out almost 75,000 traffic tickets for tinted windows alone. And that number is likely dwarfed by the number of drivers who, like Ms. Dozier, were stopped on suspicion of a minor offense and never received a ticket.[64]

Pretext stops are responsible for most of the racial disparity in traffic stops nationwide. Although popular discussions of discriminatory traffic enforcement often lump all traffic stops into one category, Charles Epp and his colleagues have shown that pretext stops are the real villain. Analyzing the results of a survey of black and white drivers in the Kansas City area, Epp finds that when the police are actually enforcing traffic safety laws, they tend to do so without regard to race.[65] But when they are carrying out investigatory or pretext stops, they are *much more likely* to stop black and other minority drivers: blacks are about two and a half times more likely to be pulled over for pretext stops.[66] Moreover, the disparities are present regardless of gender. Black men are more than twice as likely as white men, and black women are more than twice as likely as white women, to be subjected to a pretext stop.[67] In fact, black women are more likely to be pulled over for pretext stops than are white men, despite the fact that white men carry guns and commit violent crimes at much higher rates than black women do.[68]

These racial disparities are all the more troubling because the damage from a pretext stop—of a driver, a pedestrian, a loiterer—doesn't end with the stop itself or the subsequent search. Perhaps the single most destructive aspect of the pretext-stop regime is that it propels disparities in the rest of the criminal justice system. Consider Ms. Dozier. She wasn't innocent: at the time she was arrested, possession of even the smallest amount of marijuana was a crime in D.C. She had marijuana in her car, and she was arrested for it. Case closed. This is where many discussions of disparities in law enforcement end. But such a simple account fails to acknowledge the world that pretext stops create—a world in which Ms. Dozier is arrested for an offense that white drivers commit with impunity.

Appreciating how pretext stops contribute to criminal justice disparities brings clarity to important debates over racism in American policing. Police officers—including black police officers—understandably resent allegations of racism and racial profiling. In resisting such claims, however, even thoughtful police leaders overlook the damage done by pretext stops. For example, Chuck Ramsey, who served as D.C.'s police chief and more recently as the cochair of President Obama's Task Force on 21st Century Policing, rejected allegations of racial profiling by saying, "Black people commit traffic violations. What are we supposed to say? People get a free pass because they're black?"[69] But Ms. Dozier and the residents of her neighborhood are not asking for a free pass. They are just asking not to be singled out.

Pretext stops also show what FBI director James B. Comey missed in a February 2015 speech on racial bias in policing. Comey was praised for acknowledging that police officers in urban settings can be influenced by implicit, or unintentional, bias, some of which results from the fact that they "often work in environments where a hugely disproportionate percentage of street crime is committed by young men of color." Before making this point, however, he sought to defend police from accusations of intentional racism. "Why are so many black men in jail?" Comey asked. "Is it because cops, prosecutors, judges, and juries are racist? Because they are turning a blind eye to white robbers and drug dealers?" Answering his own question, he said, "I don't think so."

In some respects, Comey's speech deserved the accolades it received. The notion of implicit bias—that we all harbor attitudes and stereotypes that operate without our conscious awareness—is a powerful scientific development, and he was right to elaborate on its connections to law enforcement. To his credit, he also pointed out that poverty and other forms of social disadvantage help produce the high crime rates that police must contend with. But Comey never mentioned pretext stops—and as a result, he made the problem of racial discrimination by police seem harder to solve than it actually is. Compared with unconscious bias, or the social conditions that foster criminal behavior, pretext stops are a direct, easily remedied source of racial disparities in the criminal justice system, and they are entirely within the power of law enforcement to correct.[70]

If Comey had recognized pretext stops as a racially discriminatory practice, he would have had to revise his claim that police are not "turning a blind eye" to white drug dealers. For although he is right that no individual officer chooses to ignore criminal behavior by whites, *structurally* a pretext regime does precisely that. When Holder and the D.C. police department decided to target black communities for pretext stops, they gave a free pass to white drivers right across town with marijuana (and other drugs) safely stashed in their glove compartments.

Before she left my office, after seeing that I couldn't help her get her job back, Sandra Dozier said, "I can't believe I lost my job for this." I still can't believe it myself, but I now have a better understanding of how it happened. By the time Ms. Dozier was stopped and received her marijuana citation in 2000, D.C. and the nation had been steadily, incrementally, building the punitive criminal justice system we still live with today. Most of the pieces—the aggressive prosecutions and policing, longer sentences, prison-building, collateral consequences of convictions such as losing the right to vote or the chance to live in public housing—had been put in place, and the years since had been primarily dedicated to maintaining and tinkering with that basic architecture.

This history reveals that no single actor, or even institution, is responsible for what happened to Sandra Dozier. But it also suggests that there were many moments when D.C.—and the nation—could have pursued a different course. If the D.C. Council had chosen to decriminalize marijuana when it first considered the issue in 1975, Ms. Dozier would still have had her job. If the D.C. police hadn't targeted drivers in the city's poor black neighborhoods for pretext stops, she would still have had her job. If FedEx and other employers had a more forgiving policy toward arrests, if they were willing to look at individual circumstances rather than adopting a policy of blanket exclusion, she would still have had her job. And if America had implemented a more robust policy of urban revitalization—if it had ever undertaken a Marshall Plan for the cities—somebody with Ms. Dozier's grit and determination would have had her choice of jobs.

# EPILOGUE
## The Reach of Our Mercy, 2014–16

After forty years of increasingly punitive criminal justice policies, D.C. finally took a significant step in the other direction. In 2013 and 2014, the city council once again debated a proposal to decriminalize possession of small amounts of marijuana. Back in 1975, as we have seen, D.C. council member David Clarke had introduced decriminalization legislation, only to see the effort die in the face of fierce resistance from his fellow council member, the black nationalist pastor Doug Moore. In 2013, council member Tommy Wells took up the cause. Like Clarke, Wells sought to replace criminal penalties for possession of small amounts of marijuana with a modest civil fine. In essence, marijuana possession would be treated like a parking violation.[1] Though the two proposals were similar, the outcomes were not: decriminalization failed in 1975 but passed overwhelmingly in 2014.[2]

What changed?

In 1975, D.C. and the rest of black America were still reeling from the heroin epidemic and the unprecedented crime rates of the late 1960s. By 2014, on the other hand, America was well into what the criminologist Franklin Zimring has called "the great American crime decline."[3] Shootings were still too common, especially in the nation's poorest African American communities, but the trend lines were unmistakable: in 2012, D.C. saw 88 homicides, the lowest number since 1961 and a stunning decrease from the 485 killings that devastated the city in 1991, during the worst of the crack crisis. Drug-related killings had fallen 83 percent between 2000 and 2014. D.C.'s crime decline reflected an American trend: the national murder rate in 2014 was lower than it had been in 1960.[4]

Black Americans benefit the most when violent crime drops. Since 90 percent of D.C.'s murder victims are black, the city's homicide decline overwhelmingly saved black lives—almost four hundred in a single year. The same story can be told in other cities. In New York, for example, the crime decline of the last two decades means that almost fifteen hundred fewer people were killed each year than would have died had murder rates remained at 1990 levels. Almost two-thirds of the lives saved—a thousand lives a year—were of black and Hispanic men between the ages of fifteen and forty-four.

Just as there is no consensus as to why crime rates rose in the 1960s, there is no agreement as to why they fell during the past two decades. The tough-on-crime movement deserves some of the credit, although criminologists do not see it as the most important factor. They point to other causes, including an aging population, the end of the crack epidemic and its violent markets, and a decrease in lead exposure among children (childhood lead exposure has been linked to increased criminality).[5]

If the crime decline gave black officials the opportunity to consider less punitive alternatives, the war on crime's accumulated impact on black America turned the opportunity into an imperative. According to the most recent data, African Americans are held in state prisons at a rate five times that of whites. In eleven states, at least one in twenty adult black men is in prison.[6] The dramatic increase in criminal convictions has undermined an already depressed labor market. Jobs—never easy to find in the ghetto—have virtually disappeared for those with criminal convictions. As the sociologist Becky

Pettit concludes, "[B]y 2008, a young black man without a high school diploma was more likely to be in prison or jail than to be employed in the paid labor force."[7]

In addition to such general trends, the 2014 D.C. Council could see something more specific: the harm inflicted by marijuana criminalization had increased far beyond anything the 1975 council could have imagined. Racial disparities in marijuana arrests existed even in the 1970s, but because the War on Drugs was just beginning, their catastrophic impact on black communities wasn't yet apparent. As a result, someone like council member Doug Moore could credibly argue in 1975 that marijuana use posed a greater threat to the city's black youth than the laws prohibiting it. By 2014, this view found few adherents. Four decades into the war on marijuana, the rising arrest rates and increasing racial disparities were clearly the greater evil.[8]

Not only had many more black citizens been arrested for marijuana possession by 2014, but each arrest carried greater consequences. Technological changes meant that by 2014, records of convictions— and even arrests—were much easier for third parties to obtain than they had been in 1975. Meanwhile, new laws meant that employers, schools, housing agencies, and others could—and, in some cases, were required to—use that information against drug offenders.[9] Each of these changes was destructive enough individually, but their cumulative impact on the black community was devastating. Warrior and pretext policing led to more arrests, technological changes made the arrests impossible to escape, and legal changes turned a single arrest into a lifetime of exclusion and subordination.

Just as important to the reform effort was the fact that by 2014, advocates for decriminalization had discovered potent language to describe the drug war's devastation of black communities. Marijuana criminalization was no longer simply a bad idea with racially disparate results, as decriminalization proponents had suggested in 1975. Rather, criminalization constituted, as one witness explained during a city council hearing, "a war on the District's black neighborhoods and black residents."[10] *The New Jim Crow*, by Michelle Alexander, played a crucial role in providing advocates with a framework for understanding, and a rhetoric for criticizing, the War on Drugs. Published in 2010, the book quickly became required reading for anyone concerned about mass incarceration. Alexander's ideas profoundly influenced the D.C. Council's marijuana debates, with various witnesses citing *The New Jim Crow* and one council member explaining that the book had "compelled me to be heavily engaged in this conversation."[11]

The documented harm caused by decades of marijuana criminalization, plus powerful new arguments rooted in a commitment to racial justice, proved a winning combination for decriminalization proponents. In 1975, polls indicated that only 39 percent of black voters supported legalization, while 51 percent opposed it.[12] By 2014, a solid 58 percent of the city's black residents supported marijuana decriminalization.[13] Even the city's black churches switched sides. In 1975, black ministers had helped defeat decriminalization, arguing that marijuana was a gateway to heroin.[14] By 2014, the ministers had concluded that marijuana was instead a gateway to the criminal justice system.[15]

Marijuana decriminalization is an important victory.[16] Sandra Dozier, who lost her job at FedEx when she was arrested with $20 worth of marijuana in her glove compartment, can attest to why it matters. So can thousands of others.[17] But the victory is also a cautionary tale about the limits of recent criminal justice reform efforts.

First, as a percentage of our nation's incarcerated population, those possessing small amounts of marijuana barely register. For every ten thousand people behind bars in America, only six are there because of marijuana possession.[18] A greater concern is that criminal justice reformers increasingly separate "nonviolent drug offenders"—including those convicted of marijuana possession—from "violent criminals." In this view, nonviolent drug offenders are worthy of compassion and a chance to redeem themselves; violent offenders, by contrast, deserve what they get.

During his second term, President Barack Obama became the most prominent proponent of what we might call the nonviolent-offenders-only approach to criminal justice reform.[19] In 2015, Obama outlined his final criminal justice reform agenda in a widely anticipated speech to the NAACP's annual convention. He divided the world of criminal defendants into two groups. First, there are the nonviolent drug offenders, whose incarceration, the president said, is "the real reason our prison population is so high." Obama argued that the current system punishes these offenders too severely: "If you're a low-level drug dealer, or you violate your parole, you owe some debt to society. But you don't owe twenty years. You don't owe a life sentence."[20].

Obama contrasted the nonviolent offenders with another group: "violent criminals," who, he said, "need to be in jail." Who are these people? "Murderers, predators, rapists, gang leaders, drug kingpins—we need some of those folks behind bars."[21] In a press conference the next day, explaining why his effort to reduce mandatory minimum sentences was limited to "nonviolent drug offenses," Obama remarked, "I tend not to have a lot of sympathy when it comes to violent crime."[22]

Obama's choice to limit criminal justice reform to low-level, nonviolent drug offenders is a common one among elected officials—including African American elected officials. At the federal level, black members of the House of Representatives rallied around the Sentencing Reform Act of 2015, whose stated goal was to reduce mandatory minimums for certain low-level drug offenders while "ensuring that serious violent felons do not get out early."[23] At the state and local level, African American prosecutors such as California's Kamala Harris, Baltimore's Marilyn Mosby, and Philadelphia's Seth Williams all built reform agendas around nonviolent criminals. Defenders of the nonviolent-offenders-only approach to reform are sometimes silent about who is being left out. Other times they enlist violent offenders as a bogeyman, suggesting that leniency for nonviolent offenders will create space to lock up the violent ones for longer. As Representative Marcia Fudge (D-OH) said, "Our current system severely punishes nonviolent offenders while granting violent criminals freedom and unfettered opportunities to menace our communities."[24]

The nonviolent-offenders-only perspective is understandable, and broadly popular. I might have shared it, too, once. Until I met Dante.

Dante Highsmith was clear: "I want to go home," he said. He had just turned sixteen, and we were sitting in the legal visiting room at Oak Hill, D.C.'s juvenile prison. Light-skinned, with hazel eyes and dread-locks, Dante seemed small for his age, especially now that he was swallowed up by an oversize prison-issue sweatshirt.

I had asked Dante what he wanted to happen in his case. It was a simple question, but one that is rarely posed to young people in his shoes. As a senior lawyer had preached to me and the other new at-torneys during our orientation to juvenile court, "Everybody with power talks *at* our clients, but nobody listens *to* them. At the Public Defender Service, we listen."

I was listening closely, but I wasn't sure how to respond to Dante's request. Going home was a long shot. He was charged with armed rob-bery, and the evidence against him was strong. According to police reports, shortly after nine p.m. on an unusually frigid January night, a man was waiting for a bus on Fourteenth Street, NW, in D.C.'s Co-lumbia Heights neighborhood. He was approached by a teenage male wearing a black jacket. The teenager said, "Give it up, give it up, man. Give it up, or I'll cut you."

The man looked at the teen and saw a bulge in his pocket. Think-ing it must be a knife or, worse, a gun, the man reached into his front pocket, threw out what he had, and ran. The robber scooped up the bills, jammed them into the pocket of his jeans, and ran the other way.

He didn't get far. A woman leaving a grocery store across the street had seen what was happening. She started yelling. A security guard working in the same store gave chase, and the security guard was fast. He caught the fleeing teenager a couple of blocks later and held him for the police, who had already been called by other shoppers.

When the police came and searched the teen, they found a knife and $12 in his pocket. The police asked the suspect for his name, and he told them: "Dante Highsmith."

At the police station that night, Dante signed a brief confession. It was written in his own handwriting and contained the important details of the crime. At the bottom of the one-page confession, just above Dante's signature, he had written, "I'm sorry."

The case looked even worse once I met with the prosecutor. The legal term for our meeting was a "discovery conference," at which the prosecutor was supposed to provide police reports and other material outlining the government's evidence. But with Lynn Leslie, an African American woman who had been prosecuting juveniles for almost a decade, the discovery conferences often devolved into impromptu lectures—especially with newer public defenders like me. I had been practicing for just over a year, and Leslie seemed to delight in holding forth about the menace of crime in an effort to puncture my bubble of innocence. Dante's case, I was about to learn, would provide perfect fodder for one of her harangues.

Leslie explained that the victim was a middle-aged African American man, a laborer on his way home from work. (I would later learn that his name was Jeremy Thomas, though Leslie, like many prosecutors, referred to him as "my victim.") After describing the evidence, she said, her eyes narrowing, "Look, Forman, my victim doesn't have it easy, but he is breaking his back every day, hauling boxes, doing the right thing, providing for his family. And this is what he gets!"

I could see where this was going. The criminal justice system isn't supposed to distinguish among victims—everybody is guaranteed the law's equal protection, and the punishment shouldn't change depending on whether the victim is rich or poor, black or white, a nice guy or a jerk. That's the theory, anyway. In reality, all that does matter. In many courthouses across America, a working-class black man like Mr. Thomas might have his case overlooked. But he stood a better chance in D.C.'s majority-black courthouse, especially if he had the good fortune of having his case land on the desk of the right prosecutor. To have his case taken seriously, Mr. Thomas couldn't have done better than Lynn Leslie. She was part of a breed of race-conscious black prosecutors who prodded the system to value the lives of black victims. She was a reminder that for all my claims about punitive criminal justice being a civil rights issue, other black Americans believed just as passionately that rampant crime and violence remained the defining racial justice questions of the day. As she lectured me in her office, I could already hear her in court. "Your Honor," she would say, full of righteous fury, "nobody deserves to be accosted by some young punk, nobody deserves to be robbed, and nobody deserves to live in fear. But let me tell you, Mr. Thomas deserves it least of all."

I feared it would work, especially before certain judges. And here was the biggest obstacle Dante and I faced: the judge. Dante's case was before Judge Curtis Walker, the same judge who had invoked Dr. Martin Luther King, Jr., en route to locking up my client Brandon. I couldn't see how Dante would make out any better than Brandon had. Sure, Brandon had a gun, which was more serious than Dante's knife, but Brandon hadn't actually used it. Dante, on the other hand, had robbed somebody. Just as easily as I could hear prosecutor Leslie advocating for Dante to go to prison, I could hear Judge Walker agreeing. "Son," he would say forcefully, looking down at Dante, "Martin Luther King didn't give his life so that you could be walking around with a knife, holding up hardworking people."

None of it looked good: Dante faced strong evidence, a determined prosecutor, and a passionate judge. Now, if this had been a movie, I would proceed to find an overlooked witness who confessed to the crime and revealed that Dante had been framed, or would file a brilliant legal motion that upended the government's case. But in the miracle-free world of the public defender, a case like Dante's required me to act like a social worker. Dante would almost certainly plead guilty, and his future would depend on the sentencing hearing. I would need to persuade the judge that something other than prison was the best outcome for him, the community, and the interests of justice.

And that's where the social work came in: to do a good job at sentencing meant that I needed to look deeply into Dante's background, trying to find the moments in which he had been failed by his family, schools or other institutions, or society in general. Then, ideally, I would identify a program or combination of programs that would meet his needs and better protect society in the long term than prison would.[25] This approach can work for both adults and kids, but it is especially suited for juvenile court, where, in D.C. and most of the country, rehabilitation remains part of a judge's mandate.[26]

As I dug into Dante's background, I found a lot to work with, beginning with the trauma of his early years. Dante hadn't been arrested before, so he didn't have a juvenile case history. Nevertheless, when I went to the office that kept the child welfare files, the clerk handed me a monstrously thick binder. Opening it revealed page after page of pain. Dante had a younger brother, Jason, and the two boys had been removed from their mother's custody when Dante was eight and Jason was five. One night shortly before the removal, a caseworker had stopped by the home at ten p.m. and found Jason and Dante sitting on their front stoop, unattended. According to the boys, this wasn't unusual; they said that their mother sometimes told them to wait outside while she spent time with "mommy's friends." Their mother, Jacinda, would later admit to a caseworker that she was addicted to crack and that she occasionally left the boys outside when she was using with friends, or, a few times, when she slept with men who gave her drugs.

School documents also told a disheartening story. Dante was smart, his teachers said, but his behavior stood in the way of his learning. His educational record showed a consistent pattern of minor misconduct: a scuffle with a student here, mouthing off to a teacher there. Nothing too serious, but also not a trajectory toward educational success. The problems had started in elementary school—his first suspension was for two days in second grade, when he pushed another student; according to Dante, the student had called his mother a whore. Despite the warning signs, Dante had never received

counseling or other services over the years. The schools' only response was to suspend him for increasingly long periods.[27] Now, by
high school, Dante had been held back twice and appeared on the
cusp of dropping out.

There were a few bright spots. When Dante and Jason were taken
from their mother, they were placed with their grandmother, Jacinda's mother, instead of being sent into the foster care system. Jacinda's
mother was often sick and couldn't manage teenage boys as well
as she would have liked, but she was caring, drug-free, and fiercely
protective of her grandsons. As for school, Dante was a star in his carpentry and woodshop class, and a visit to his and Jason's bedroom revealed the fruits of his labor: carvings and other half-finished projects
were crammed into every corner. The pièce de résistance was a slab
of wood almost five feet high with the letters J-A-S-O-N carved across
the top. Dante had given it to his little brother for his thirteenth birthday. I could see how much Jason adored his older brother when he
showed me the carving, saying it was "my best birthday present ever."

Until this arrest, Dante had avoided the criminal justice system.
So why now? Why this night? Why this robbery? The first few times
we met, I avoided talking to him about the crime itself. But once we
had developed more of a relationship and I thought he trusted me, I
asked him about it. His story was one I had heard before, and it rang
true.

A group of guys who lived on Dante's block and the two adjoining
ones called themselves the "Thirteenth Street Mob," though, like many
names for neighborhood crews in D.C., theirs was preposterously ambitious. The "mob" was about ten guys, and though Thirteenth Street
stretched for miles, they all came from a three-block stretch. However, if you were a teenager living on one of those blocks, they were in
charge, and you crossed them at your peril. Dante found this out himself when he was twelve and his grandmother sent him to the grocery
store for a box of cereal. He had the bad fortune of running into three
members of the crew on his way out of the store. They were older
than he was, and bigger, and when they demanded the cereal, he

had no choice but to give it to them. He returned home to his grand-mother empty-handed and in tears.

Now that Dante was about to turn sixteen himself, he was given the chance to join the gang. He told me that he had been on the fence. Standing around on the corner with the guys seemed like a waste of time, but he liked the sense of camaraderie, and the protection. "It's just easier if you know somebody has your back," he explained.[28] The other members of the crew told him what he had to do: rob somebody at the bus stop and bring the money back to the group, who would be waiting in the alley behind the corner store. So that's what he did—or tried to do.

I began to imagine a path forward. When I asked Dante what he thought would help keep him out of trouble and away from the neighborhood crew, he didn't hesitate. "Something to do after school. I need something to keep me off the corner." Ideally, he said, it would involve working with his hands. The carvings I had seen backed that up.

I started working the phones. The social workers at the Public Defender Service kept a list of programs for our juvenile clients, and I focused on the few that had any connection to crafts or trades. I quickly ran into two problems. First, there were far more Dantes in D.C. than programs for them, so the waiting lists were often long and the first answer was invariably no. (At PDS, we often lamented that there were never waiting lists for prison—just for alternatives to prison.) But I was used to hearing no, and I figured I could keep calling until I wore somebody down or a spot opened up. But the second problem was more difficult. All the programs had rules about whom they would accept, and while the rules varied, one was consistent: only nonviolent offenders were eligible. Although some charges left room for argument (I recall a lengthy debate with a program officer over whether burglary was a crime of violence), Dante's charge—armed robbery—met nobody's definition of nonviolent.

Call after call yielded the same result. I would speak to an intake coordinator at this job training program, or a counselor at that alternative education program. I would describe Dante's woodworking talent and his bedroom stuffed with carvings. I would explain how he had overcome enormous family obstacles, that he was teetering on the verge of success, and how this one opportunity could prove transformative for him. Time and again the answer came back: "I'm sorry, sir, we have criteria, and we don't accept people charged with violent offenses like armed robbery."

President Obama's 2015 speech to the NAACP won lavish praise from racial justice advocates. "We finally have the president we thought we elected: one who talks directly and forcefully about race and human rights," wrote the Georgetown professor Michael Eric Dyson.[29] I understand why reformers would be so pleased to finally—finally!—see an American president discussing any sort of leniency. But when Obama and others insist that "nonviolent drug offenders" are the only appropriate beneficiaries of criminal justice reform, all I can hear are the counselors telling me they can't consider Dante for their program.

Basing criminal justice reform on leniency for nonviolent drug offenders reinforces a deeply problematic narrative. First, consider the numbers. America's incarceration rates for nonviolent drug offenders are unprecedented and morally outrageous, but they are not "the real reason our prison population is so high." Roughly 20 percent of America's prisoners are in prison on drug charges. As a result, even if we decided today to unlock the prison door of every single American behind bars on a drug offense, tomorrow morning we'd wake up to a country that still had the world's largest prison population.

And to be clear, when advocates speak of "nonviolent drug offenders," they are not talking about all, or even most, of the five hundred thousand incarcerated on drug offenses. As we saw in chapter 5, the drug trade—especially during the crack era—was extraordinarily violent. Some of the people involved had no connection to violence, but it wasn't easy—pacifists didn't survive for long. In arguing for mercy and compassion for nonviolent drug offenders, and only for them, advocates are pursuing an approach that excludes not just the majority of prisoners, but even the majority of incarcerated drug offenders.

The narrow scope of this style of reform was confirmed by the Department of Justice's 2014 clemency initiative. Attorney General Eric Holder made headlines when he announced that the Justice Department would consider recommending that the president commute some of the extraordinarily long sentences given to people convicted of drug crimes, mostly from the late 1980s and 1990s.[30] Holder's initiative was welcome news—the sentences it would target were indeed much too long, and because crack offenses were penalized more harshly than powder cocaine offenses, African Americans suffered the most. But the guidelines were quite restrictive. Eligibility was limited to federal prisoners who had already served ten years, had no significant criminal history, were "nonviolent, low-level" offenders, and had "no history of violence prior to or during their current term of imprisonment." In excluding anybody with a history of violence, the Justice Department guidelines rendered most federal prisoners ineligible for clemency.

Defenders of the nonviolent-offenders-only approach suggest that it is just a start. Reform must begin with nonviolent offenders, they say, but others might benefit later. President Obama's senior adviser, Valerie Jarrett, suggested as much when, in 2016, she told National Public Radio, "If we can begin with the nonviolent drug offenders, it's an important first step. It doesn't mean that we wouldn't come back if research indicated that we should tailor other parts of our judicial system. But let's start with where we have consensus and move forward and not let the perfect be the enemy of the good."[31]

I am sympathetic to this perspective—and not only because of the political realities Jarrett cites. I have described mass incarceration as the result of a series of small decisions, made over time, by a disparate group of actors. If that is correct, mass incarceration will likely have to be undone in the same way. So it makes sense for advocates to start with the least culpable or threatening individuals.

But criminal justice reform's first step—relief for nonviolent drug offenders—could easily become its last. To see how, look no further than the president's own language. When Obama declared that he has "no sympathy" or "no tolerance" for those who have committed violent offenses, he effectively marked this larger group of violent offenders as permanently out-of-bounds. Such talk draws no distinctions and admits no exceptions. It allows for no individual consideration of the violent offense. The context, the story, the mitigating factors—none of it matters. Any act of violence in your past casts you as undeserving forever.

Obama should have understood the flaw in this approach. He frequently cited *The Wire*, David Simon's account of the crack years in Baltimore, as one of his favorite television shows, and in 2015 he invited Simon to the White House to discuss criminal justice issues. But *The Wire* would seem an odd choice for a president espousing the nonviolent-offenders-only approach to reform. Other than Bubbles the heroin addict, none of the show's main characters would have been eligible for clemency under the Department of Justice's guidelines. Yet despite the show's rampant violence, most viewers, including apparently Obama himself, don't think of the show as being primarily about a bunch of ruthless thugs. Why not? Because their violent acts are not the only things we know about them. We know them fully, as people, not just by their charge sheets or criminal records. Obama said as much, telling Simon, "But part of the challenge [of criminal justice reform] is going to be making sure, number one, that we humanize what so often on the local news is just a bunch of shadowy characters, and tell their stories. And that's where the work you've done has been so important."[32]

Just so. And other defenders of the nonviolent-offenders-only approach would do well to remember the point. People who have committed a violent offense make up 53 percent of the nation's state prisoners, and of those, more are incarcerated for Dante's crime—robbery—than for any other.[33] But the label "violent offender," tossed out to describe a shadowy group for whom we are supposed to have no sympathy, encourages us to overlook their individual stories. It causes us to separate those other people—the ones who did something violent, the ones who belong in cages—from the rest of us. It leads us, as Bryan Stevenson has written, to define people by the worst thing they have ever done.[34] And it ensures that we will never get close to resolving the human rights crisis that is 2.2 million Americans behind bars.

Finally, somebody said yes. It wasn't anybody from the list of programs I had been using; it wasn't even my phone call that made the difference. Dante's mother, Jacinda, was the one who found an opportunity for her son. Jacinda was now in recovery and attending a Narcotics Anonymous group that met at her church. She didn't have custody of her boys, but she was allowed to visit them as often as she wanted. In our conversations, Jacinda was remarkably open about her failings as a mother and about how those shortcomings had hurt Dante. At our first meeting, she told me that she was determined to step up now. I had heard this promise often from other parents, and I knew how hard it could be to keep. But Jacinda was doing it. She showed up for all of Dante's court dates, spoke up on his behalf to social workers and the judge, and called me regularly for news about the case.

After I told her that everybody was turning Dante down because he was charged with a violent offense, Jacinda started asking around herself. A friend from her Narcotics Anonymous group told her about Pastor Gaffney, a Pentecostal minister who had just started a carpentry, counseling, and life skills program for teenage boys. It was a tiny operation with no track record of success, but the offerings aligned well with Dante's needs. Dante liked the idea as well. This was good, since his sentencing date loomed in two weeks and we didn't have any other options to present.

My elation at his being accepted into the program was tempered by the thought of one man: Judge Walker. Just because Dante had been accepted didn't mean that Judge Walker would approve. I thought

I could make the case that Dante was a good candidate for rehabilitation. But I could also hear Lynn Leslie's rebuttal. Sure, she would
say, rising up to address Judge Walker, this young man *says* he has
never done anything like this before, he *says* he was barely part of the
gang, but we only have his word for that. And yes, she would say,
Dante is a juvenile, but just barely. If he had robbed Mr. Thomas a
week later, after he turned sixteen, he would have been transferred to
adult court and faced a fifteen-year prison sentence. Leslie might even
press further and try to use Dante's youth against him. It was a common move in courts during the 1990s, when the theme of juvenile
"super-predators" had captured the nation's attention. In 1996, the
year of Dante's sentencing, the former federal drug czar William Bennett and colleagues were warning that "America is now home to
thickening ranks of juvenile 'super-predators'—radically impulsive,
brutally remorseless youngsters, including ever more preteenage
boys, who murder, assault, rob, burglarize, deal deadly drugs, join
gun-toting gangs, and create serious communal disorders."[35] Who
was to say that Dante wasn't one of them?

But even if Judge Walker agreed with me that Dante had potential, Lynn Leslie would always have her trump card: justice for the
victim. And judges often agreed with prosecutors that justice for
the victim meant punishing the defendant with the criminal system's signature offering: prison.

I decided I had no choice but to visit the man Dante had robbed.
I wanted to tell him what we were going to propose at sentencing.
Even more important, I wanted him to learn about Dante. He saw
this young man only through the lens of that one terrible night, and
I wanted him to know that Dante was more than that. Talking to victims was something lawyers in my office did sometimes, but not often,
because it hardly ever worked. We rarely got past the front door,
since many victims don't welcome the defender of the person who
harmed them. It could also backfire. Even if I handled myself profes-
sionally and appropriately, there was always a risk that the victim
would perceive my visit as unwanted pressure, or even coercion. If

he did, he could tell the prosecutor, who might take it up with Judge Walker, who might in turn punish Dante for my sins—real or perceived.

Despite those risks, I had to try. It seemed like Dante's only chance. Lynn Leslie would surely factor Mr. Thomas's views into her sentencing recommendation, and Judge Walker would just as surely consider them when making his decision. If Mr. Thomas came to court demanding a prison sentence, that outcome was almost inevitable.

The address I had for Mr. Thomas turned out to be the first floor of a row house just off North Capitol Street. It was on one of those blocks—common throughout the city—where you could see the Capitol and other landmarks just a mile or two in the distance but still be among dilapidated buildings and trash-filled streets that seemed worlds away. It was a Sunday around six p.m.—prime time for finding witnesses at home (except during football season, because interrupting a Washington Redskins game was a good way to antagonize someone). There was an empty hole where the doorbell should have been, so I knocked, tentatively at first, then louder. A teenage boy answered, and seconds later a man who looked to be about fifty years old joined him. It was Mr. Thomas.

I told him that I was the lawyer representing the boy who had robbed him, quickly adding that I knew some things about the case that I thought he'd want to know. "Could I come in? For just a couple of minutes?" I asked. He hesitated briefly, then opened the door and showed me in, emphasizing that it would have to be quick because he was making dinner.

After directing me to an oversize sofa, Mr. Thomas sat in a matching armchair across from me. The room was dominated by a large television console with family photographs on top. Two boys, including the one who had answered the door, were in most of them.

As soon as we were seated, I made my pitch, barely pausing for breath. I told Mr. Thomas what I had learned about Dante's childhood: that his mother had been addicted to crack and had left him unsupervised deep into the night. I told him that the robbery that day had been Dante's initiation into a small-time neighborhood crew that had offered him a sense of family and belonging that he hadn't gotten at home. I said that Dante was good with his hands and that we had found a church-based trade program that was willing to take him. This all spilled out so quickly that I feared I wasn't making much sense, but I plowed ahead to my request: Would he consider telling the judge that he was okay with Dante going to this program instead of prison?

I wrapped up my spiel by giving Mr. Thomas a copy of the police report containing Dante's confession. Defense lawyers don't typically volunteer damaging evidence, but since Dante had already pleaded guilty, I figured little harm could come of it. And I wanted Mr. Thomas to see the apology in Dante's own words. As I handed him the single sheet of paper, I told him that I had never seen a client apologize to his victim on the night of a robbery. That Dante had done so, I said, reflected on his character. Then I handed Mr. Thomas a letter Dante had written to him, which I planned to present in court at the sentencing hearing. In the letter, Dante had apologized again, writing, "What I did to you was wrong. But I'm not a bad person. If you forgive me, I won't let you down."

Mr. Thomas took the papers from me, and after looking them over quickly, he stood, excused himself, and left the room. I hadn't been expecting this, and had no idea what to think. Was he going to call the prosecutor and complain right then and there? My fretting was interrupted by voices from the kitchen; there were two male voices, and one was definitely Mr. Thomas's. Then his voice stopped, and I heard only a younger voice, which I assumed was that of the boy who had answered the door. The young man's voice was low but firm, and snatches of it made their way out to me. I heard bits of Dante's confession to the police. At first I was confused, and then I caught on: the son must be reading the material to his dad. He read the confession first, then Dante's apology letter. After a few minutes, Mr. Thomas came back. This time he didn't sit down, telling me, "Sir, I will think about what you said. Now I have to finish making dinner." He didn't seem angry, but I could tell there was no point in trying to prolong my visit.

The two weeks leading up to the sentencing hearing were torture. I replayed my conversation with Mr. Thomas over and over again, wondering if I could or should have said something different. As hard as it was for me to wait and hope and do nothing, at least I had a slate of other cases to consume me. Dante and his mother had only one, and they each called me almost daily for updates. Jacinda was full of ideas; the night before the sentencing, she called offering to visit Mr. Thomas herself. I told her I appreciated how much she wanted to help, but I was confident that Judge Walker would not look favorably on this.

The next morning, the hallway outside the courtroom contained its usual bustle of lawyers, clients, family members, witnesses, social workers, and other court personnel. Victims or other key government witnesses were often escorted to court by somebody from the prosecutor's office, but I had been in the hallway for just a minute or two when I saw Mr. Thomas waiting on a bench. He was wearing a black suit and was sitting alone.

I went to talk to him. I hadn't expected to see him, and I hadn't thought about what I might say. I fumbled around incoherently until he saved me by interrupting. "I've been thinking about what you told me the other day," he said, before reaching into his pocket and fishing out some papers—Dante's confession and his apology letter. "This boy asked me to forgive him," he said, pointing at the letter, "and I'm not sure that I can." He looked past me, toward the courtroom door we would both soon enter, and said, "But I can try."

I exhaled deeply and thanked him. Just then, Lynn Leslie appeared. She seemed annoyed to see that I was talking to the victim, and I excused myself. As I left to find Dante's family members, I said a little prayer, hoping that Mr. Thomas wouldn't change his mind.

He didn't. When the case was called, Lynn Leslie and I each made our arguments. She asked the judge to send Dante to Oak Hill for at least two years. I argued for probation and the carpentry program we had found. But the voice that mattered most was Mr. Thomas's. He told the judge just what he had told me in the hallway about forgiveness. He said that he had prayed on the matter and had ended up asking himself what he would want if his son stood in Dante's shoes. For that reason, he said, he could support our plan. He could support not sending Dante to prison.

Judge Walker prized efficiency, and he acted quickly after listening to Mr. Thomas. There was no Martin Luther King speech. He just looked directly at Dante, saying, "I hope what Mr. Forman said about you is right. I hope you never forget Mr. Thomas. Because I wouldn't do this but for his grace." Holding up a copy of the apology letter Dante had written—the same one Mr. Thomas had brought to court—Judge Walker said, "Son, this is a nice letter, but these are just words, and I've seen a lot of nice words over the years. So don't thank him with a letter. Thank him with your actions."

Ever since the day of Dante's sentencing, I've wondered what our criminal justice system would look like if we tried to approach it the way Mr. Thomas did. What if we came to see that justice requires accountability, but not vengeance? What if we came to understand that equal protection under the law, including equal protection for black victims too long denied it, doesn't have to mean the harshest available punishment? What if we endeavored to make the lives of black victims matter without policies that lead to the mass incarceration of black defendants? What if we strove for compassion, for mercy, for forgiveness? And what if we did this for everybody, including people who have harmed others?

From a policy perspective, this would mean expanding recent reform proposals: instituting pretrial diversion programs to funnel people into drug treatment instead of prison, funding public defenders adequately, giving discretion back to judges by eliminating mandatory minimums, building quality schools inside juvenile and adult prisons, restoring voting rights to people who have served their sentences (or, better yet, allowing people to vote while incarcerated), and welcoming—not shunning and shaming—those who are returning from prison. These ideas would have been ridiculed as hopelessly naïve or softheaded as recently as a few years ago. But now, for the first time in forty years, they are getting a hearing. The collective work ahead is to deepen and broaden these efforts, all the while ensuring that they don't remain limited to the category of nonviolent offenders.

The election of Donald Trump, whose "law and order" campaign promised a retreat from the limited reforms instituted by the Obama administration, need not herald the demise of these efforts. Though the federal government gets most of the media attention, cities, counties, and states are where the action is on matters of crime and punishment. Policing is almost entirely a local affair, and almost 90 percent of American prisoners are in state and local jails, not federal ones. For those of us who seek to create a more humane criminal justice system, the message is clear: We must redouble our efforts at the state and local levels.

As important as policy change is, however, it is only part of the story. Our personal choices matter, too. Dante avoided incarceration only because of Mr. Thomas's individual decision to speak up for him. So too with Pastor Gaffney: when he decided to start a carpentry program for struggling teens and then allowed an armed robber to join, he made choices that changed Dante's life forever.

Our challenge as Americans is to recognize the power each of us has in our own spheres to push back against the harshness of mass incarceration. I was reminded of this recently while speaking to an audience at Yale about our criminal justice system. When I finished, a young woman said, "I'm persuaded by this whole conversation, and I'd like to do something, but I'm not a lawyer. I'm a student in the School of Management. What can I do?"

Well, a lot. I told her the stories of Sandra Dozier and Dante Highsmith. And then I asked: As a future corporate leader, what if she were to move her company away from a blanket policy of terminating all employees arrested while on probationary status, and toward a more forgiving, tailored, and individualized approach? Or, if she became an entrepreneur, what about starting something like Los Angeles's Homeboy Industries, which trains and hires former gang members and previously incarcerated individuals?

None of this will be easy. But then, it wasn't easy for Mr. Thomas. When the prosecutor Lynn Leslie requested jail time for Dante on his behalf, she was asking that D.C.'s criminal system, in the person of Judge Walker, do precisely what it had been built to do, and Mr. Thomas would have been well within his rights to concur. After all, much of that system had been constructed in the name of victims just like him. They don't deserve a life limited by racism and economic inequality. And, as the prosecutor pointed out, they certainly don't deserve to be robbed on their way home from work. This made Mr. Thomas's decision to give Dante another chance all the more admirable.

Individual choices like Mr. Thomas's matter immensely to the people involved, even if they barely touch the system as a whole. So too with many of the policy changes I have described, each of which reforms only one corner of our vast criminal justice apparatus. Against the scale of the world's largest prison system, with its grotesque racial disparities, such incremental moves might appear meager. But mass incarceration, as we have seen, was *constructed* incrementally, and it may have to be dismantled the same way.

A few years ago I was in downtown D.C., coming out of the Metro, the city's subway system. As I passed by a construction site, I heard a voice from above: "Mr. Forman!" I looked up and recognized Dante. It took me a second: it had been more than fifteen years since his sentencing hearing, and I hadn't kept up with him. Once he was put on probation, I had moved on. I knew he hadn't been rearrested while I was a public defender, since I would have been assigned to his case if he had. But other than that, I had no idea how things had worked out for him.

But there he was: Dante, filled out, with a goatee. He was a man now, with a hard hat and a construction job.

We didn't talk for long—he was at work, and I was late to a meeting. And though he would have been too polite to admit it, I suspect he didn't want to extend the conversation as much as I did. Public defenders relish these rare moments of connection with former clients who seem to be doing well. But our clients often feel differently. For many of them, and maybe for Dante, seeing their old lawyer can remind them of one of the most powerless moments in their lives.

But I did get the bare outlines of Dante's story: he had finished the carpentry program and gotten his GED. It hadn't been easy to find or keep a job. But he had stayed out of trouble and hadn't been arrested again. Eventually, he had gotten hired on a construction team, and now was working steadily. And he had a son of his own.

I didn't want to keep him, but as I was leaving, I told him that I still thought sometimes about his case. I said I still remembered Mr. Thomas, and how he had tried to forgive. "Me too," Dante said slowly. "Me too." Then he turned away and went back to work.

# Notes

## Introduction

1. See, e.g., Robert E. Pierre, "Oak Hill Center Emptied and Its Baggage Left Behind," *Washington Post*, May 29, 2009; Anne Hoffman, "D.C.'s Juvenile Justice, Then and Now," *All Things Considered*, October 26, 2012.
2. William Sabol and James P. Lynch, "Sentencing and Time Served in the District of Columbia Prior to Truth in Sentencing" (Urban Institute, 2001), 4. Ninety-one percent of those convicted of felony offenses were men. Ibid.
3. Marc Mauer and Tracy Huling, *Young Black Americans and the Criminal Justice System: Five Years Later* (Sentencing Project, 1995).
4. See, e.g., Michelle Alexander, *The New Jim Crow: Mass Incarceration in the Age of Colorblindness* (New Press, 2010).
5. Justice Policy Institute, "The Punishing Decade: Prison and Jail Estimates at the Millennium" (2000), 3, 5.
6. Douglas Martin, "James Forman Dies at 76; Was Pioneer in Civil Rights," *New York Times*, January 12, 2005.
7. "He imbued the organization with a camaraderie and collegiality that I've never seen in any organization then or since," recalled Julian Bond, SNCC's communications director at the time and later the chairman of the NAACP. Joe Holley, "Civil Rights Leader James Forman Dies," *Washington Post*, January 11, 2005.
8. Marc Mauer, *Race to Incarcerate* (New Press, 1999), 121.
9. Clarence W. Hunter, "Search Begins to Fill Superior Court Slot," *Washington Afro-American*, April 19, 1986.

10. Nazgol Ghandnoosh, *Race and Punishment: Racial Perceptions of Crime and Support for Punitive Policies* (Sentencing Project, 2014), 9.

11. There are important exceptions to the tendency to overlook black actors. See, e.g., Randall Kennedy, *Race, Crime, and the Law* (Vintage Books, 1998), 370–72; Lisa Miller, *The Perils of Federalism* (Oxford University Press, 2008), 147–66; Vanessa Barker, *The Politics of Imprisonment: How the Democratic Process Shapes the Way America Punishes Offenders* (Oxford University Press, 2009), 149–51; Michael Javen Fortner, *Black Silent Majority: The Rockefeller Drug Laws and the Politics of Punishment* (Harvard University Press, 2015); John Clegg and Adaner Usmani, "The Racial Politics of the Punitive Turn" (unpublished manuscript, June 2016).

12. See, e.g., David A. Sklansky, "Not Your Father's Police Department: Making Sense of the New Demographics of Law Enforcement," *Journal of Criminal Law and Criminology* 96, no. 3 (2006): 1209–1243.

13. Between 1970 and 2011, the number of black elected officials increased nationwide by 800 percent—from 1,469 to 10,500. Juliet Eilperin, "What's Changed for African Americans Since 1963, by the Numbers," *Washington Post*, August 22, 2013.

14. *Capitol View Civic Association Newsletter* 4, no. 6, May 1979. Washingtoniana Collection, CA Box 11, Martin Luther King Jr. Memorial Library, Washington, D.C.

15. Craig K. Lisk and Fifty Residents to Marion Barry and Other Elected Officials, November 28, 1988, David A. Clarke Papers, Box 47, Folder 21, Special Collections Research Center, George Washington University Library.

16. See, e.g., former U.S. Attorney and New York mayor Rudolph Giuliani, who said this on *Meet the Press*: "I find it very disappointing that you're not discussing the fact that 93 percent of blacks in America are killed by other blacks." He added, "What about the poor black child that is killed by another black child? Why aren't you protesting that?" "Giuliani & Dyson Argue Over Violence in Black Communities," *Meet the Press*, November 23, 2014. Giuliani's argument is not a new one. The historian Khalil Gibran Muhammad describes such comments as "playing the violence card," a rhetorical move dating to at least the late 1800s, in which dominant groups delegitimize discrimination claims from ethnic and racial minorities by pointing to violence within their communities. Khalil Gibran Muhammad, "Playing the Violence Card," *New York Times*, April 6, 2012; Muhammad, *The Condemnation of Blackness: Race, Crime, and the Making of Modern Urban America* (Harvard University Press, 2010), 97, 132.

17. This has been an important theme in the work of the political scientist Lisa Miller. Lisa L. Miller, "Black Activists Don't Ignore Crime," *New York Times*, August 5, 2016.

18. In fact, Giuliani's criticism ignores the fact that, as we will see in chapter 4, the term "black-on-black crime" was first used by black commentators.

19. I disagree with the political scientist Michael Fortner, who argues that "mass incarceration had less to do with white resistance to racial equality and more

to do with the black silent majority's confrontation with the 'reign of criminal terror' in their neighborhoods." Fortner, *Black Silent Majority*, 23.

20. See, e.g., Michelle Alexander, *The New Jim Crow*, 205–206; Elizabeth Hinton, Jullily Kohler-Hausmann, and Vesla Weaver, "Did Blacks Really Endorse the 1994 Crime Bill?," *New York Times*, April 13, 2016; Miller, *Perils of Federalism*, 147–66.

21. Ta-Nehisi Coates highlights the importance of class to black politics on matters of crime and punishment in "Black and Blue: Why Does America's Richest Black Suburb Have Some of the Country's Most Brutal Cops?," *Washington Monthly*, June 2001.

22. Bruce Western, *Punishment and Inequality in America* (Russell Sage Foundation, 2006), 26–27.

23. I acknowledge the existence of "linked fate" across classes within black America. Michael C. Dawson, *Behind the Mule: Race and Class in African-American Politics* (Princeton University Press, 1994). But the *degree* to which blacks see their fates as linked varies based on context. As Cathy Cohen argues in her study of the black political class's response to the AIDS and HIV crisis, "[N]ot every black person in crisis is seen as equally essential to the survival of the community, as an equally representative proxy of our own individual interests, and thus as equally worthy of political support by other African Americans." Cathy J. Cohen, *The Boundaries of Blackness: AIDS and the Breakdown of Black Politics* (University of Chicago Press, 1999), xi. My claim is that those accused of crime—who are disproportionately though not exclusively poor—have often been viewed as less worthy of political support by other African Americans. I discuss this further in James Forman, Jr., "The Black Poor, Black Elites, and America's Prisons," *Cardozo Law Review* 32 (2011): 791.

24. Daniel J. Freed, "The Nonsystem of Criminal Justice," in *Report to the Task Force on Law and Law Enforcement* (Violence Commission, vol. 13, 1969).

## 1. Gateway to the War on Drugs

1. Michael H. Tonry, *Malign Neglect: Race, Crime, and Punishment in America* (Oxford University Press, 1995), 82.

2. See, e.g., Michael Tonry and Matthew Melewski, "The Malign Effects of Drug and Crime Control Policies on Black Americans," in Michael Tonry, ed., *Thinking About Punishment: Penal Policy Across Space, Time and Discipline* (Ashgate Publishing, 2009), 81, 104–105.

3. Ibid., 105–109.

4. "Behind the D.C. Numbers: The War on Marijuana in Black and White," ACLU, June 2013, 4.

5. Harry S. Jaffe and Tom Sherwood, *Dream City: Race, Power and the Decline of Washington, D.C.*, rev. ed. (Argo-Navis, 2014), 12.

6. "Three Mayors Speak of Their Cities," *Ebony*, September 1974, 35. Gloria Wolford, "Kenneth A. Gibson Elected in Newark," *Baltimore Afro-American*, June 27, 1970.

7. District of Columbia Home Rule Act, D.C. CODE § 1–201 (1973).

8. For important discussions of how Congress has limited D.C.'s local autonomy,

see Michael K. Fauntroy, *Home Rule or House Rule? Congress and the Erosion of Local Governance in the District of Columbia* (University Press of America, 2003) and Ronald Walters and Toni-Michelle C. Travis, eds., *Democratic Destiny and the District of Columbia* (Lexington Books, 2010).

9. "Mayor, City Council Take Oath Today," *Washington Post*, January 2, 1975; La-Barbara Bowman, "Mayor, Council Sworn In," *Washington Post*, January 3, 1975; Jaffe and Sherwood, *Dream City*, 55; Ernest Holsendolph, "Elected City Officials Inaugurated in Washington," *New York Times*, January 3, 1975. For a discussion of George Clinton and the *Chocolate City* album, see Natalie Hopkinson, *Go-Go Live: The Musical Life and Death of a Chocolate City* (Duke University Press, 2012).

10. Jonetta Rose Barras, "The Strange World of David Clarke," *Washington City Paper*, September 29, 1995; Elizabeth Becker, "One-Time Allies Now Vie for Ward One Council Seat," *Washington Post*, October 28, 1974; Jacqueline Trescott, "David Clarke, the City Council's Big Little Man: Tempering Temper with Compassion," *Washington Post*, February 7, 1983; Michael Abramowitz, "A Civil Rights Champion of Unrelenting Intensity," *Washington Post*, August 31, 1990.

11. Greg Mize, interview by author, January 2014, 19; Barras, "The Strange World of David Clarke."

12. Jerry V. Wilson, *The War on Crime in the District of Columbia, 1955–1975* (U.S. Department of Justice, 1978), 77, Table 7-21.

13. Carroll Kilpatrick, "Nixon Labels Drug Abuse Crisis for U.S.," *Boston Globe*, June 18, 1971.

14. Michael Massing, *The Fix* (University of California Press, 2000), 137.

15. Stuart Auerbach, "Penalty End Asked On Home 'Pot' Use," *Washington Post*, March 23, 1972.

16. Fred P. Graham, "National Commission to Propose Legal Private Use of Marijuana," *New York Times*, February 13, 1972; National Commission on Marihuana and Drug Abuse, *Marihuana: A Signal of Misunderstanding* (1972), 91.

17. Massing, *The Fix*, 136.

18. Lily Rothman, "The Conservative Case for Legalizing Marijuana," *Time*, February 26, 2015.

19. James T. Wooten, "Carter Seeks to End Marijuana Penalty for Small Amounts," *New York Times*, August 3, 1977. Carter's statement turned out to be the high-water mark for the marijuana decriminalization movement. As Michael Massing explains, "a fierce political backlash against pot was brewing," and President Reagan's War on Drugs was imminent. Massing, *The Fix*, 142.

20. *Washington Star-News*, December 6, 1974.

21. Bill No. 1-44, Legislative Services Office, D.C. City Council, 1, 2.

22. D.C. Code, Sec. 33-423 (1975).

23. Timothy S. Robinson, "Halleck Loses Struggle to Keep D.C. Judgeship," *Washington Post*, May 21, 1977; Eugene L. Meyer and Timothy S. Robinson, "Judge Halleck Held Qualified, Reappointment Left to Ford," *Washington Post*, September 20, 1975.

24. *Reform of Marijuana Laws: Hearing on Bill 1-44 Before the Commission on the Judiciary and Criminal Law*, D.C. City Council (July 16, 1975, morning session), 47. Legislative Services Office, D.C. City Council.

25. Washington Urban League, "An Examination of Differential Patterns in the Arrest and Disposition of Marijuana Possession Cases in Washington, D.C." (1975).

26. *Reform of Marijuana Laws: Hearing on Bill 1-44* (July 16, 1975, morning session), 77.

27. Ibid., 47, 53, 58.

28. *Reform of Marijuana Laws: Hearing on Bill 1-44* (July 16, 1975, afternoon session), 3.

29. Ibid., 3–7.

30. *Reform of Marijuana Laws: Hearing on Bill 1-44* (July 16, 1975, morning session), 32.

31. Robert L. DuPont and Richard N. Katon, "Development of a Heroin-Addiction Treatment Program: Effect on Urban Crime," *Journal of the American Medical Association* 216 (May 24, 1971), 1320–1321.

32. William L. Claiborne, "City 'Heroin Epidemic' Cited," *Washington Post*, February 5, 1971; William L. Claiborne, "Heroin Treatment in D.C. Extended by 2 Years," *Washington Post*, January 11, 1972; William L. Claiborne, "D.C. Heroin Addicts May Total 18,000," *Washington Post*, December 19, 1970; Suzannah Lessard, "Busting Our Mental Blocks on Drugs and Crime," *Washington Monthly*, June 1971.

33. Claiborne, "City 'Heroin Epidemic' Cited"; Anne Hebald, "10,400 Using Heroin," *Washington Post*, August 10, 1970. A study conducted by researchers at American University found that the typical Washington, D.C., heroin addict began using the drug before he turned nineteen. James Q. Wilson, *Thinking About Crime* (Vintage, 1985; rev. ed.), 203; Whitney M. Young, "Two Big Reasons Why They're Cracking Down on the Drug Threat," *Washington Afro-American*, March 17, 1970.

34. Wilson, *Thinking About Crime*, 205.

35. When Albert Biderman and his team asked D.C. residents whether they had done anything to protect themselves against the dangers of crime, 38 percent spontaneously suggested that they stayed off the streets at night. Albert D. Biderman et al., *Report on a Pilot Study in the District of Columbia on Victimization and Attitudes Toward Law Enforcement* (Bureau of Social Science Research, 1967), 128–29. The most common measures taken to secure homes were improving door locks and adding bars on windows. Ibid; Young, "Two Big Reasons"; Ronald Kessler, "The Heroin Economy: Millions a Day," *Washington Post*, May 12, 1970; Haim G. Ginott, "Between Parent and Teenager: Addiction," *Washington Post*, September 18, 1969.

36. Robert L. Asher, "The Methadone Treatment: Using a Drug to Fight a Drug: Pros and Cons," *Washington Post*, November 17, 1970.

37. Comptroller General of the United States, "Narcotic Addiction Treatment and Rehabilitation Programs in Washington, D.C." (April 20, 1972), 10–11.

38. Joe Mack, Jr., "Trio Fights Dope Use in D.C.," *Chicago Daily Defender*, January 16, 1971.

39. *Federal Drug Abuse and Drug Dependence Prevention, Treatment, and Rehabilitation Act of 1970: Hearing on S. 3562 Before the Special Subcommittee on Alcoholism and Narcotics of the S. Comm. on Labor and Public Welfare*, 91st Congress 530 (1970) (statement of Col. Hassan Jeru-Ahmed, director, Blackman's Development Center, Washington, D.C.), 544. Even this minimal use of methadone was controversial within Hassan's organization. See Gary Lindsay, "Black Man's Army in War Against Drug Abuse," *Washington Afro-American*, October 11, 1969.

40. Statement of Hassan Jeru-Ahmed before Senate Subcommittee, 530.

41. Ibid., 508.

42. William Raspberry, "Methadone Use: Another Blunder," *Washington Post*, May 11, 1974.

43. Statement of Hassan Jeru-Ahmed before Senate Subcommittee, 530; Mack, "Trio Fights Dope Use"; Lindsay, "Black Man's Army."

44. A doctor who worked with heroin addicts in New Haven, Connecticut, described a similar hostility to methadone among Black Panthers in that city; they viewed methadone as "a sort of Band-Aid on the ghetto, an attempt to avoid the total revolution they believed would soon happen." Kathleen J. Frydl, *The Drug Wars in America, 1940–1973* (Cambridge University Press, 2013), 336.

45. Lindsay, "Black Man's Army."

46. Statement of Hassan Jeru-Ahmed before Senate Subcommittee, 544.

47. Flyer published by the Blackman's Development Center urging the community to unite against heroin suppliers and dealers. Statement of Hassan Jeru-Ahmed before Senate Subcommittee, 516. Hassan's anger at black drug dealers was seconded by the editors of *The Hilltop*, Howard University's student newspaper. After a drug bust on campus in March 1972, the editors proclaimed that "drugs, especially hard drugs, are one of the most detrimental forces against the development of a great Black race." Accordingly, "[t]he Hilltop finds no disagreement with the apprehension and arrests of those degenerate individuals who peddle the drug sickness upon future Black leadership." Editorial, "A Note on a Drug Bust," *The Hilltop*, March 17, 1972. A majority of students shared this antipathy toward drugs and those who sold them, at least according to a poll conducted a few months earlier by the paper. *The Hilltop*'s poll revealed that 92 percent of students thought there was a drug problem on campus; moreover, "all students believe that the Administration should put more pressure on drug pushers and eighty-eight percent of those surveyed think that students themselves should put more pressure on pushers." Pat Johnson, "Students Favor Crackdown on Drugs," *The Hilltop*, November 5, 1971.

48. Jaffe and Sherwood, *Dream City*, 94.

49. Statement of Hassan Jeru-Ahmed before Senate Subcommittee, 539–40; Mack, "Trio Fights Dope Use in D.C."; Lindsay, "Black Man's Army"; Eugene L. Meyer, "Hassan Praised as Drug Informer," *Washington Post*, December 20, 1973. Michael Fortner argues that Harlem black activists rejected root-cause solutions: "[M]any African-American activists . . . would dismiss the significance of social programs (or a lack thereof)." Michael Javen Fortner, *Black*

*Silent Majority: The Rockefeller Drug Laws and the Politics of Punishment* (Harvard University Press, 2015), 66. He says that Harlem's black silent majority "derided the structural solutions proposed and mocked the sociology that validated those solutions. To them, those were ideas without relevance or remedy." Ibid., 171. I find contrary evidence in D.C. Most D.C. activists were like Hassan, who embraced structural *and* individual explanations for crime and solutions to crime. My conclusions are similar to those of Khalil Gibran Muhammad, who argues, "[D]espite their elitism, many black reformers tended to offer 'root cause solutions' alongside their class-infused cultural critique of black criminality." Khalil Gibran Muhammad, *The Condemnation of Blackness: Race, Crime, and the Making of Modern Urban America* (Harvard University Press, 2010), 10.

50. Meyer, "Hassan Praised."

51. Statement of Hassan Jeru-Ahmed before Senate Subcommittee, 539.

52. Mack, "Trio Fights Dope Use"; Lindsay, "Black Man's Army."

53. Known as "Murder City," Detroit saw youth gangs, including an infamous heroin ring that earned $7.5 million a week, and homicides reaching their peak in 1974 of 714—almost two a day. "Police Chief Helps to Change Detroit's Image: His Crime Prevention Program Turns 'Murder City' to Model City," *Deseret News*, February 6, 1983.

54. "New Spirit in Detroit," *The Nation*, January 19, 1974. A Detroit native and Howard Law graduate, Keith was part of the first generation of black judges to be appointed to the federal bench; in 1974 he received the Spingarn Medal, the NAACP's highest honor.

55. "New Spirit in Detroit."

56. Fortner, *Black Silent Majority*; Vanessa Barker, *The Politics of Imprisonment: How the Democratic Process Shapes the Way America Punishes Offenders* (Oxford University Press, 2009), 146–49.

57. Rev. Oberia D. Dempsey, "Drug Addicts," *Amsterdam News*, letter to the editor, February 1, 1969.

58. "Rev. Dempsey Tells Harlem to Arm Itself," *Baltimore Afro-American*, May 1, 1971.

59. Barker, *The Politics of Imprisonment*, 151. Others called for interdiction—for example, an ambitious young candidate for Congress named Charles Rangel led a march from Harlem to the French embassy, demanding that the French government stop the flow of heroin from that country. "Rangel Pickets Embassy," *Amsterdam News*, June 20, 1970.

60. Orde Coombs, "Letter to a Black Boy Murdered in New York City," *Essence*, December 1970, 54.

61. Ibid.

62. William Raspberry, "Eliminating the Pusher," *Washington Post*, December 29, 1971.

63. The former SNCC activist Ivanhoe Donaldson said, "I wanted to live in a black city, a place to call my home." Jaffe and Sherwood, *Dream City*, 109.

64. Juan Williams, "The Many Facets of Douglas Moore," *Washington Post*, September 5, 1978; Juan Williams, "Moore Paints Self as Poor's Champion," *Washington Post*, August 16, 1978.

65. Williams, "Moore Paints Self as Poor's Champion"; Bart Barnes, "Moore Emphasis: Black Nationalism," *Washington Post*, March 15, 1971; Megan Rosenfeld, "Barry, Moore Lead Parties in At-Large City Council Races," *Washington Post*, September 11, 1974.

66. "9 Democrats, 3 Republicans Vie for Nominations to Fill At-Large Council Seats," *Washington Post*, September 1, 1974.

67. R. C. Newell, "Jail Inmates Endorse Candidates," *Washington Afro-American*, June 15, 1974.

68. Douglas B. Feaver and Megan Rosenfeld, "Tucker, 2 Moores, Hobson Sr., Barry Lead City Council Race," *Washington Post*, November 6, 1974.

69. The Kerner Commission, *Report of the National Advisory Commission on Civil Disorders* (1968), 161.

70. Ibid. In New York State, black and Latino legislators echoed Moore's skepticism when, in 1971, they resisted efforts to soften marijuana laws. That year, the state assembly narrowly rejected a decriminalization bill; the opposition included eight of the nine black and Puerto Rican representatives. Francis X. Clines, "Assembly Retains Marijuana Laws: Bipartisan Vote Rejects Bill to Reduce Penalties," *New York Times*, May 19, 1971.

    Six years later, in 1977, the assembly took up the issue again, with the case for decriminalization led by State Senator Franz Leichter, who represented Manhattan's majority-white Upper West Side. Vander Beatty, a state senator representing Brooklyn, echoed D.C.'s Doug Moore and John Fauntleroy in his belief that decriminalization was meant to protect the state's white suburban and rural youth: "[I've] never seen all the enthusiasm about this bill when all the little black youths in the ghetto were going to jail and knocking around every street corner," he said. State Senator Israel Ruiz, Jr., from the Bronx, agreed, arguing that "a lot of people are going to get hurt" by decriminalization. In a passionate challenge to Leichter delivered from the floor of the senate, he declared, "One of these days, Senator Leichter, instead of giving political statements for your West Side so-called liberals, come into my district and I will show you kids smoking pot one right after the other, sitting on stoops." He continued: "You try to talk to them and they will not even talk back to you because they are in never-never land, and if you tell me marijuana is not harmful, sir, I would respectfully call you a liar." Ultimately, however, opposition proved futile. Under pressure from the legislature's Democratic leaders, even Senator Beatty voted yes, but with a bitterness that bordered on animosity: "Tonight I am going to cast a 'yes' vote to bail out white, middle-class Americans." Senate Floor Debate on Calendar Bill No. 694, NYLS Senate Debate Transcripts: 1977 Chapter 360, 10, 477, 545.

71. Gil Scott-Heron, "Comment #1," in *Small Talk at 125th and Lenox: A Collection of Black Poems* (World Publishing, 1970), 15–16.

72. Stokely Carmichael (Kwame Ture), "Definitions of Black Power," in Thomas R. West and James W. Mooney, eds., *To Redeem a Nation: A History and Anthology of the Civil Rights Movement* (Brandywine Press, 1993), 246.

73. *Reform of Marijuana Laws: Hearing on Bill 1-44* (July 16, 1975, morning session), 42.

74. Diane Quander, "Howard's Drug Week Crys [*sic*] 'Respect Yourself,'" *The Hill-top*, November 5, 1971.

75. Carmen Fields, "Atlanta Mayor Jackson Brings Message to Boston Youths: Any Man Can," *Boston Globe*, July 13, 1975. Jackson was speaking of marijuana, but the Howard *Hilltop* had made a similar point about harder drugs. After the two students died from apparent drug overdoses in October 1971, *The Hilltop* ran a series of angry editorials. "How many more lives will heroin, LSD, and mescaline be responsible for taking before Black people realize that 'tripping' and revolution and 'getting high' and survival do not mix?" the editors asked. Editorial, "Gasp for Freedom-Helena," *The Hilltop*, October 22, 1971. A week later, the editors called drugs "genocidal," proclaiming that the campus "drug-culture operates to the detriment of and is diametrically opposed to all that is Black and revolutionary." Editorial, "Drugs Win . . . Again," *The Hilltop*, October 29, 1971.

76. Stokely Carmichael, *Stokely Speaks: Black Power Back to Pan-Africanism* (Random House, 1971), 209. Howard's Professor Bowden agreed with Carmichael, call-ing the drug scene a form of genocide and saying, "there must be an individual responsibility on the part of Black people to recognize what the MAN is doing and a refusal to let him succeed in the destruction of Black people." Diane Quander, "Howard's Drug Week Crys [*sic*] 'Respect Yourself.'"

77. *Reform of Marijuana Laws: Hearing on Bill 1-44* (July 16, 1975, morning session), 49.

78. Don Freeman, "Marijuana Legalization & Black Mental Health: The Black Community & Marijuana Legalization" 12 (1975), Legislative Services Office, D.C. City Council.

79. Paul A. Quander to the Committee on Judicial and Criminal Law, July 8, 1975, Legislative Services Office, D.C. City Council.

80. *Reform of Marijuana Laws: Hearing on Bill 1-44* (July 16, 1975, morning session), 44.

81. Leah Y. Latimer, "Grateful Grads and Memories at Armstrong's 80th Anniver-sary," *Washington Post*, September 17, 1981.

82. Andrew Barnes, "Expand Aid for Convicts, D.C. Warned," *Washington Post*, February 7, 1971.

83. Laura A. Kiernan, "Public Defender Unit Accused of Bias," *Washington Post*, October 13, 1978.

84. Charles J. Ogletree, Jr., *All Deliberate Speed: Reflections on the First Half-Century of Brown v. Board of Education* (Norton, 2004), 84.

85. *Reform of Marijuana Laws: Hearing on Bill 1-44* (July 16, 1975, evening session), 6.

86. Ibid., 4–5. Moore's and Fauntleroy's arguments came from a well-established line of thinking in the black community. Almost every African American can remember having a parent, teacher, or minister say that because of racism, past and present, "you have to be twice as good to make it." Sometimes the argument is motivational—as in, you need to study twice as hard if you are going to impress the teacher or get into Harvard. Sometimes it's cautionary—as in, you can't afford to talk back to a police officer or you will get locked up or shot. Moore and Fauntleroy were deploying the cautionary version of this argument, warning that for blacks, the simple misstep of marijuana

experimentation carried dramatic risks of a life of addiction, crime, and degradation. But they were also taking the argument into a new arena—after all, it is one thing to advise your grandson or exhort your congregation, quite another to use that same argument as the foundation for criminal justice policy.

87. "A Statement by (Rev.) Andrew Fowler in [*sic*] behalf of the Committe [*sic*] of One Hundred Ministers and Baptist Ministers Conference of Washington, D.C. and Vicinity Before the City Council," July 16, 1975, Legislative Services Office, D.C. City Council.

88. Ibid., 4.

89. "A Presentation Made by the Reverend Samuel George Hines on Behalf of the Second Precinct Clergymen's Association at a Hearing at the City Council on Wednesday," July 16, 1975. Legislative Services Office, D.C. City Council.

90. Statement of Hassan Jeru-Ahmed before Senate Subcommittee, 536.

91. *Reform of Marijuana Laws: Hearing on Bill 1-44* (July 16, 1975, evening session), 10.

92. *Reform of Marijuana Laws: Hearing on Bill 1-44* (July 16, 1975, morning session), 49.

93. Ibid.

94. Helen Dewar, "Diggs Tests Veto Views on Pot Bill," *Washington Post*, October 14, 1975.

95. Milton Coleman, "A Solitary Battle: Doug Moore Is Running Against Hostile Establishment," *Washington Post*, March 29, 1978.

96. LaBarbara Bowman, "Ministers Oppose Bills: Targets Are Pot, Bets, Homosexual Bonds," *Washington Post*, September 24, 1975.

97. Jay Mathews, "Legal Marijuana Opposed," *Washington Post*, August 1, 1975.

98. Ibid.

99. Bowman, "Ministers Oppose Bills."

100. LaBarbara Bowman, "Clergymen Turned Tide," *Washington Post*, October 23, 1975.

101. LaBarbara Bowman, "D.C. Council Vice Chairman Tucker Seeks Step-Up," *Washington Post*, October 26, 1974.

102. Ibid.

103. Bowman, "Clergymen Turned Tide."

104. Linda Newton Jones, "Baptist Ministers Endorse Washington for Second Time," *Washington Post*, July 30, 1974.

105. There were three defections from the original eight council members who supported the bill: Sterling Tucker, William Spaulding, and James Coates. Bowman, "Clergymen Turned Tide."

106. Ibid.

107. And the fact that many of them did so in good faith also does not fit easily with standard accounts of the War on Drugs. For example, Michael Tonry, an influential early critic of the drug war, has argued that "[t]here was no basis on which policymakers could have believed in good faith that the key strategies of the War on Drugs would be so successful as to justify the burdens they would impose on minority citizens." Tonry, *Malign Neglect*, 116.

108. Randall Kennedy, *Race, Crime, and the Law* (Vintage Books, 1998), 17. Kennedy

borrows the term "politics of respectability" from the historian Evelyn Brooks Higginbotham. Evelyn Brooks Higginbotham, *Righteous Discontent: The Women's Movement in the Black Baptist Church, 1880–1920* (Harvard University Press, 1993).

109. Statement by Andrew Fowler, 4.

110. During the deliberations over the bill, the Washington Urban League submitted research showing that prosecution patterns in marijuana possession cases already suggested "a policy toward leniency if not decriminalization." Washington Urban League, "Differential Patterns," 7. Indeed, the Urban League found that an astonishing 75 percent of marijuana cases processed in 1973 by the D.C. Superior Court were dismissed by prosecutors. Clarke's opponents cited these practices to argue that the consequences of prohibition were not so grave. Judge Fauntleroy, for example, said, "I believe that in this city, those who have been arrested for possession of small amounts of marijuana usually are steered into one of several drug counseling programs, and if they successfully complete these programs, the charges against them are dropped." *Reform of Marijuana Laws: Hearing on Bill 1-44* (July 16, 1975, evening session), 15.

111. Wilson, *The War on Crime in the District of Columbia*, 77.

## 2. Black Lives Matter

1. Jerry V. Wilson, *The War on Crime in the District of Columbia, 1955–1975* (U.S. Department of Justice, 1978), 67, Graph 7-11. Vesla Weaver, "Frontlash: Race and the Development of Punitive Crime Policy," *Studies in American Political Development* 21 (Fall 2007): 230.

2. Michael Flamm, *Law and Order: Street Crime, Civil Unrest, and the Crisis of Liberalism in the 1960s* (Columbia University Press, 2005), 42.

3. Ibid., 44.

4. Ibid., 180.

5. Carl Bernstein, "The Guns of D.C.: Dodge City on the Potomac," *Washington Post*, May 11, 1969.

6. Milton Viorst, "Blame the Fear on a Few Thugs," *Washington Star*, February 3, 1973.

7. "Malcolm X in D.C. with Solution to Crime Rate," *Daily Defender*, May 13, 1963, 5.

8. As the political scientist Vesla Weaver explains about the 1960s, "Crime did rise quite substantially and the homicide rate, by far the most unbiased measure of violent crime, saw a precipitous rise." Weaver, "Frontlash," 234.

9. Federal Bureau of Investigation, "Uniform Crime Report 1960," Table 5—Index of Crime, 1960, Standard Metropolitan Statistical Areas, 53–77; Federal Bureau of Investigation, "Uniform Crime Report 1970," Table 5—Index of Crime, 1970, Standard Metropolitan Statistical Areas, 82–97. For discussions of the national trends see William J. Stuntz, *The Collapse of Criminal Justice* (Belknap Press of Harvard University Press, 2011), 18–20; David Garland, *The Culture of Control* (University of Chicago Press, 2001), 90; and Gary LaFree, *Losing Legitimacy: Street Crime and the Decline of Social Institutions in America* (Westview Press, 1998), 20.

10. See, e.g., Eric C. Schneider, *Smack: Heroin and the American City* (University of Pennsylvania Press, 2008); Jessica Wolpaw Reyes, "Lead Exposure and Behavior: Effects on Antisocial and Risky Behavior Among Children and Adolescents," *Economic Inquiry* 53, no. 3 (2015): 1583, 1599, and Table 7; Barry Latzer, *The Rise and Fall of Violent Crime in America* (Encounter Books, 2016); Dana Goldstein, "Too Old to Commit Crime?," *The Marshall Project*, March 20, 2015; Claude Fischer, "A Crime Puzzle: Violent Crime Declines in America," *Berkeley Blog*, June 16, 2010.

11. Office of Criminal Justice Plans and Analysis, "Government of the District of Columbia, April 1992 Homicide Report," Table A-2, 35; John A. Wilson, untitled document, in John A. Wilson Papers, Box 57, Folder 16, Special Collections Research Center, George Washington University Library.

12. *Gun Control: Public Hearing Before the Committee on Judiciary & Criminal Law of the District of Columbia Council* (June 6, 1975), 12, Legislative Services Office, D.C. City Council.

13. Gary Kleck, "Homicide, Capital Punishment, and Gun Ownership: An Aggregate Analysis of U.S. Homicide Trends from 1947 to 1976" (Ph.D. diss., University of Illinois, 1979), 124.

14. Sixty percent of all armed robberies involved handguns, as did the vast majority of the city's firearm-related homicides. *Gun Control: Public Hearing* (June 6, 1975), 96.

15. Cartoon, *Washington Afro-American*, January 18, 1975.

16. Editorial, "Why Not an Anti-Crime Drive?" *Washington Afro-American*, January 18, 1975.

17. *Newsletter, North Michigan Park Civic Association*, March 1976, Washingtoniana Collection, CA Box 14, Martin Luther King Jr. Library, Washington, D.C.

18. "Attack Set on Crime," *Washington Afro-American*, October 4, 1975.

19. Larry Coleman, "Death, Crime Haunt Homecoming," *The Hilltop*, October 27, 1972.

20. "Crime Conference Set for Howard University," *Washington Afro-American*, December 6, 1975.

21. According to the *Afro*, "More than half of the community is barricaded behind double and triple-locked doors, barred windows and doors, and seemingly one out of every four homes is displaying a burglar alarm. Even the church windows are barred in many areas." Editorial, "Crime and Fear in the Streets," *Washington Afro-American*, November 22, 1975.

22. R. C. Newell, "Kung-Fu: Alive and Well, Growing in the Inner-City," *Washington Afro-American*, August 14, 1976.

23. Gregory Kearse, "Crime and Armament," *Washington Afro-American*, August 31, 1974.

24. In a 1967 survey, for example, 51 percent of whites said they feared for their personal safety; 65 percent of blacks said the same. Flamm, *Law and Order*, 96.

25. Winston Groom, "New Report on D.C. Crime: Profile of a Frightened City," *Washington Star*, September 22, 1975.

26. Jody Beck and Charles A. McAleer, "Neighbor Due at Crime Parley Is Slain," *Washington Star*, April 7, 1976.

27. *Handguns, S. 2507: Hearing Before the Subcommittee to Investigate Juvenile Delinquency of the Senate Judiciary Committee*, 92nd Congress (1971) (statement of Lloyd Cutler, former executive director, National Commission on Causes and Prevention of Violence), 59.

28. Patricia Camp, "Stray Shot Kills Youth, 14, in Van," *Washington Post*, July 20, 1975.

29. Editorial, "Time to End This Self-Destruction," *Washington Afro-American*, May 22, 1976; Editorial, "Concerned Citizens Fight Crime," *Washington Afro-American*, July 19, 1975.

30. John A. Wilson, untitled document, Wilson Papers, Box 24, Folder 7.

31. Peter Perl, "A Bridge He Could Not Cross," *Washington Post Magazine*, November 1993.

32. Ibid.

33. "D.C. Council Chairman John Wilson, 49, Dies at Home in Apparent Suicide," *Jet*, June 1993, 14.

34. Hollie I. West, "Politics and John Wilson," *Washington Post*, March 9, 1975.

35. Camp, "Stray Shot Kills Youth," Wilson Papers, Box 24, Folder 7.

36. Roy Wilkins, *Standing Fast: The Autobiography of Roy Wilkins* (Viking, 1982), 65.

37. That is how South Carolina governor Cole Blease explained a pardon decision. Black women also suffered from Blease's racism. "Adultery seems to be their most favorite pastime," he said. "I have . . . very serious doubt as to whether the crime of rape can be committed upon a negro." Douglas Blackmon, *Slavery by Another Name* (Doubleday, 2008), 305.

38. Editorial, "Wilson's Gun Proposal," *Washington Star*, February 15, 1975.

39. As chapter 1 explores, a striking feature of the marijuana decriminalization debate was the lack of participation from the mostly black victims of marijuana enforcement.

40. *Gun Control Legislation, Bills 1-24 and 1-42: Public Hearing Before the Committee on Judiciary & Criminal Law of the District of Columbia Council* (June 7, 1975) (statement of Richard Ware), 23, Legislative Services Office, D.C. City Council.

41. Gary Kleck, "Homicide, Capital Punishment, and Gun Ownership: An Aggregate Analysis of U.S. Homicide Trends from 1947 to 1976" (Ph.D. diss., University of Illinois, 1979), 47.

42. *Gun Control Legislation, Bills 1-24 and 1-42*, 220.

43. Ibid., 24.

44. In the election, Fauntroy defeated, among others, future council member Doug Moore.

45. As D.C.'s nonvoting delegate to Congress, Fauntroy could not vote on a bill's final passage, but he had the right to vote in committee and the right to introduce legislation.

46. *Gun Control: Public Hearing* (June 6, 1975), 11.

47. Editorial, "Handguns Must Go!" *Washington Star*, February 3, 1975.

48. *Gun Control: Public Hearing* (June 6, 1975) (written testimony from Rev. Stanford J. Harris on behalf of the Capitol Hill Group Ministry).

49. *Gun Control: Public Hearing* ( June 6, 1975), 15.

50. Ibid., 97.

51. "Pragmatism in Gun Control," *Washington Star*, June 21, 1975.

52. William Raspberry, "What About the Old Gun Law?" *Washington Post*, June 16, 1975.

53. John A. Wilson, "International Comparisons," Wilson Papers, Box 24, Folder 7.

54. John A. Wilson, untitled document, Wilson Papers, Box 24, Folder 7.

55. Letter from John Wilson, April 9, 1976, Wilson Papers, Box 63, Folder 1; Dick Gregory, *Dick Gregory's Political Primer* (Harper & Row, 1972), 322.

56. Editorial, "Black Crime and 'Ills of Society,'" *Washington Afro-American*, June 14, 1975.

57. *Gun Control: Public Hearing* ( June 6, 1975), 15.

58. Ibid., 17.

59. *Gun Control Legislation, Bills 1-24 and 1-42* ( June 7, 1975), 25.

60. Nicholas Johnson, *Negroes and the Gun: The Black Tradition of Arms* (Prometheus Books, 2014), 285.

61. Douglas Wells, "Jackson Calls for Stiff, Swift Gun Abuse Penalties in Georgia," *Atlanta Daily World*, September 3, 1972.

62. *Firearms Legislation, Part 6: Hearing Before Subcommittee on Crime of the House Committee on the Judiciary*, 94th Congress (1975) (statement of Maynard Jackson, mayor, City of Atlanta), 1905.

63. Robert Sherrill, *The Saturday Night Special* (Penguin Books, 1975), 34–35.

64. *Firearms Legislation, Part 2, Chicago: Hearing Before Subcommittee on Crime of the House Committee on the Judiciary*, 94th Congress (1975) (statement of Rev. Russ Meek, president, Search for Truth, Inc.), 691.

65. *Firearms Legislation, Part 3, Detroit: Hearing Before Subcommittee on Crime of the House Committee on the Judiciary*, 94th Congress (1975) (statement of Erma Henderson, councilwoman, Detroit City Council), 1045–1046.

66. John A. Wilson, untitled document, Wilson Papers, Box 24, Folder 7.

67. "Time to End This Self-Destruction," *Afro-American*.

68. "Even though we have the biggest police department of any city this size in the country, and the Constitution talks about equal protection under the law, when a guy comes to my home, if I don't have an equalizer, then by the time I wait and call the police, I will not have had equal protection of the law." *Gun Control Legislation, Bills 1-24 and 1-42* ( June 7, 1975), 79.

69. Council member Arrington Dixon also expressed this concern, though in a more understated fashion. At the hearing, he asked Fauntroy to assess the "impact of disarming the citizens of the District of Columbia when surrounding jurisdictions may, in fact, not be disarmed." *Gun Control: Public Hearing* ( June 6, 1975), 29.

70. Coleman Young, *Hard Stuff: The Autobiography of Coleman Young* (Viking, 1994), 286. This quote is from 1986, but Young's opposition to gun control dates back to at least 1974. See, e.g., Tom Opre, "Present Handgun Laws Effective . . . If Enforced," *Detroit Free Press*, March 3, 1974. Opposing his police commissioner's support for gun control, Young said, "Perhaps some people do have a need for

handguns in their homes." Tyrone Powers, a black FBI agent stationed in Detroit while Young was mayor, agreed: "I thought it ludicrous for African American people to talk about gun control, with these violent, well-trained [white supremacist] groups preparing to wipe us off the face of the Earth . . . Mayor Coleman Young of Detroit was right when he refused to disarm his city of African American residents who were surrounded by hostile gun-toting suburbanites." Tyrone Powers, *Eyes to My Soul: The Rise or Decline of a Black FBI Agent* (Majority Press, 1986), 286.

71. The relationship between African Americans and gun ownership is the subject of three recent books: Nicholas Johnson, *Negroes and the Gun;* Charles Cobb, *This Non-Violent Stuff'll Get You Killed* (Basic Books, 2014); and Akinyele Omowale Umoja, *We Will Shoot Back: Armed Resistance in the Mississippi Freedom Movement* (New York University Press, 2014). Other important discussions include Akhil Reed Amar, *The Bill of Rights: Creation and Reconstruction* (Yale University Press, 1998), 262–66, and Robert J. Cottrol and Raymond T. Diamond, "The Second Amendment: Toward an Afro-Americanist Reconsideration," *Georgetown Law Journal* 80 (1991): 309–61.

72. Robin West, *Progressive Constitutionalism* (Duke University Press, 1995), 23.

73. Senator Clark, 39th Congress, 1st Session. *Congressional Globe* 833 (February 14, 1866).

74. Johnson, *Negroes and the Gun,* 99.

75. Ta-Nehisi Coates, "The Case for Reparations," *The Atlantic,* June 2014.

76. Nicholas Johnson, David Kopel, George Mocsary, and Michael O'Shea, *Firearms Law and the Second Amendment: Regulation, Rights and Policy* (Aspen Publishers, 2012), 290–92. Mississippi prohibited blacks from owning firearms, ammunition, dirks, or bowie knives. Stephen P. Halbrook, *Freedmen, the Fourteenth Amendment, and the Right to Bear Arms, 1866–1876* (Praeger, 1998), 2, 12.

77. Blackmon, *Slavery by Another Name,* 81–82.

78. Herbert Shapiro, *White Violence and Black Response* (University of Massachusetts Press, 1988), 6–7, 12–13, 16, 21.

79. David F. Krugler, *1919, The Year of Racial Violence: How African Americans Fought Back* (Cambridge University Press, 2014), 11.

80. Krugler, *1919, The Year of Racial Violence,* 66–98.

81. Blackmon, *Slavery by Another Name,* 357–59; A. Scott Berg, *Wilson* (Putnam, 2013), 349; James Chace, *1912: Wilson, Roosevelt, Taft & Debs—The Election That Changed the Country* (Simon & Schuster, 2004), 43, 243–44. According to Chace, "Woodrow Wilson was in essence a white supremacist, holding a romantic view of the courtesy and graciousness of the antebellum southern plantation owners, as well as accepting uncritically the post-Reconstruction South that arranged to keep the black Americans in their place." Ibid., 43.

82. "Mr. Trotter and Mr. Wilson," *The Crisis,* January 1915, 119.

83. J. E. Cutler, "Race Riots in D.C.," Memo for the Director of Military Intelligence, "Negro Subversion" file, 10218-350, RG 165, National Archives. Quoted in Delia Cunningham Mellis, "'The Monsters We Defy': Washington, D.C., in the Red Summer of 1919" (Ph.D. diss., CUNY, 2008), 81.

84. Randolph's disagreement with Du Bois was rooted in Du Bois's support for World War I. In 1918 Du Bois urged black Americans "to forget our special grievances and close our ranks shoulder to shoulder with our own white fellow citizens and the allied nations that are fighting for our democracy." Harlem radicals such as Randolph were highly critical of Du Bois's statement. Andrew E. Kersten, *A. Philip Randolph: A Life in the Vanguard* (Rowan & Little-field, 2007), 20.

85. Ida B. Wells, *Southern Horrors: Lynch Law in All Its Phases* (New York Age Print, 1892), 71; Manning Marable, *Malcolm X: A Life of Reinvention* (Viking, 2011), 304.

86. Johnson, *Negroes and the Gun*, 13.

87. James Forman, *The Making of Black Revolutionaries* (University of Washington Press, 1985), 376.

88. Howell Raines, *My Soul Is Rested: Movement Days in the Deep South Remembered* (Putnam, 1977), 267.

89. Johnson, *Negroes and the Gun*, 251.

90. Adam Winkler, *Gunfight: The Battle Over the Right to Bear Arms in America* (W. W. Norton, 2011), 245.

91. Ibid., 252.

92. Sherrill, *The Saturday Night Special*, 52.

93. Jaffe and Sherwood, *Dream City*, 71. Accounts of Carmichael's precise words vary; guns remain a theme in all of them. Here's how the historian Michael Flamm tells the story: "'Go home and get your guns,' Carmichael told a crowd after the looting had begun. 'When the white man comes he is coming to kill you. I don't want any black blood in the street. Go home and get you a gun.'" Flamm, *Law and Order*, 146.

94. Sanders Beburo, "Stokely: Education before Destruction," *The Hilltop*, November 15, 1968.

95. Leon Dash and Phil Casey, "'Front' Raps Gun Control as 'Racist,'" *Washington Post*, August 10, 1968.

96. Adrienne Manns, "New Officers Named, Others to be Ousted," *Washington Afro-American*, October 5, 1968; Lawrence Feinberg and Reed Hundt, "Montgomery Rejects Strict Gun Curbs," *Washington Post*, September 7, 1968.

97. Firearms Control Regulations Act of 1975 (D.C. Council Act No. 1-142).

98. The only poll, conducted by Georgetown University in March 1976, asked residents whether they would support a law "prohibiting the sale of handguns." Sixty-nine percent of the city's residents said yes, with 82 percent of whites and 62 percent of blacks expressing approval. Robert A. Hitlin, director of the Georgetown University Poll, to Gregory Mize, Committee on the Judiciary and Criminal Law, Council of the District of Columbia, March 25, 1976, in Wilson Papers, Box 27, Folder 7.

99. *Firearms Legislation, Part 2, Chicago*, 688.

100. Richard Ryan, "Blacks, Victims Leading Pressure for Handgun Control Legislation in Congress," *Boston Globe*, April 13, 1975.

101. "Dravidian Students Develop an Outer Hardness, Inner Peace," *Ebony*, June 1970, 108.

102. *Firearms Legislation, Part 2, Chicago*, 694.

103. Sixty-five percent of blacks said they would have to be prepared to defend their homes themselves, compared with 52 percent of whites. Only 23 percent of blacks said they could rely on the police alone, compared with 40 percent of whites. Hazel Erskine, "The Polls: Gun Control," *Public Opinion Quarterly* 36, no. 3 (1972): 467.

104. Fred Steeple, "Push for Strong Gun Laws Eyed Cautiously by Atlanta Solons," *Atlanta Daily World*, December 6, 1974.

105. *Gun Control Legislation, Bills 1-24 and 1-42* (June 7, 1975), 80.

106. Ibid., 79.

107. Ibid., 79–80.

108. According to Conyers,

    [I]t is clear that we are in an arms race within our country. This fact was not quite clear to many people inside our black communities when I began hearings on this subject two years ago. There was some ambivalence among blacks about surrendering weapons to a government and a country against which they feel they might need to use those weapons in self-defense. It was very commonly stated, "Why should I give up my gun? I may need it to defend myself against the police or against the government!" I have witnessed, however, the sharp change in the black community on the question of gun control. As we began to separate fact from fiction and to understand that we were the greatest victims of gun violence, we as a people began to come around. In fact, there are not many black people in the city who do not know someone who has been injured or killed in senseless handgun violence.

    John Conyers, "Crime as a Concern of Congress," in Herrington J. Bryce, ed., *Black Crime: A Police View* (U.S. Department of Justice, 1977), 22.

109. Randall Kennedy, *Race, Crime, and the Law* (Vintage Books, 1998), 48.

110. *Gun Control Legislation, Bills 1-24 and 1-42* (June 7, 1975), 22.

111. Ibid., 26.

112. Citing the rising black death rate, Wilson argued that "the black community is not surviving by means of the vigilante system." John A. Wilson, untitled document, Wilson Papers, Box 24, Folder 7.

113. (My emphasis.) Cobb, *This Non-Violent Stuff'll Get You Killed*, 47.

114. Which is not to say that the promised protection was always forthcoming. In subsequent chapters I will discuss how, at times, law enforcement continued to underserve black neighborhoods, especially low-income ones. But for now the point is about motive, and the promise of change. In the mid-1970s the black political class had just taken office, and black citizens were willing to give them a chance.

115. Jacqueline Bobo, "Black Women's Films," in Alma M. Garcia, ed., *Contested Images: Women of Color in Popular Culture* (AltaMira Press, 2012), 39. Almost

thirty years later, her declaration was turned into a song by the group Sweet
Honey in the Rock, whose founder, Bernice Johnson Reagon, had been a
SNCC worker. Sweet Honey in the Rock, "Ella's Song," in *Breaths*, Songtalk
Publishing Company, 1988.

116. "2 Whites Seized in Negro Slayings," *New York Times*, November 7, 1964.

117. Congress typically pushed D.C. in a punitive direction, especially in the 1980s
and 1990s. But the unique politics of gun control worked in the opposite direction, as congressional opposition to gun regulation served to stop D.C.'s leaders from passing a more punitive law.

118. *Firearms Legislation, Part 6, Atlanta*, 1909.

119. See *Gun Control: Public Hearing* ( June 6, 1975) (statement of Kay Campbell Mc-
Grath, Woman's National Democratic Club) (gun control supporter endorsing
mandatory minimums), 76; *Gun Control Legislation, Bills 1-24 and 1-42* ( June 7,
1975) (statement of Michael Parker, general counsel to NRA Institute for Legislative Action) ("[W]e are not going to make any real progress on the crime
problem until we start getting tough with the criminals"), 12; and *Gun Control
Legislation, Bills 1-24 and 1-42* ( June 7, 1975) (statement of William Saunders,
principal of Eastern High School) (proposing mandatory sentences and stringent penalties for those who use guns in a crime), 74.

120. *Gun Control Legislation, Bills 1-24 and 1-42* ( June 7, 1975), 80–86. The Capitol
View Civic Association, representing a majority-black neighborhood, agreed
with Moore. While they opposed taking guns from home and store
owners—who should retain the right "to use their firearms freely against
criminals and burglars who intrude on their property"—they endorsed legislation "to require an automatic, immediate jail sentence everytime [*sic*] a person is convicted of using a gun while committing a crime." *Capitol View Civic
Association, Inc. Newsletter*, January 1972, Washingtoniana Collection, CA Box 11,
Martin Luther King Jr. Memorial Library, Washington, D.C.

121. *Firearms Legislation, Part 3, Detroit*, 877.

122. Thomas Marvell, "The Impact of Enhanced Prison Terms for Felonies
Committed with Guns," *Criminology* 33 (1995): 259.

123. "Black Opinion Poll Presses for Strict Gun Control," *Chicago Metro News*, October 30, 1976.

124. *Firearms Legislation, Part 6, Atlanta*, 1906.

125. William Taaffe, "House Panel Kills Anti-Handgun Bill," *Washington Star*, October 30, 1975.

126. Flamm, *Law and Order*, 103.

127. Dan T. Carter, *The Politics of Rage: George Wallace, The Origins of the New Conser-
vatism, and the Transformation of American Politics* (Louisiana State University
Press, 2000), 313.

128. Nancy E. Marion, *A History of Federal Crime Control Initiatives, 1960–1993* (Praeger, 1994), 70.

129. Allen J. Matusow, *The Unraveling of America: A History of Liberalism in the 1960s*
(University of Georgia Press, 1984), 401.

130. Garland, *Culture of Control*, 76 (discussing the politics of the late 1970s, in which

"welfare policies for the poor were increasingly represented as expensive luxuries that hardworking taxpayers could no longer afford").

## 3. Representatives of Their Race

1. National Organization of Black Law Enforcement Officials (NOBLE), *Justice by Action* (Turner Publishing, 1998), 8.

2. Thomas A. Johnson, "Black Police Officials Establish Organization in Effort to Expand Influence in Criminal Justice Field," *New York Times*, September 9, 1976.

3. NOBLE, *Justice by Action*, 8; Johnson, "Black Police Officials Establish Organization."

4. Athelia Knight and Eugene Robinson, "Barry Picks Maurice Turner to be D.C. Police Chief," *Washington Post*, May 1, 1981.

5. James Baldwin, "Fifth Avenue, Uptown: A Letter from Harlem," *Esquire*, July 1960.

6. An indispensable historical account is W. Marvin Dulaney, *Black Police in America* (Indiana University Press, 1996).

7. National Park Service, National Register of Historic Places, "Armstrong Manual Training Center," July 17, 1996, 6, 7.

8. Alison Stewart, *First Class: The Legacy of Dunbar, America's First Black Public High School* (Lawrence Hill Books, 2013), 2.

9. National Park Service, "Armstrong Manual Training Center," 8.

10. Sally E. Hadden, *Slave Patrols: Law and Violence in Virginia and the Carolinas* (Harvard University Press, 2001), 3–4.

11. Ibid., 4.

12. Gilbert King, *Devil in the Grove: Thurgood Marshall, the Groveland Boys, and the Dawn of a New America* (HarperCollins, 2012), 17, 91, 139–41.

13. Hadden, *Slave Patrols*, 71.

14. Dulaney, *Black Police in America*, 13. Although we typically think about the Fourteenth Amendment's Equal Protection Clause as protecting criminal defendants, central to the original vision was the promise of protection *from* violence. Many Reconstruction legislators argued that the Fourteenth Amendment was necessary to ensure that all citizens, including recently freed slaves, would receive state protection from private violence. See, e.g., James Forman, Jr., "Juries and Race in the Nineteenth Century," *Yale Law Journal* 113 (2004): 917.

15. Harold N. Rabinowitz, *Race Relations in the South, 1865–1890* (University of Georgia Press, 1996), 42.

16. V. L. Wharton, *The Negro in Mississippi, 1865–1890* (Harper and Row, 1965), 167–68. See also Hubert Williams and Patrick V. Murphy, "The Evolving Strategy of Police: A Minority View," *Perspectives on Policing* 13 (January 1990).

17. U.S. Congress, Senate, Municipal Election in Jackson, Mississippi, 50th Congress, 1st sess., 1988, S. Misc. Doc. 166.

18. Dulaney, *Black Police in America*, 17.

19. Ibid. Population data from "Area, Natural Resources, and Population," *Statistical Abstract of the United States 1910* (U.S. Census Bureau, 1910), 36–42.

20. Dulaney, *Black Police in America*, 17, 23; Robert M. Fogelson, *Big-City Police* (Harvard University Press, 1977), 124.

21. The Urban League survey can be found in National Urban League, "Negro Police Officers in 76 of the Largest United States Cities" (1932), Box 6: A37, Part 6: Southern Regional Office, General Office File, 1919–1979, Urban League Papers, Library of Congress. The NAACP survey can be found in "NAACP Negro police questionnaire, 1948–49," Box II: A451, NAACP Papers, Library of Congress.

22. Charles Kirk Pilkington, "The Trials of Brotherhood: The Founding of the Commission on Interracial Cooperation," *Georgia Historical Quarterly* 69, no. 1 (Spring 1985): 55, 57.

23. Untitled report on the need for black police officers in Atlanta, Southern Regional Council (undated, appears to be from 1936), Box 6: A69, Part VI: Southern Regional Office, General Office File, 1919–1979, Urban League Papers.

24. Ibid.

25. Ibid.

26. NAACP, *Wanted: Negro Police for Negro Districts in Atlanta*, November 1937, Box 1: G44, NAACP Papers, Library of Congress.

27. Marion E. Jackson, "Sentiment Mounts for Negro Police," *Atlanta Daily World*, July 23, 1947.

28. "Speakers Voice Sentiment for Negro Police," *Atlanta Daily World*, September 24, 1947.

29. "Pleas for Negro Police Heard Here Wednesday," *Atlanta Daily World*, November 27, 1947.

30. William Gordon, "Atlanta Council in Wrangle Over Hiring of Negro Police," *Chicago Defender*, December 6, 1947.

31. Dulaney, *Black Police in America*, 43.

32. "Atlanta Gets Race Police with Limited Power," *New Journal and Guide*, December 6, 1947.

33. "Atlanta Council in Wrangle Over Hiring of Negro Police."

34. Atlanta City Council Minutes, December 1, 1947, pp. 86–87, Row 5, Section B, Shelf 5, Volume 45 of Atlanta City Council 10/6/1947–5/2/1949, Kenan Research Center, Atlanta History Center; "Council, Hartsfield Give Okay to Negro Police," *Atlanta Daily World*, December 2, 1947.

35. "The Long Awaited Dream Comes True," *Atlanta Daily World*, December 3, 1947.

36. Martha G. Fleming, "Atlantans Pay Tribute to City's First Black Police," *Atlanta Daily World*, November 6, 1977; Atlanta City Council Minutes, December 1, 1947, p. 87.

37. Fleming, "Atlantans Pay Tribute to City's First Black Police."

38. Dulaney, *Black Police in America*, 56; NOBLE, *Justice by Action*, 10.

39. C. Lamar Weaver, "New Police Welcomed to Active Duty," *Atlanta Daily World*, May 2, 1948.

40. "Throngs Thrilled by New Atlanta Officers," *Atlanta Daily World*, April 4, 1948.

41. Weaver, "New Police Welcomed to Active Duty."

42. Brian N. Williams and J. Edward Kellough, "Leadership with an Enduring Impact: The Legacy of Chief Burtell Jefferson of the Metropolitan Police Department of Washington, D.C.," *Public Administration Review* 66 (November/December 2006): 813.

43. *To Secure These Rights: The Report of the President's Committee on Civil Rights* (Government Printing Office, 1947), 89.

44. Kenesaw M. Landis, *Segregation in Washington: A Report of the National Committee on Segregation in the Nation's Capital, November 1948*, 83.

45. Coates, "The Case for Reparations."

46. Constance McLaughlin Green, *The Secret City: A History of Race Relations in the Nation's Capital* (Princeton University Press, 1967), 319; Martha Derthick, *City Politics in Washington, D.C.* (Joint Center for Urban Studies of the Massachusetts Institute of Technology and Harvard University, 1962), 122. In 1906, Kelly Miller, the founder of Howard University's Sociology Department, discussed how trade unions kept blacks in low-paying jobs. "The trades unions, either by the letter of the law or by the spirit in which it is executed, effectually bar the negro from the more remunerative pursuits of trade and transportation. The negro workman is thus compelled to loiter around the outer edge of industry and to pick up such menial work or odds-and-ends pursuits as white men do not care to undertake." Kelly Miller, "The Economic Handicap of the Negro in the North," *Annals of the American Academy of Political and Social Science* 27 (May 1906): 84. Little had changed in forty years.

47. Ben Segal, "The Practices of Craft Unions in Washington, D.C., with Respect to Minority Groups," in *Civil Rights in the Nation's Capital: A Report on a Decade of Progress* (National Association of Intergroup Relations Officials, 1959), 34.

48. Green, *The Secret City*, 319.

49. Landis, *Segregation in Washington*, 63.

50. Ibid., 64.

51. Williams and Kellough, "Leadership with an Enduring Impact," 814.

52. Robert F. Levey, "Policeman Came Along at the 'Right Time.'" *Washington Post*, September 9, 1976.

53. Williams and Kellough, "Leadership with an Enduring Impact," 814.

54. Ibid., 815.

55. Ibid., 814.

56. Edward Peeks, "2 Killings Provoked Probe," *Washington Afro-American*, October 26, 1957.

57. Elsie Carper and Alfred E. Lewis, "Police Assignments Not Determined by Race, Eight Top Officials Testify," *Washington Post*, October 23, 1957.

58. Edward Peeks, "Chief Murray Says He's All for Integrated Police, But . . ." *Washington Afro-American*, October 22, 1957. A similar story could be told in Detroit. In 1960 Willis F. Ward, chief of the Civil Division in the U.S. Attorney's Office in Detroit, complained that the police department's "high echelon

police officials" mandated segregated squad cars. "If for any reason the partner of the colored policeman does not make duty on a certain day, the colored officer must work alone, sometimes walking a beat. However, his counterpart, the white policeman, is given a white partner to assume his patrolling duties in the scout car." According to Ward, this was just one manifestation of the core problem: black police "are segregated and treated apart from the rest of the force in work assignments, and they are often humiliated by their superiors when they express dissatisfaction in this regard." *Hearings Before the United States Commission on Civil Rights*, Detroit, Michigan, December 14, 15, 1960, 387.

59. In this respect, freedom of choice here was even more nefarious than in the school desegregation context—and it was plenty bad there too, as the Supreme Court recognized in *Green v. County School Board of New Kent County* (391 U.S. 430, 1968). In *Green*, the Court struck down a plan by which New Kent County proposed to end formal school segregation by saying that students could now choose to attend either the formerly black school or the formerly white school. The Court appreciated how social context (including threats) constrained free choice, pointing out that no white students had chosen to attend the formerly black school and few black students had chosen to attend the formerly white school. Freedom of choice in the police context made integration even less likely; not only did a black officer have to agree to work with a white one, he had to find a white partner willing to work with him.

60. William M. Kephart, *Racial Factors and Urban Law Enforcement* (University of Pennsylvania Press, 1957), 9.

61. Ibid., 83.

62. Ibid., 78, 79.

63. Donald J. Black and Albert J. Reiss, Jr., "Patterns of Behavior in Police and Citizen Transactions," *Studies of Crime and Law Enforcement in Major Metropolitan Areas*, vol. 2 (U.S. Government Printing Office, 1967), 135.

64. Edward Peeks, "Victory Is Seen in All-Out Fight," *Washington Afro-American*, August 17, 1957. See also Burtell Jefferson, "Policies for Increasing the Number of Black Police Executives," in Herrington J. Bryce, ed., *Black Crime: A Police View* (National Institute of Law Enforcement and Criminal Justice, Law Enforcement Assistance Administration, U.S. Department of Justice, 1997), 132–33.

65. Peeks, "Victory Is Seen in All-Out Fight."

66. Ibid.

67. Edward Peeks, "Promotion Plan Called 'Devils,'" *Washington Afro-American*, September 7, 1957.

68. Levey, "Policeman Came Along at the 'Right Time.'"

69. Bill Davidson, "The Mess in Washington: A City in Trouble," *Saturday Evening Post*, July 13, 1963; Elsie Carper and Alfred E. Lewis, "Police Bias Is Denied by Murray," *Washington Post*, November 1, 1957.

70. Ina R. Friedman, *Black Cop: A Biography of Tilmon B. O'Bryant, Assistant Chief of Police, Washington, D.C.* (Lodgepole Press, 1997), 93–94.

71. Ibid.

72. Burtell Jefferson, "Policies for Increasing the Number of Black Police Executives," 132–34.

73. William Raspberry, "Few Negroes in Upper Police Ranks," *Washington Post*, September 16, 1966. Inspired by the way in which O'Bryant and Jefferson had used the objective civil service examination to help African American officers advance in a racist police department, integrationists later considered it a great victory when in 1967 this exam—essentially the same exam later at issue in *Washington v. Davis*—was officially given the same weight as more subjective measures of officers' performance. Alfred E. Lewis, "District Police Revamp Tests for Promotion," *Washington Post*, July 3, 1967.

74. Jefferson, "Policies for Increasing . . . ," 133.

75. Edward Peeks, "Fireworks Will Go Off at Probe," *Washington Afro-American*, September 14, 1957.

76. Edward Peeks, "Ruthless Slaying Triggered Split," *Washington Afro-American*, July 6, 1957; Edward Peeks, "Behind the Charges of Police Brutality," *Washington Afro-American*, June 29, 1957.

77. "Back Move to Oust Police Chief," *Washington Afro-American*, June 15, 1957.

78. D.C. Branch, NAACP, "Information in the Nature of Partial Documentation, Particulars and Evidence in the Matter of Metropolitan Police Department and Chief Robert V. Murray," exhibit 1: Blanche Price affidavit of February 11, 1957, NAACP Papers, Washington Bureau, Box IX: 226, Folder 6, Library of Congress.

79. Ibid., exhibit 5: Results of Blanche Price investigation in letter of March 21, 1957.

80. Ibid., exhibit 2: Claude H. Anderson affidavit of March 31, 1957.

81. Ibid., exhibit 15: Testimony Isaac Williams, Jr.

82. Untitled report on need for black police officers in Atlanta, Southern Regional Council (undated, appears to be from 1936), Box 6: A69, Part VI: Southern Regional Office, General Office File, 1919–1979, Urban League Papers, Library of Congress.

83. Edward Peeks, "Race Prejudice Laid to Officers," *Washington Afro-American*, August 3, 1957.

84. Ibid.

85. (My emphasis.) Editorial, "How to Settle the Brutality Issue," *Washington Afro-American*, July 20, 1957.

86. Elsie Carper, "Chief Murray Is Exonerated of Police Bias," *Washington Post*, November 8, 1957.

87. Ibid.

88. Landis, *Segregation in Washington*, 88.

89. Davidson, "The Mess in Washington."

90. Editorial, "Who Got Hurt?," *Washington Afro-American*, November 16, 1957.

91. Elliott M. Rudwick, *The Unequal Badge: Negro Policemen in the South* (Southern Regional Council, 1962), 9–10.

92. Task Force on the Police, President's Commission on Law Enforcement and Administration of Justice, *Task Force Report: The Police* (Government Printing Office, 1967), 170, citing U.S. Civil Rights Commission, *Administration of Justice Staff Report* (U.S. Government Printing Office, 1963), ch. 11, 26.

93. Fogelson, *Big-City Police*, 283.

94. Edward Peeks, "D.C. Needs More Colored Cops in Top Jobs to Fight Crime, Says Lawson," *Washington Afro-American*, April 27, 1963; Chuck Stone, "Crisis in the D.C. Police Dept.: One Reason Crime Is Rising," *Washington Afro-American*, June 1, 1963.

95. Stone, "Crisis in the D.C. Police Dept."

96. "Raise a Negro to Captain by Aug. 28, Police Urged," *Washington Post*, August 23, 1963.

97. Editorial, "O'Bryant's Curious Statement," *Washington Afro-American*, August 24, 1963.

98. Jerry V. Wilson, *The War on Crime in the District of Columbia, 1955–1975* (U.S. Department of Justice, 1978), 32.

99. "Davidson, Eugene C." (2015), Paper 51, Moorland-Spingarn Research Center, Manuscript Division, Howard University; Bruce Weber, "Chuck Stone, a Fiery, Trusted Columnist in Philadelphia, Dies at 89," *New York Times*, April 7, 2014.

100. Friedman, *Black Cop*, 36–37; Williams and Kellough, "Leadership with an Enduring Impact," 813–14.

101. Harry Jaffe and Tom Sherwood, *Dream City: Race, Power, and the Decline of Washington, D.C.*, rev. ed. (Argo-Navis, 2014), 12–13.

102. John Lewis, *Washington Afro-American*, October 12, 1968.

103. Ibid.

104. Warren Weaver, Jr., "Powell Says Riots Can End if Mayor Meets 5 Demands," *New York Times*, July 23, 1964.

105. Martin Arnold, "Murphy Appoints a Negro to Head Harlem Precinct," *New York Times*, August 15, 1964; John Sibley, "2 Harlem Demands Accepted by Mayor," *New York Times*, August 7, 1964.

106. Governor's Commission on the Los Angeles Riots, *Violence in the City—An End or a Beginning?* (Los Angeles, 1965), 1–2.

107. Bill Lane, "Negro Policemen," *Los Angeles Sentinel*, May 12, 1966.

108. Bill Lane, "Truth a Casualty," *Los Angeles Sentinel*, August 19, 1965.

109. Editorial, "Why the Rioting?," *Los Angeles Sentinel*, August 19, 1965.

110. "Upgrade Officers—Wilkins," *Los Angeles Sentinel*, November 4, 1965.

111. Bill Robertson, "Militants 'By-Passed' at Police Commission Meet," *Los Angeles Sentinel*, June 16, 1966.

112. Michael Flamm, *Law and Order: Street Crime, Civil Unrest, and the Crisis of Liberalism in the 1960s* (Columbia University Press, 2005), 54–55.

113. President's Commission on Law Enforcement and Administration of Justice, *The Challenge of Crime in a Free Society* (Government Printing Office, February 1967), 107.

114. Ibid., 101–102.
115. *Report of the National Advisory Commission on Civil Disorders* (Government Printing Office, 1968), 165–66.
116. Ibid., 166.
117. Black United Front, "Proposal for Neighborhood Control of the Police in the Black Community," September 25, 1968, Papers of Frank Smith, Jr., Box 18, Folder 7, Special Collections Research Center, George Washington University Library, 6.
118. Ibid., 9.
119. Ibid., 6.
120. Jaffe and Sherwood, *Dream City*, 34.
121. Ibid., 93.
122. "Police Critic Barry Recruits for Force," *Washington Post*, September 25, 1970.
123. Eugene Beard, Lee P. Brown, and Lawrence E. Gary, Institute for Urban Affairs and Research, *Attitudes and Perceptions of Black Police Officers of the District of Columbia Metropolitan Police Department* (Howard University, 1976), 18.
124. Campbell Gibson and Kay Jung, "Historical Census Statistics on Population Totals by Race, 1790 to 1990, and by Hispanic Origin, 1970 to 1990, for Large Cities and Other Urban Places in the United States" (U.S. Census Bureau, Population Division, 2005), Table 23; Paul Delaney, "Recruiting of Negro Police Is a Failure in Most Cities," *New York Times*, January 25, 1971; "Michigan Police Fail in Year-Long Effort to Recruit Negroes," *New York Times*, October 20, 1968.
125. Delaney, "Recruiting of Negro Police Is a Failure."
126. Alfred E. Lewis, "Police Score a Beat," *Washington Post*, September 20, 1970; see also Irna Moore, "Negro Police Recruits Now Outnumber Whites," *Washington Post*, December 21, 1969.
127. Task Force on the Police, President's Commission on Law Enforcement and Administration of Justice, *Task Force Report: The Police* (Government Printing Office, 1967), 167.
128. Ibid.
129. Ibid.
130. Donald J. Black and Albert J. Reiss, Jr., "Patterns of Behavior in Police and Citizen Transactions," in *Studies of Crime and Law Enforcement*, vol. 2, 135, Table 25. When Peter Moskos, a former Baltimore police officer turned professor, interviewed white and black officers in 1999, he encountered black officers who sounded a similar refrain. One told him, "People out here are lazy. L-A-Z-Y. Waiting in the cheese line. Being poor is no excuse for being ignorant. I made it in this country. It can be done. But you got to work for it." Peter C. Moskos, "Two Shades of Blue: Black and White in the Blue Brotherhood," *Law Enforcement Executive Forum* 8 (2008): 57, 74.
131. Black and Reiss, "Patterns of Behavior in Police and Citizen Transactions," 137.
132. James D. Bannon and G. Marie Wilt, "Black Policemen: A Study of Self-Images," *Journal of Political Science and Administration* 1, no. 1 (1973): 23–24.

133. Kephart, *Racial Factors and Urban Law Enforcement*, 119.

134. Nicholas Alex, *Black in Blue: A Study of the Negro Policeman* (Appleton-Century-Crofts, 1969), 158.

135. Mark R. Killingsworth, "Black Police Put Job Ahead of Skin Color," *Washington Post*, August 22, 1968. In 1999, a black officer told Peter Moskos that while he was arresting a black suspect, the suspect pleaded, "Brother, you got to understand." The officer responded, "I'm not your brother! I'm not your cousin! I'm not your 'homie.' And no, I don't understand where you're 'coming from.'" Moskos, "Two Shades of Blue," 57, 74.

136. "Black policemen were motivated to enter police work more by the lack of alternative opportunities and by the relative absence of discrimination in civil-service employment than by any positive characteristics to be found in police work itself." Joseph Bensman, foreword to Alex, *Black in Blue*, xviii.

137. Alex, *Black in Blue*, 34–36, 43.

138. Ibid.

139. Beard, Brown, and Gary, *Attitudes and Perceptions of Black Police Officers*, 14–16, Tables 2.4–2.6; 19, Table 2.7.

140. "The Anguish of Blacks in Blue," *Time*, November 23, 1970; Booker Griffin, "'L.A.'s Finest' Finally Opening Up and Talking," *Los Angeles Sentinel*, September 14, 1972.

141. James Lardner, "New Police Chief Sworn In," *Washington Post*, January 14, 1978.

142. Washington's silence on race was not unusual. During the 1974 race for mayor, Washington's chief opponent, Clifford Alexander, had called for the appointment of a black police chief. Washington responded, "We want a chief for the whole," not only the city's black majority. Bill Watson, "Who Will Be Police Chief," *Washington Afro-American*, August 10, 1974.

143. Williams and Kellough, "Leadership with an Enduring Impact," 818.

144. Beard, Brown, and Gary, *Attitudes and Perceptions of Black Police Officers*, 24–26.

145. Ibid., 41, 65, 68.

146. Paul W. Valentine, "Hiring Bill Is Enacted Over Veto," *Washington Post*, January 20, 1976. Marion Barry, another prominent figure in the fight to hire additional black officers, linked this cause with another dear to him, the requirement that city employees live in the District. As Barry explained, "Police officers have about the greatest community contact of any of our government's public servants. Yet the vast majority live in other communities, often bringing with them a suburban sense of values which may conflict with urban value systems." Marion Barry, "Residence for D.C. Employees," *Washington Informer*, April 1, 1976.

147. John Wilson notes on Affirmative Action Plan, Wilson Papers, Box 20, Folder 17; William Raspberry, "Affirmative Action: How Much Is Enough?" *Washington Post*, February 23, 1976. Justin McCrary has pointed out that for those departments that did not join D.C. in voluntarily adopting affirmative action programs, court-ordered hiring mandates constituted "arguably the most aggressive affirmative action program ever implemented in the United States."

Justin McCrary, "The Effect of Court-Ordered Hiring Quotas on the Composition and Quality of Police," *American Economic Review* 97, no. 1 (2007): 318.

148. Williams and Kellough, "Leadership with an Enduring Impact," 819, 820.

149. Editorial, "Our Weekly Review," *Washington Bee*, August 6, 1887.

150. Lardner, "New Police Chief Sworn In."

151. Burtell Jefferson to John Ray, May 14, 1981, Legislative Services Office, D.C. City Council.

152. Robert C. Maynard, "Black Police Vow Solidarity," *Washington Post*, June 7, 1970.

153. Beard, Brown, and Gary, *Attitudes and Perceptions of Black Police Officers*, 91.

154. Thomas A. Johnson, "Black Police Officials Establish Organization in Effort to Expand Influence in Criminal Justice Field," *New York Times*, September 9, 1976.

155. Herrington J. Bryce, ed., *Black Crime: A Police View*, 157. Like Doug Moore and Stokely Carmichael, NOBLE attributed lax drug law enforcement to racist indifference to black suffering. They also regarded police brutality as a manifestation of racism. Today, when we contemplate the toll that the War on Drugs has taken on black communities and consider how easily aggressive policing can turn deadly, it is hard to imagine demanding less brutality and stricter drug enforcement in the same breath. But that's precisely what NOBLE was doing.

## 4. "Locking Up Thugs Is Not Vindictive"

1. Ms. Willis's case was more than two years old and had been transferred to me from a senior lawyer who had left the office. So it was even worse: she had been downgraded.

2. Ms. Willis had two previous convictions for selling small amounts of drugs. Even one previous conviction would have qualified her for the sixty-year maximum. D.C. Code Ann. § 48-904.08 (West 1981).

3. National Institute on Drug Abuse, *Principles of Drug Addiction Treatment: A Research-Based Guide*, National Institutes of Health, 3rd ed., U.S. Department of Health and Human Services (October 1999, revised December 2012), 9, 12–13.

4. The maximum penalty for first-time offenders was a $1,000 fine and one year's imprisonment. For second/subsequent offenders, the maximum penalty was a $10,000 fine and ten years' imprisonment. Judiciary Committee Report on Bill 4-123, the District of Columbia Controlled Substances Act of 1981, April 8, 1981, Legislative Services Office, D.C. City Council, 2, 5. Keith Richburg, "Referendum Sought on Mandatory Sentences for Drug Dealers," *Washington Post*, June 29, 1981.

5. 14th Street Coalition to Mayor Marion S. Barry, Jr., June 19, 1979, in John A. Wilson Papers, Box 53, Folder 21, Special Collections Research Center, George Washington University Library.

6. John A. Wilson, statement on Bill 4-184 and PR 4-38, undated, Wilson Papers, Box 25, Folder 11.

7. Loretta Tofani, "Pitching Dope," *Washington Post*, August 19, 1979.

8. Ibid.

9. Ron Shaffer, "Man Tries to Drive Out Anacostia Drug Sellers," *Washington Post*, July 23, 1978.

10. Jim Mantell, "Crime Protest Rally Set for Shaw Area," *Washington Afro-American*, June 6, 1981.

11. *Capitol View Civic Association Newsletter* 4, no. 6, May 1979. Washingtoniana Collection, CA Box 11, Martin Luther King Jr. Memorial Library, Washington, D.C.

12. Loretta Tofani, "D.C. Residents Patrol 'Turf,' Hunt Thieves," *Washington Post*, November 25, 1979.

13. A different neighborhood association, along the upper reaches of Sixteenth Street, home to many of the city's black professionals, reported that a rash of rapes and burglaries had "left us shivering in apprehension." Neighbors, Inc., to Law Enforcement Assistance Administration, December 30, 1977, CA Box 2, Crime Watch Proposal folder, Washingtoniana Collection, Martin Luther King Jr. Memorial Library, Washington, D.C.

14. Tofani, "D.C. Residents Patrol 'Turf,' Hunt Thieves."

15. Ibid.

16. Vincent Taylor, "Residents 'Fed-Up' with Drug Traffic," *Washington Afro-American*, October 17, 1981.

17. A concerned citizen to city council members, June 12, 1979, Wilson Papers, Box 53, Folder 21.

18. Editorial, "Drug Epidemic Raises Questions," *Washington Afro-American*, April 4, 1981. Echoing the concerns raised by Doug Moore, Stokely Carmichael, and other black nationalists a decade earlier, the *Afro* editors worried "if the ready and easy availability of marijuana, heroin and synthetic drugs on the streets, and in some instances in our prisons, is part of a larger plan to keep blacks and other minorities 'in their place.'"

19. Everett W. Scott, D.C. Federation of Civic Associations, to David A. Clarke, February 14, 1979, Clarke Papers, Box 42, Folder 1. ("[W]e recognize that a person is presumed innocent, but we also recognize statistics showing many of these people while out on bail commit a second offense.") Crime was a constant issue at the D.C. Federation of Civic Associations Executive Committee meetings in 1979. Minutes of Civic Associations, CA Box 16, Washingtoniana Collection, Martin Luther King Jr. Memorial Library, Washington, D.C.

20. Editorial, "Crime Statistics and D.C.," *Washington Afro-American*, January 8, 1977.

21. Special Report, "'Revolving Door' Justice: Why Criminals Go Free," *U.S. News & World Report*, May 10, 1976, p. 39. (The magazine conceded that "D.C.'s record of sending 6 out of 10 convicted felons to jail or prison indicates its judges may be sterner than those in many other cities.")

22. Edward M. Kennedy, "Punishing the Offenders," *New York Times*, December 6, 1975.

23. Carl T. Rowan, "Locking Up Thugs Is Not Vindictive," *Washington Star*, April 23, 1976.

24. Nicholas C. McBride, "Drive Against Drug Trade Draws Critics," *Washington Afro-American*, July 16, 1983.

25. Courtland Milloy, "Campaign Trail Tougher Than Toms Creek Fields of John Ray's Boyhood," *Washington Post*, September 10, 1982.

26. *Report on the Committee of the Judiciary on Bill 4-123*, 5, John Ray to Members of D.C. City Council re: Bill 4-123, May 18, 1981; Burtell Jefferson to John Ray, May 14, 1981, Legislative Services Office, D.C. City Council.

27. Joanne Ostrow, "Ray Asks Citizen Support for City Anticrime Bills," *Washington Post*, March 26, 1981; John Ray to Members of D.C. City Council re: Bill 4-123.

28. Keith B. Richburg and Eugene Robinson, "Witnesses Decry D.C. Crime, Differ on Ways to Combat It," *Washington Post*, March 14, 1981.

29. Testimony of Jerome Page on Criminal Code Reform Bills to the Committee on the Judiciary, D.C. City Council, March 13, 1981, Legislative Services Office, D.C. City Council.

30. The U.S. Attorney for D.C. occupies a unique position, serving as both the District's chief local prosecutor and a federal prosecutor.

31. Keith B. Richburg, "D.C. Officials Split on Crime Penalties," *Washington Post*, March 13, 1981.

32. Ibid.

33. United States Sentencing Commission, *Special Report to Congress: Mandatory Minimum Penalties in the Federal Criminal Justice System* (August 1991). D.C. would be a leader among states as well. In 1980, only five states had mandatory minimums for selling drugs, and about twenty had them for possessing or using a gun during a crime. Richard S. Morelli, Craig Edelman, and Roy Willoughby, *A Survey of Mandatory Sentencing in the U.S.*, Criminal Justice Statistics Division, Pennsylvania Commission on Crime and Delinquency (Washington, D.C.: National Criminal Justice Reference Service, 1981).

34. Keith B. Richburg, "City Council Adopts Drug Code Without Mandatory Sentences," *Washington Post*, May 20, 1981. The vote totals are ambiguous. It appears that Ray had one ally for mandatory minimums on the city council, Nadine Winter.

35. Michael Javen Fortner, *Black Silent Majority: The Rockefeller Drug Laws and the Politics of Punishment* (Harvard University Press, 2015); Vanessa Barker, *The Politics of Imprisonment: How the Democratic Process Shapes the Way America Punishes Offenders* (Oxford University Press, 2015), 146–49.

36. James H. Cleaver, "PCP Growth Goes 'Crazy,'" *Los Angeles Sentinel*, May 15, 1980.

37. "WGG Founder's Celebration to Salute Top Leaders," *Los Angeles Sentinel*, June 9, 1997.

38. Inventory of the Maxine Waters Papers, 1976–1990, Online Archives of California, Collection No. LP411.

39. "Waters Attacks PCP," *Los Angeles Sentinel*, March 30, 1978. In 1990 Waters would be elected to Congress, where she served—and continues to serve—as a reliable opponent of tough-on-crime measures.

40. Editorial, "The Ultimate Low," *Los Angeles Times*, July 10, 1978; "The Lawmakers," *Los Angeles Sentinel*, May 4, 1978.

41. Ed Davis, "L.A. Becomes PCP Capital of World," *Los Angeles Sentinel*, October 25, 1979.

42. Editorial, "An Open Letter to PCP Dealers & Other Dogs!," *Los Angeles Sentinel*, September 25, 1980.

43. Ed Davis, "Pushers: The Grandfathers of PCP Crimes," *Los Angeles Sentinel*, September 11, 1980.

44. Jim Cleaver, "*Sentinel* Declares World War III on PCP," *Los Angeles Sentinel*, August 28, 1980.

45. Ed Davis, "Cochran Seeks New PCP Law," *Los Angeles Sentinel*, November 25, 1979. Cochran never abandoned his antidrug stance; in his 2003 memoir he explained that he would not represent people in major drug cases, because he "didn't want to have anything to do with the drugs that were poisoning our community." Johnnie Cochran, Jr., and David Fisher, *A Lawyer's Life* (Thomas Dunne Books/St. Martin's Press, 2002), 207.

46. *Ebony*, August 1979. Though the *Ebony* special issue was the most high-profile invocation of "black on black crime," the term had long been used by black writers. In 1970, for example, Rev. Jesse Jackson accused the Chicago police of "allowing black-on-black murder to grow." Black police officers also used the term frequently in the 1970s, explaining that blacks in law enforcement were determined to take "black on black crime" more seriously. Jesse Jackson, "Black and White Crime," *Chicago Tribune*, August 19, 1970; Renault Robinson, "Black Watch," *Chicago Defender*, November 27, 1971 ("The Members of the Afro-American Patrolmen's League are against crime—especially Black-on-Black crime"); see "Black on Black Crime Rising," New York *Amsterdam News*, January 29, 1978 (noting that "Black-on-Black crime account[ed] for almost 60 percent" of rising homicide rates).

47. Ed Davis, "Cochran Denounces Black Crime Apologists," *Los Angeles Sentinel*, February 14, 1980.

48. Davis, "Cochran Seeks New PCP Law"; Davis, "Cochran Denounces Black Crime Apologists."

49. American Civil Liberties Union, "Memorandum to the Legislative Committee of the National Capitol Area ACLU on the Proposed Mandatory Sentencing Initiative for the District of Columbia," Legislative Services Office, D.C. City Council.

50. Laura A. Kiernan, "Officials Divided on Merits of Mandatory Sentencing," *Washington Post*, August 25, 1982.

51. Tom Sherwood, "Petitions Ask Fixed Terms for Some Crimes," *Washington Post*, March 5, 1982.

52. Vincent Taylor, "Groups Fight Initiative," *Washington Afro-American*, September 7, 1982; Laura A. Kiernan, "Voters in D.C. Back Mandatory Sentence Plan,"

*Washington Post*, September 3, 1982; Tom Sherwood, "Sentencing Initiative Is Opposed," *Washington Post*, April 1, 1982.

53. Charles F. Ruff, "Mandatory Minimum Sentence Initiative," *District Lawyer* (September/October 1982), 28; Laura A. Kiernan, "Charles F. C. Ruff Quits as Chief Prosecutor Here," *Washington Post*, October 24, 1981.

54. Laura A. Kiernan, "Mandatory Sentence Measure Opposed," *Washington Post*, September 8, 1982.

55. Laura A. Kiernan, "District Voters Decide Tuesday on Initiative 9," *Washington Post*, September 12, 1982.

56. Juan Williams, "Jefferson Resigning as Ray's Campaign Manager," *Washington Post*, August 3, 1982.

57. Kiernan, "Voters in D.C. Back Mandatory Sentence Plan."

58. Ibid.

59. Juan Williams, "Heroin in My Neighborhood," *Washington Post*, August 12, 1981.

60. Edward D. Sargent, "Neighborhood Enjoys Day of Freedom in Drug Sweep: Dealers 'Busy Again' After D.C. Drug Sweep," *Washington Post*, July 18, 1983; Vincent Taylor, "Ray Releases Paper on Crime-Fighting," *Washington Afro-American*, May 4, 1982.

61. Vincent Taylor, "Ray Releases Paper on Crime-Fighting"; Juan Williams, "Ray, at 14th & W, Outlines Plans to Curb Crime," *Washington Post*, April 29, 1982.

62. Juan Williams, "Ray, at 14th & W, Outlines Plans to Curb Crime."

63. Laura A. Kiernan and Al Kamen, "Mandatory Sentence Proposal Strongly Backed in D.C. Vote," *Washington Post*, September 15, 1982.

64. Calculated by the author based on data provided by the D.C. Board of Elections.

65. Ibid.

66. Kiernan and Kamen, "Mandatory Sentence Proposal Strongly Backed."

67. Benjamin J. Lambiotte, "Retribution or Rehabilitation? The Addict Exception and Mandatory Sentencing After *Grant v. United States* and the District of Columbia Controlled Substances Amendment Act of 1986," *Catholic University Law Review* 37 (1988): 733, 734.

68. "Crime and Justice Report for the District of Columbia," November 1985, John A. Wilson Papers, Box 12, Table 8.

69. Ibid., Box 9, Table 4.

70. United States Sentencing Commission, *Special Report to the Congress: Mandatory Minimum Penalties in the Federal Criminal Justice System* (1991).

71. Attorney General Eric Holder, Remarks, Annual Meeting of the American Bar Association's House of Delegates, San Francisco, August 12, 2013.

72. Ostrow, "Ray Asks Citizen Support."

73. *Problems in Urban Centers: Oversight Hearings Before the House Committee on the District of Columbia*, 96th Congress 314, 328 (1980) (statement of Burtell Jefferson, chief of D.C. Metropolitan Police).

74. Rowan, "Locking Up Thugs."

75. Jerome Page, Testimony on Criminal Code Reform Bills, 4.

76. A 1984 survey of 1,200 black Americans by *Ebony* magazine is illustrative. Pollsters asked, "Do you think the federal government should be spending *more, less,* or is it spending about the *right* amount now on the following items?" Overwhelming majorities of black voters said the government should spend more on job training (89 percent), education (87 percent), and enforcement of antidiscrimination laws (70 percent). Kenneth B. Clark and Kate Clark Harris, "What Do Blacks Really Want?," *Ebony,* January 1985, 113. Eight years later, a survey of African American opinion by the Joint Center for Political and Economic Studies would reach similar conclusions. When asked "Do you think that the government should provide more job training, education, and child care for poor people?" 95 percent said yes. When asked "Is the government spending too much, too little, or about the right amount of money on education?" 85 percent of the respondents said "too little." And when asked "Some people think that the Great Society programs of the 1960s are the cause of the problems of America's cities. Others think that twelve years of (Ronald) Reagan/(George) Bush neglect is the reason for America's urban problems. Which of these statements comes closest to your own views?" 71 percent cited Reagan/Bush neglect, compared with 13 percent who blamed Great Society programs. Support for such "root cause" solutions did little to dampen enthusiasm for tough-on-crime measures, however. When asked "How much do you support mandatory sentences for anyone convicted of selling any amount of drugs?" 73 percent of respondents in the 1992 Joint Center survey supported mandatory sentences, while 24 percent opposed them. The Joint Center for Political and Economic Studies, *Voices of the Electorate Among the African-American Population,* July 1992, accessed September 9, 2016, http://ropercenter .cornell.edu/.

77. Kevin K. Gaines, *Uplifting the Race: Black Leadership, Politics, and Culture in the Twentieth Century* (University of North Carolina Press, 1996); Evelyn Brooks Higginbotham, *Righteous Discontent: The Women's Movement in the Black Baptist Church, 1880–1920* (Harvard University Press, 1993).

78. Elijah Anderson, "The Code of the Streets," *The Atlantic,* May 1994.

79. "New Drug Clinics Funded," *Washington Star,* April 28, 1977.

80. David Clarke to Chief Burtell Jefferson, August 18, 1978, Clarke Papers, Box 150, Folder 19, Special Collections Research Center, George Washington University Library.

81. Burtell Jefferson to David Clarke, September 29, 1978. Clarke Papers, Box 150, Folder 19.

## 5. "The Worst Thing to Hit Us Since Slavery"

1. Seth Stoughton, "Law Enforcement's 'Warrior' Problem," *Harvard Law Review Forum,* April 10, 2015, 227; *Final Report of the President's Task Force on 21st Century Policing* (Office of Community Oriented Policing Services, Washington, D.C., 2015), 1.

2. Lenese Herbert, "Can't You See What I'm Saying? Making Expressive Conduct

a Crime in High-Crime Areas," *Georgetown Journal on Poverty Law & Policy* 9, no. 1 (2002): 135–37.

3. Khalil Gibran Muhammad, *The Condemnation of Blackness* (Harvard University Press, 2010).

4. James Baldwin, "Fifth Avenue, Uptown: A Letter from Harlem," *Esquire*, July 1960.

5. Cheryl Devall, "Jackson Calls Himself 'General' in Drug War," *Chicago Tribune*, May 23, 1988.

6. Ronald Reagan, "A Vision for America," televised address (November 3, 1980).

7. Pub. L. No. 97-35 (June 1981). See also Ronald Reagan, "Address Before a Joint Session of Congress on the Program for Economic Recovery," televised address (February 18, 1981); Robert Moffitt and Douglas A. Wolf, "The Effect of the 1981 Omnibus Budget Reconciliation Act on Welfare Recipients and Work Incentives," *Social Science Review* 61 (1987): 249–52 (outlining the OBRA changes to AFDC eligibility and payout calculations); Publ. No. 97-35 Sec 104(a) (codified at 7 U.S.C. 2013) (restricting participation in the food stamp program by rendering ineligible for food stamps households whose gross income was 130 percent of the poverty line); Zachary D. Smith, "District Facing Hardship," *Washington Afro-American*, March 11, 1984 (explaining that the District was to lose millions in federal aid to Medicare and AFDC).

8. House Committee on Ways and Means, 98th Congress, *Effects of the Omnibus Budget Reconciliation Act of 1981 (OBRA) Welfare Changes and the Recession on Poverty*, 12, Table 1 (Comm. Print 1984); U.S. Government Accountability Office, GAO/PEMD-85-4, *An Evaluation of the 1981 AFDC Changes: Final Report*, 28, Table 4. (1985).

9. John E. Jacob, "The State of Black America, 1985," *Los Angeles Sentinel*, January 24, 1985.

10. Harry S. Jaffe and Tom Sherwood, *Dream City: Race, Power, and the Decline of Washington, D.C.*, rev. ed. (Argo-Narvis, 2014), 209.

11. Mark Kleiman, *Against Excess: Drug Policy for Results* (Basic Books, 1993), 296; David Sklansky, "Cocaine, Race and Equal Protection," *Stanford Law Review* 47 (1995): 1291.

12. Sklansky, "Cocaine, Race and Equal Protection," 1291.

13. Peter Reuter et al., "Drug Use and Drug Programs in the Washington Metropolitan Area" (Greater Washington Research Center, 1988), vi.

14. Tracie Reddick, "Communities Move Against Drug Dealers," *Washington Times*, March 1, 1988.

15. Devall, "Jackson Calls Himself 'General.'"

16. Editorial, "The War Goes On," *Los Angeles Sentinel*, March 24, 1988. Like the term "black-on-black crime," the analogy between crack and slavery originated with African American writers and politicians, but it didn't remain there. Beginning in the late 1980s, for example, the Partnership for a Drug Free America, whose public information campaigns included the "This Is Your Brain on Drugs" series, compared drug use with slavery in messages to black audiences. These ads shifted their accusatory attention from drug dealers

to drug users. The organization ran a full-page advertisement in the *Afro-American*—entitled "Yo Slave!"—featuring a black hand holding vials of crack. "The dealer is selling something you don't want," the ad warned. "You'll pay more than just cash money. You'll trade in your hopes, your dreams, even your self-respect. Now, do you really want to buy?" Finally, in bold letters, the group ran the campaign's tagline: "Addiction is Slavery." "Yo, Slave!" *Afro-American*, October 20, 1990. The partnership also produced a television ad furthering the analogy between crack and slavery. "Almost four hundred years ago," begins the gravel-voiced narrator, "African Americans were brought to this continent in chains, stripped of their dignity, torn from their families." Accompanying this somber account is a scene of African villagers being dragged away with chains around their necks. From there, the ad leaps forward in time and pivots to drugs, as a shot of a female slave's hopeful candle dissolves into the image of a lighter heating a crack pipe. "Don't dishonor them," the narrator commands, "by becoming a slave to heroin, cocaine, and crack." As he speaks, chains appear around the necks of two young black men in a deep nod. Unlike their ancestors, we're meant to conclude, these men unwittingly shackled themselves. Partnership for a Drug Free America. *Drug Abuse as the New Slavery*, YouTube video, 1991.

17. Linda Wheeler, "1 D.C. Homicide Closes '87, 2nd Brings in the New Year," *Washington Post*, January 2, 1988; Sari Horwitz, "Weapons, Drugs and Youths: Formula for the District's Deadliest Month," *Washington Post*, February 2, 1988; "District of Columbia Neighborhood Report Crime Watch," *Washington Post*, January 14, 1988.
18. Isaac Fulwood, "Washington's Year of Shame," *Washington Post*, January 1, 1989.
19. Horwitz, "Weapons, Drugs and Youths"; "District of Columbia Neighborhood Report Crime Watch," *Washington Post*.
20. "District of Columbia Neighborhood Report Crime Watch," *Washington Post*.
21. Eric Charles May and Anne Simpson, "District of Columbia Neighborhood Report Crime Watch," *Washington Post*, January 21, 1988.
22. Horwitz, "Weapons, Drugs and Youths."
23. "2 Slayings Reported in District," *Washington Post*, January 12, 1988.
24. Horwitz, "Weapons, Drugs and Youths"; Lynne Duke, "Last Days of Slain NE Woman Puzzle Family," *Washington Post*, January 21, 1988.
25. "1988 Homicide Toll Reaches 24 in D.C.," *Washington Post*, January 21, 1988.
26. Horwitz, "Weapons, Drugs and Youths."
27. "Body Found in Car in NE," *Washington Post*, January 27, 1988; "January 1988 Homicides in the District," *Washington Post*, February 2, 1988.
28. Sari Horwitz, "D.C. Homicides Equal Record: NW Barbershop Slaying Is 32nd Killing in Single Month," *Washington Post*, January 28, 1988.
29. Weil Martin and Sari Horwitz, "3 Fatal Shootings Bring D.C.'s Bloodiest Month to an End: 3 Slayings in 1 Day in D.C. Bring January Total to a Record 37," *Washington Post*, February 1, 1988; Horwitz, "Weapons, Drugs and Youths."

30. Martin and Horwitz, "3 Fatal Shootings."

31. Horwitz, "Weapons, Drugs and Youths."

32. Fulwood, "Washington's Year of Shame."

33. David M. Kennedy, *Don't Shoot: One Man, a Street Fellowship, and the End of Violence in Inner-City America* (Bloomsbury, 2011), 11.

34. Mike Tidwell, *In the Shadow of the White House*, quoted in Patrick Symmes, "Swift and Certain," *Washington City Paper*, January 28, 1994.

35. Albert Herring, interview with author, February 18, 2014, 11. Herring spoke in his individual capacity, not as a representative of the U.S. Department of Justice.

36. U.S. Department of Justice, "The Chances of Lifetime Murder Victimization, 1997," in *Crime in the United States*, Uniform Crime Reports (1999); Jaffe and Sherwood, *Dream City*, 379. In 1991, 467 black citizens were killed in D.C., compared with 18 whites. Hamil Harris, "Homicide: 467 Black; 18 White," *Washington Afro-American*, January 4, 1992.

37. Harris, "Homicide: 467 Black; 18 White."

38. Ibid. See also Andrew Papachristos, Anthony Braga, and David Hureau, "The Concentration and Stability of Gun Violence at Micro Places in Boston, 1980–2008," *Journal of Quantitative Criminology* 26, no. 1 (2010): 33–53, explaining that in Boston 50 percent of all gun violence over three decades occurred on just 3 percent of city streets.

39. Jonetta Rose Barras and Clara Jeffery, "Poor Record," *Washington City Paper*, November 4, 1994.

40. Centers for Disease Control and Prevention, *Nonfatal and Fatal Firearm-Related Injuries—United States, 1993–1997* (Morbidity and Mortality Weekly Report, 1999); Peter Reuter, *Money from Crime: A Study of the Economics of Drug Dealing in Washington* (RAND Drug Policy Research Center, 1990), 97. Jill Leovy writes, "[T]here are about four or five injury shootings for every fatal one in South Los Angeles." Jill Leovy, *Ghettoside: A True Story of Murder in America* (Random House, 2015), 49.

41. Molly Moore, "D.C. Trauma Trains Medic for the Gulf," *Washington Post*, November 8, 1990.

42. Patrick Sharkey, "The Acute Effect of Local Homicides on Children's Cognitive Performance," *Proceedings of the National Academy of Sciences* 107, no. 26 (2010).

43. Elijah Anderson, *Code of the Street: Decency, Violence, and the Moral Life of the Inner City* (W. W. Norton, 1999), 317; Ta-Nehisi Coates describes his difficulty in making it through the day as a middle schooler in West Baltimore in *Between the World and Me* (Random House, 2015), 26–28.

44. John A. Rich, *Wrong Place, Wrong Time: Trauma and Violence in the Lives of Young Black Men* (Johns Hopkins University Press, 2009), ix–xvii.

45. Kennedy, *Don't Shoot*, 10.

46. Rick Christie, "Atlanta Business Sector's Pick for Mayor Quits, Leaving Field to Maynard Jackson," *Wall Street Journal*, August 9, 1989.

47. Lisa L. Miller, *The Myth of Mob Rule: Violent Crime and Democratic Politics* (Oxford University Press, 2016), 133–42.

48. Sklansky, "Cocaine, Race, and Equal Protection," 1286; Naomi Murakawa, *The First Civil Right: How Liberals Built Prison America* (Oxford University Press, 2014), 113–47.

49. David Morrison, "Anti-Crack Bias," *Washington City Paper*, September 8, 2000.

50. Michael Isikoff, "Getting Too Tough on Drugs," *Washington Post*, November 4, 1990.

51. Sklansky, "Cocaine, Race and Equal Protection," 1294.

52. David Cole, *No Equal Justice: Race and Class in the American Criminal Justice System* (New Press, 1999), 141–45.

53. NOBLE, *Justice by Action*, 14.

54. Joint Center for Political and Economic Studies, *Black Elected Officials: A National Roster*, xv, xxxi (University Press of America, 1991).

55. Phil McCombs, "Regardie, Zeroing in on Barry: War of Words Heats Up Over 'Nightline' Clip," *Washington Post*, March 3, 1989.

56. Marion Barry, Remarks to the National Press Club, on March 23, 1989, as broadcast by C-Span.

57. Tom Sherwood, "Aides Warned Barry of Backlash on Crime," *Washington Post*, November 29, 1988.

58. Christie, "Atlanta Business Sector's Pick for Mayor Quits."

59. "Woman Gets 10 Years in Heroin Case," *Atlanta Journal-Constitution*, January 15, 1992; Larry Copeland, "Drug Czar Proposed by Lomax Also Plans to Hire 300 More Police," *Atlanta Journal-Constitution*, May 24, 1989.

60. Adam Gelb, "3 Deputies in Line for Chief's Job; Hard Nosed Candidate Favored," *Atlanta Journal-Constitution*, July 15, 1990.

61. Devall, "Jackson Calls Himself 'General' in Drug War."

62. Lynn Norment, "Charles Rangel: The Front-Line General in the War on Drugs," *Ebony*, March 1989, 128.

63. Nicholas Benton, "Drug War Ravages Nation's Capital," *The Executive Intelligence Review*, December 9, 1988; Sari Horwitz and Michael York, "Police Mum on Probe of Drug Killings; D.C. Police Closemouthed on Investigation of Drug-War Killings," *Washington Post*, November 22, 1988.

64. Nelson F. Kofie, "Race, Class, and the Struggle for Neighborhood in Washington, D.C.," in Graham Russell Hodges, ed., *African American History and Culture* (Garland, 1999), 111.

65. *Gun Control: Public Hearing Before the Committee on Judiciary & Criminal Law of the District of Columbia Council* (June 6, 1975), 14, Legislative Services Office, D.C. City Council.

66. Sari Horwitz and Athelia Knight, "Barry Announces 3-Pronged Attack on Drugs, Violence," *Washington Post*, February 13, 1988.

67. Jon Cohen, "The Force May Not Be with You," *Washington City Paper*, December 16, 1988; Carlos Sanchez, "Firepower on Streets Rises: D.C. Police Take 9mm Gun from Boy, 12," *Washington Post*, January 20, 1988.

68. Ron Harris, "Blacks Feel Brunt of Drug War," *Los Angeles Times*, April 22, 1990.

69. Brian N. Williams and J. Edward Kellough, "Leadership with an Enduring Impact: The Legacy of Chief Burtell Jefferson of the Metropolitan Police Department of Washington, D.C.," *Public Administration Review* 66 (November/December 2006): 816, 817.

70. Ed Bruske, "Plea Bargains Erode Drug Law's Intent," *Washington Post*, May 12, 1986.

71. Sari Horwitz, "D.C. Drug Crackdown Nets 23,000 Arrests," *Washington Post*, August 21, 1987.

72. Linda Wheeler, "D.C. Tops Country in Drug Arrests," *Washington Post*, September 24, 1987.

73. Lisa Daugaard's work with LEAD in Seattle, as well as the problem-oriented policing movement, both show that police don't have to adopt such a narrow view. Sara Jean Green, "LEAD Program for Low-Level Drug Criminals Sees Success," *Seattle Times*, April 8, 2015; Herman Goldstein, "Improving Policing: A Problem-Oriented Approach," *Crime & Delinquency* 25 (1979): 236–58.

74. Wil Haygood, "Locked Up Inside," *Washington Post*, December 18, 2005.

75. Herbert, "Can't You See What I'm Saying?," 137.

76. Michael York and Pierre Thomas, "Taking It to the Streets," *Washington Post*, December 15, 1991.

77. Ibid.

78. William Chambliss, "Policing the Ghetto Underclass: The Politics of Law and Law Enforcement," *Social Problems* 41, no. 2 (1944): 179.

79. Ibid.

80. New York City police chief Ray Kelly reportedly used a similar rationale to defend the city's stop-and-frisk policy in 2010. New York senator Eric Adams stated in an affidavit in *Floyd v. New York* that in July 2010 he met with Commissioner Kelly to discuss proposed legislation regarding stop-and-frisk practices and that during the meeting, "Commissioner Kelly stated that the NYPD targets its stop-and-frisk activity at young black and Latino men because it wants to instill the belief in members of these two populations that they could be stopped and frisked every time they leave their homes, so that they are less likely to carry weapons." *Floyd v. City of N.Y.*, 283 F.R.D. 153, 163 n.40 (S.D.N.Y. 2012).

81. Chambliss, "Policing the Ghetto Underclass," 179.

82. York and Thomas, "Taking It to the Streets."

83. Carolyn Johns-Gray to David Clarke, September 23, 1989, David A. Clarke Papers, Special Collections Research Center, George Washington University Library.

84. Sari Horwitz, "When Officers Go Too Far," *Washington Post*, November 19, 1998.

85. *Cox v. District of Columbia*, 821 F. Supp. 1 (Dist. Ct. D.C. 1993).

86. D.C. recently revised its asset forfeiture laws. For a history of D.C. legislation, see D.C. Council Committee on the Judiciary and Public Safety, *Report on Bill 20-48, "Civil Asset Forfeiture Amendment Act of 2014"* (November 12, 2014).

87. John Ward Anderson, "15 Vehicles Seized in D.C. Drug Cases," *Washington Post*, September 3, 1986.

88. Pam McClintock, "Barry: Take Cars from Drug Users," *Washington Times*, October 5, 1989.

89. Marion Barry, Remarks to the National Press Club on March 23, 1989, as broadcast by C-Span; Sari Horwitz and Nathan McCall, "Barry Hopes to Seize Cars in Which Drugs Are Found," *Washington Post*, September 29, 1989.

90. John Ward Anderson, "'Clean Sweep' Takes Drug Effort to the Streets," *Washington Post*, September 27, 1986.

91. Judith J. Scott, "Operation Clean Sweep to Continue," *Washington Afro-American*, May 2, 1987.

92. Editorial, "Declaring War—Again," *Washington Afro-American*, September 6, 1986.

93. Scott, "Operation Clean Sweep to Continue."

94. Grace Huey, troop leader, to David Clarke, February 3, 1988, Clarke Papers, Box 21, Folder 14.

95. Albert Herring, interview with author, February 18, 2014, 18.

96. Ibid.

97. Ibid.

98. William Choyke, "User Unfriendly," *Washington City Paper*, May 31, 1985.

99. Ibid.

100. Marjorie Hoyer, "Punish Dealers, Users Swiftly, Bennett Urges," *Washington Post*, May 4, 1989; "Drug Czar: Go After Casual Users, Parents," *Chicago Tribune*, May 4, 1989.

101. Lt. Lowell K. Duckett, Chairman, D.C. Black Police Caucus, to Mayor Marion Barry, February 3, 1989, Clarke Papers, Box 39, Folder 1.

102. Larry D. Payne, "Cops Selling PCP?," *Washington Afro-American*, September 20, 1986.

103. Editorial, "Continue the Drug War . . . ," *Washington Afro-American*, September 20, 1986.

104. William Raspberry, "Go After the Drug Buyers Too," *Washington Post*, September 2, 1987.

105. Committee Report, Committee on Human Services, District of Columbia Substance Abuse Treatment and Prevention Act of 1989 (Bill 8-77), 3.

106. John Ward Anderson, "Prisoners Lost Control of Uprising, Probers Told," *Washington Post*, July 13, 1986; Nancy Lewis, "Barry, Prison Chief, Cited for Contempt," *Washington Post*, March 13, 1987.

107. *Inmates of Occoquan v. Barry*, 650 F. Supp. 619, 620, 621, 635 (D.D.C. 1986).

108. The trial judge would eventually call Barry's bluff, holding him and his communications director in contempt and fining each $50,000. Lewis, "Barry, Prison Chief, Cited for Contempt."

109. Rita McWilliams, "Death Row," *Washington City Paper*, October 19, 1990, 24.

110. Courtland Milloy, "A General in the Drug Wars," *Washington Post*, December 11, 1988.

111. "Cracked: A City Running Scared," *Washington Post*, June 18, 1995.

112. Keith A. Harriston, "Fulwood Resigns As Police Chief; D.C. Homicide Rate Cited in Decision," *Washington Post*, September 9, 1992.

113. *Jet*, October 26, 1992; Leroy Mobley, "The Real Black on Black Crime," *Afro-American Red Star*, November 7, 1992.

114. I propose such a model in James Forman, Jr., "Community Policing and Youth as Assets," *Journal of Criminal Law & Criminology* 95 (2004): 1.

### 6. What Would Martin Luther King, Jr., Say?

1. U.S. Department of Justice Civil Rights Division, *Investigation of the Ferguson Police Department* (2015), 10–15.

2. Stop data collected by the Maryland State Police between 1995 and 1997 revealed that 95.6 percent of drivers from whom police requested permission to search gave their consent. Data provided by the Ohio Highway Patrol for 1987–91 and 1995–97 show consent rates of 88.3 percent and 93.1 percent, respectively, for the two periods. Ilya D. Lichtenberg, "Voluntary Consent or Obedience to Authority: An Inquiry into the Consensual Police-Citizen Encounter" (unpublished Ph.D. diss., Rutgers University, October 1999), 160–64, 386, Table 7-1). A different study on stops conducted statewide by the Maryland State Police from January 1995 to June 2000 found that police obtained consent to search 96 percent of the time they requested it. Samuel R. Gross and Katherine Y. Barnes, "Road Work: Racial Profiling and Drug Interdiction on the Highway," *Michigan Law Review* 101 (2002): 658, 672. When the Illinois State Police sought consent to search as part of a highway interdiction program in 1992, motorists consented more than 98 percent of the time. *Chavez v. Illinois State Police*, 251 F.3d 612, 621–22 (7th Cir. 2001).

3. Pamela K. Lattimore et al., *Homicide in Eight U.S. Cities: Trends, Context, and Policy Implications* (National Institute of Justice, 1997), 14.

4. U.S. Department of Justice Bureau of Justice Statistics, *Criminal Victimization and Perceptions of Community Safety in 12 Cities, 1998* (1999), 9.

5. General Social Survey (GSS), 1994.

6. Paul Duggan, "D.C. Residents Urged to Care, Join War on Guns," *Washington Post*, January 14, 1995.

7. Ibid.

8. Ruben Castaneda and David Montgomery, "In King's Name, a Mandate," *Washington Post*, January 17, 1994.

9. "Jackson Addresses Alabama Prisoners," *Philadelphia Tribune*, March 14, 1995.

10. William J. Clinton, "Remarks to the Convocation of the Church of God in Christ in Memphis (November 13, 1993)," Administration of William J. Clinton, 2359.

11. Ibid., 2360.

12. Michelle Alexander and Donna Murch have excoriated President Clinton for his role in facilitating mass incarceration. Michelle Alexander, "Why Hillary Clinton Doesn't Deserve the Black Vote," *The Nation*, February 10, 2016; Donna Murch, "The Clintons' War on Drugs: When Black Lives Didn't Matter," *The New Republic*, February 9, 2016. Jamelle Bouie has argued that the politics of the 1994 crime bill were complicated, detailing how some African Americans supported the law and others were ambivalent. Jamelle Bouie,

"The Messy, Very Human Politics of Bill Clinton's Crime Bill," *Slate*, April 11, 2016.

13. Duggan, "D.C. Residents Urged to Care."

14. Eric Holder interview with Derek McGinty, *The Derek McGinty Show*, WAMU, November 24, 1994, p. 7.

15. There have been many Operation Ceasefires around the country, as this is a common name for programs combatting gun violence.

16. New York Police Department, Police Strategy No. 1, *Getting Guns Off the Streets of New York* (1994).

17. Lawrence W. Sherman and Dennis P. Rogan, "Effects of Gun Seizures on Gun Violence: 'Hot Spots' Patrol in Kansas City," *Justice Quarterly* 12, no. 4 (1995), 680–81.

18. Charles R. Epp, Steven Maynard-Moody, and Donald Haider-Markel, *Pulled Over: How Police Stops Define Race and Citizenship* (Chicago: University of Chicago Press, 2014), 32.

19. Edmund F. McGarrell et al., "Reducing Firearms Violence Through Directed Police Patrol," *Criminology and Public Policy* 1, no. 1 (2001): 119–48. A *New York Times* story explained, "Police departments here [Indianapolis] and in Kansas City, Mo., have tried something police departments never did before to get illegal guns off the streets: They have focused on the guns in the way they have long focused on drugs and drunken drivers. Elementary as it sounds, it works." Fox Butterfield, "A Way to Get the Gunmen: Get the Guns," *New York Times*, November 20, 1994.

20. Nancy Lewis, "Holder Says Gun Campaign Will Enlist 50 Officers; U.S. Attorney to Be Host of Summit This Week," *Washington Post*, March 8, 1995.

21. Both pedestrians and vehicles would be targeted, but Holder said that vehicles would be the principal focus because vehicle searches had proved most fruitful in the Kansas City experiment. Eric Holder interview with Diane Rehm, *The Diane Rehm Show*, National Public Radio, January 25, 1995, 6–7.

22. Lewis, "Holder Says Gun Campaign Will Enlist 50 D.C. Officers."

23. Nancy Lewis, "Under the Gun: 3rd Police District Squad Gets There First to Get the Weapons Off the Street," *Washington Post*, June 16, 1995.

24. *Whren v. United States*, 517 U.S. 806 (1996), 813. Michelle Alexander, *The New Jim Crow: Mass Incarceration in the Age of Colorblindness* (New Press, 2010), 108; David Cole, *No Equal Justice: Race and Class in the American Criminal Justice System* (New Press, 1999), 39; Paul Butler, "The White Fourth Amendment," *Texas Tech Law Review* 43 (2010): 250.

25. Holder interview with Rehm, 6.

26. Though he did elsewhere. In an interview with the *Washington Post* reporter Nancy Lewis, Holder said police would focus on heavily tinted windows. According to Lewis, Holder's Operation Ceasefire would "target vehicles, especially those in violation of safety standards, such as being operated with improper lights or heavily tinted windows, as well as pedestrians who meet a specific profile that might indicate that they are carrying a weapon." Nancy Lewis, "Special Teams to Draw Bead on Illegal DC Guns," *Washington Post*, June 6, 1995.

27. Holder interview with Rehm, 6–7.

28. Ibid., 7.

29. In 1973 the Supreme Court held that police need not inform drivers of their right to refuse to be searched. *Schneckloth v. Bustamonte*, 412 U.S. 218 (1973).

30. Charles Remsberg, *Tactics for Criminal Patrol: Vehicle Stops, Drug Discovery and Officer Survival* (Calibre Press, 1995), 212, 215.

31. American Civil Liberties Union of Illinois, "CPD Traffic Stops in 2013: Searches of Cars by Consent: Contraband Finds Per Search, by Type," December 2014; Sgt. Greg Stewart and Emily Covelli, "Stops Data Collection: The Portland Police Bureau's Response to the Criminal Justice Policy and Research Institute's Recommendations," Portland Police Bureau, February 13, 2014; Larry K. Gaines, "An Analysis of Traffic Stop Data in Riverside, California," *Police Quarterly* 9, no. 2 (June 2006): 210, 216, 224, 225.

32. Remsberg, *Tactics for Criminal Patrol*, 69.

33. Sherman and Rogan, "Effects of Gun Seizures on Gun Violence," 683; McGarrell et al., "Reducing Firearms Violence," 131, Table 2.

34. In the Chicago study from 2013, while police found weapons in 0.5 percent of consent searches, they found drugs in 9.5 percent of consent searches; and 83.3 percent of the time drugs were found, the amounts were small (ten grams or less). In Portland, police retrieved weapons in 4.7 percent of all searches and drugs in 22.0 percent of all searches. And in Riverside, California, police found weapons in 1.1 percent of searches and drugs in 8.4 percent. (In all three cities, cars driven by whites were significantly more likely to be found with drugs in them than those driven by blacks or Hispanics.) ACLU of Illinois, "CPD Traffic Stops in 2013"; Stewart and Covelli, "Stops Data Collection," 27, Table 21; Larry Gaines, "An Analysis," 225, Table 7.

35. Lewis, "Holder Says Gun Campaign Will Enlist 50 D.C. Officers"; Ruben Castaneda, "DC Tops States in Arrests for Weapon Offenses, U.S. Says," *Washington Post*, November 13, 1995.

36. Metropolitan Police Department, *MPDC 1998 Annual Report: Investing in Public Safety for Today and Tomorrow* (1999), 19.

37. DeNeen Brown, "District Weekly: A Suburb Thrives in the City but Despite Affluence, Ward 3 Faces Problems," *Washington Post*, June 16, 1994.

38. Robert L. Wilkins, "Comments of the Public Defender Service for the District of Columbia Concerning Public Oversight Hearing on the Impact of the Joint Gun Initiative Conducted by the Metropolitan Police Department, the U.S. Attorney's Office, and the Bureau of Alcohol, Tobacco and Firearms," October 25, 1995, p. 2.

39. Ibid., 3.

40. Councilman Bill Lightfoot worried that the gun squads were targeting young black men. Nancy Lewis, "Officials Say D.C. Anti-Gun Program Seems to Be Working," *Washington Post*, October 26, 1995.

41. Wade Henderson, "NAACP Washington Lobby: More Than Just Black and White," *About . . . Time Magazine*, October 31, 1994.

42. Lenese C. Herbert, "Et in Arcadia Ego: A Perspective on Black Prosecutors'

Loyalty Within the American Criminal Justice System," *Howard Law Journal* 49 (2005): 513.

43. Paul Butler, "Brotherman: Reflections of a Reformed Prosecutor," in Ellis Cose, ed., *The Darden Dilemma* (HarperPerennial, 1997), 1–2.

44. Bill Gifford, "Good Cop: Eric Holder, Liberal Crime-Fighter," *The New Republic*, May 1, 1995, 16.

45. Robert E. Pierre, "Police Hail the Success of Gun Drive," *Washington Post*, July 18, 1996.

46. Jeffrey Goldberg, "The Color of Suspicion," *New York Times*, June 20, 1999.

47. Michael Isikoff and Tracy Thompson, "Getting Too Tough on Drugs: Draconian Sentences Hurt Small Offenders More Than Kingpins," *Washington Post*, November 4, 1990.

48. Ron Harris, "Blacks Feel Brunt of Drug War," *Los Angeles Times*, April 22, 1990.

49. David Cole, "The Paradox of Race and Crime: A Comment on Randall Kennedy's 'Politics of Distinction,'" *Georgetown Law Journal* 83 (1995): 2562, note 68; Charisse Jones, "Crack and Punishment: Is Race the Issue?" *New York Times*, October 28, 1995.

50. Nkechi Taifa, "Laying Down the Law, Race by Race," *Legal Times*, October 10, 1994.

51. See chapter 2, "Black Lives Matter."

52. Benjamin Levin is a must-read on this topic. Levin demonstrates how liberals, including many racial justice advocates, have come to see guns as a category unto themselves, one to which none of the normal over-punishment concerns apply. Benjamin Levin, "Guns and Drugs," *Fordham Law Review* 84 (2016): 2173.

53. Paul Duggan, "D.C. Votes More Leeway for Judges; Mandatory Sentences in Drug Cases Altered," *Washington Post*, December 7, 1994.

54. "United States: Call in the Feds," *The Economist* (April 3, 1999); Daniel C. Richman, "Project Exile and the Allocation of Federal Law Enforcement Authority," *Arizona Law Review* 43, no. 2 (2001): 369–412.

55. Frank Lynn, "New Yorkers Face a Busy Election Day," *New York Times*, November 6, 1988. In October 1990 Johnson told the *Amsterdam News* that "we are sending many cases to federal courts where gun and drug convictions have a five-year mandatory sentence." Jesse H. Walker, "Bronx DA Defends Self, Office and His Borough," *Amsterdam News*, October 13, 1990; Bob Kappstatter, "DA Guns for More 1-Year Terms," *Daily News*, September 29, 1995.

56. In 1997, Paul Butler brilliantly and poignantly described being singled out for surveillance by black officers while walking three blocks from his home in a well-off, integrated D.C. neighborhood. Paul Butler, "Walking While Black," *Legal Times*, November 10, 1997.

57. Ronald Weitzer, Stephen Tuch, and Wesley Skogan, "Police–Community Relations in a Majority-Black City," *Journal of Research in Crime and Delinquency* 45, no. 4 (2008): 419; Ronald Weitzer, "Citizens' Perceptions of Police Misconduct: Race and Neighborhood Context," *Justice Quarterly* 16, no. 4 (1999): 820–22.

58. Ronald Weitzer, interview by author, March 10, 2014.

59. Weitzer, "Citizens' Perceptions of Police Misconduct," 830.

60. Ibid., 841–42.

61. Ibid., 841.

62. David K. Shipler, *The Rights of the People* (Knopf, 2011), 48, 57.

63. Ibid., 72–73. The Gun Recovery Unit had distilled its philosophy down to a simple, if remarkable, idea. According to the unit's training material, "[F]or too long police officers have been trained to view the Constitution of the United States and its judicial interpretations as placing rigid restrictions on what law enforcement can do on the street while shielding criminals from detection." Instead, the Constitution should be understood "as a law enforcement sword rather than a shield." Ibid., 41.

64. Police Reform Organizing Project, *Nearly 2,000,000 Per Year Punitive Interactions Between the NYPD and New Yorkers*, August 2015, 3,5.

65. Epp, Maynard-Moody, and Haider-Markel, *Pulled Over*, 13–14, 65–66, 72.

66. Ibid., 14, 72–73.

67. Ibid., 67, figure 3.3.

68. Ibid.

69. Jeffrey Goldberg, "The Color of Suspicion."

70. I do not suggest that this is the *only* source of disparity. Rather, my claim is that this is *a* source of disparity, and one that police are uniquely positioned to correct.

## Epilogue

1. In pursuing decriminalization, D.C. is part of a national trend. Bill Keller, "How to Legalize Pot," *New York Times*, May 19, 2013 (Colorado and Washington had already legalized marijuana by 2013); Mark A. R. Kleinman, "Marijuana Legalization Doesn't Have to Lead to Commercialization," *New York Times*, September 9, 2015 (D.C., Washington, Colorado, Oregon, and Alaska had legalized marijuana by 2015). National polling data show a dramatic shift in attitudes regarding marijuana criminalization: in 1969, just 12 percent of Americans were in favor of legalizing marijuana possession; in 2003, the number had grown to 34 percent, and by 2014 a majority of Americans (51 percent) favored legalization. Lydia Saad, "Majority Continues to Support Pot Legalization in U.S.," *Gallup*, November 6, 2014.

2. The council passed the measure by a vote of 11–1 in February 2014, and it took effect one year later, on February 26, 2015.

3. Franklin E. Zimring, *The Great American Crime Decline* (Oxford University Press, 2007).

4. Uniform Crime Reports, Federal Bureau of Investigation.

5. See, e.g., Zimring, *The Great American Crime Decline*; Philippe Bourgois, "Crack and the Political Economy of Social Suffering," *Addiction Research and Theory* 11, no. 1 (2003): 32–33; Malcolm Gladwell, "N.Y. Crack Epidemic Appears to Wane; Seeing Drug's Destructiveness, Younger People Are Turning Away," *Washington Post*, May 31, 1993; Katherine Boo, "Crack's Crash: Teens Are Rejecting the Drug That Ruled D.C.," *Washington Post*, August 28, 1994, A1.

6. Ashley Nellis, *The Color of Justice: Racial and Ethnic Disparities in State Prisons* (The Sentencing Project, 2016), 3; *Report of the Sentencing Project to the United Nations Human Rights Committee Regarding Racial Disparities in the United States Criminal Justice System* (2013), 1.

7. Becky Pettit, *Invisible Men: Mass Incarceration and the Myth of Black Progress* (Russell Sage Foundation, 2012), 64; see also Bruce Western, *Punishment and Inequality in America* (Russell Sage Foundation, 2006), 85–107.

8. ACLU report, *Behind the D.C. Numbers: The War on Marijuana in Black and White* (2013), 4.

9. James B. Jacobs, *The Eternal Criminal Record* (Harvard University Press, 2015). Evidence of the dramatic growth of collateral consequences can be seen in the legislation. In 1975 Clarke's bill simply proposed to replace a criminal penalty with a civil fine. Wells, by contrast, added various provisions, including some that would have seemed nonsensical to the 1975 council. For example, the 2014 act provided that "no person shall be rendered ineligible for public assistance by reason of a civil violation of . . . [the Marijuana Possession Decriminalization Amendment Act]." Marijuana Possession Decriminalization Amendment Act of 2014, D.C. Act 20-305, §402 (2014). In 1975 it would have been unheard of to deny an individual welfare because she had been arrested for drug possession.

10. D.C. Council, Committee on the Judiciary and Public Safety, *Public Hearing Before the Committee on the Simple Possession of Small Quantities of Marijuana Decriminalization Amendment Act of 2013*, October 24, 2013, 55.

11. *Public Hearing on Marijuana Decriminalization Amendment Act of 2013* (statement of council member David Grosso), 3, 50. Additional evidence of Alexander's influence can be seen in the fact that a citizens' group called the New Jim Crow Group for Change had formed in response to her book. A member of the group spoke at the hearing in support of decriminalization. Ibid., 84–85.

12. Jay Mathews, "Legal Marijuana Opposed," *Washington Post*, August 1, 1975.

13. As in 1975, a black-white gap in support remained, as 73 percent of the city's white residents supported decriminalization. Polling also revealed a class gap: those with incomes over $100,000 were more likely to support decriminalization (71 percent support) than those with incomes less than $50,000 (61 percent). There was also a gender gap, with men more likely to support than women, and black women the group least supportive (51 percent in favor; 45 percent against). *Washington Post* D.C. Poll, January 9–14, 2014.

14. For example, Andrew Fowler, the head of the powerful Committee of One Hundred Ministers, said in 1975 that "[t]he young users of marijuana will be easily susceptible to the harder drugs." "A Statement by (Rev.) Andrew Fowler in [*sic*] behalf of the Commite [*sic*] of One Hundred Ministers and Baptist Ministers Conference of Washington, D.C., and Vicinity Before the City Council," July 16, 1975.

15. Council of the District of Columbia Committee on the Judiciary and Public Safety Committee Report: *Report on Bill 20-409, Marijuana Possession Decrimi-*

*nalization Amendment Act of 2014*, January 15, 2014, 14, 19. Not all black church leaders were persuaded. Some still believed that decriminalization would hurt young people by making it easier for them to smoke marijuana. See ibid., 14 (summarizing testimony of Elder Bernard Howard from Sanctuary of Praise), 18 (summarizing testimony of Yvonne L. Williams, chair of Bible Way Church).

16. Wells celebrated, calling his legislation "a first step in remedying the failed war on drugs." Steven Nelson, "D.C. Council Endorses Pot Decriminalization as Legalization Fight Looms," *U.S. News & World Report*, February 4, 2014.

17. In 2010 alone, 5,115 people in D.C. were arrested for marijuana possession. More than 90 percent of those arrested were black. See ACLU, *The War on Marijuana in Black and White* (2013), 43.

18. Nonviolent, small-quantity (i.e., 10 ounces or less) marijuana possessors represent .06 percent, or 6 in 10,000, of all prisoners. Eric Sevigny and Jonathan Caulkins, "Kingpins or Mules," *Criminology and Public Policy* 3 (2004): 421. See also John F. Pfaff, "The War on Drugs and Prison Growth: Limited Importance, Limited Legislative Options," *Harvard Journal on Legislation* 52 (2015), 173.

19. As Marie Gottschalk notes, "Some opponents of the war on drugs have supported easing up on drug offenders and other nonviolent offenders in order to get tough with the 'really bad guys.'" Marie Gottschalk, *Caught: The Prison State and the Lockdown of American Politics* (Princeton University Press, 2015), 167.

20. Barack Obama, Speech to NAACP, July 14, 2015.

21. Ibid.

22. Barack Obama, "Press Conference by the President, July 15, 2015" (Office of the Press Secretary, 2015).

23. Press Release, October 8, 2015, "House Judiciary Committee Unveils Bipartisan Sentencing Reform Legislation."

24. Press Release, "Fudge, Delahunt, Issa, Rooney, Introduce Bill to Review Nation's Criminal Justice System," April 28, 2010.

25. Miriam Gohara, "Grace Notes: A Case for Making Mitigation the Heart of Noncapital Sentencing," *American Journal of Criminal Law* 41 (2014): 41; National Juvenile Defender Center, "Role of Juvenile Defense Counsel in Delinquency Court," Spring 2009.

26. Kristin N. Henning, "What's Wrong with Victims' Rights in Juvenile Court?: Retributive v. Rehabilitative Systems of Justice," *California Law Review* 97 (2009): 1107–1170.

27. Dante's early experience with suspension is all too common. Black students are disproportionately suspended from schools and subjected to more frequent and harsher punishment, beginning as early as preschool. Sarah E. Redfield and Jason P. Nance, *School-to-Prison Pipeline: Preliminary Report*, American Bar Association, February 2016, 27–30.

28. Victor Rios describes the dilemma Dante faced in *Punished: Policing the Lives of Black and Latino Boys* (NYU Press, 2011), 55. Jose, one of the young men in Rios's study, joins a gang for protection, though he ends up being further victimized by rival gang members as a result.

29. Michael Eric Dyson, "President Obama's Racial Renaissance," *New York Times*, August 1, 2015.

30. Matt Apuzzo, "Justice Dept. Starts Quest for Inmates to Be Freed," *New York Times*, January 30, 2014.

31. *All Things Considered*, "White House Adviser on 'Devastating Consequence' of Solitary Confinement," January 26, 2016.

32. "President Obama Interviews the Creator of 'The Wire' David Simon," transcript available at Medium.com, March 27, 2015.

33. E. Ann Carson, *Prisoners in 2014* (Bureau of Justice Statistics, 2015), 16.

34. Bryan Stevenson, *Just Mercy: A Story of Justice and Redemption* (Spiegel & Grau, 2014), 17–18.

35. William Bennett et al., *Body Count: Moral Poverty . . . And How to Win America's War Against Crime and Drugs* (Simon & Schuster, 1996), 26–27.

# Acknowledgments

I am grateful to my agent, David McCormick, who saw what I hoped to do, and to my brilliant editor, Alex Star, who helped me to do it.

I am blessed to have good friends and colleagues who took time from their own busy lives to read and comment on drafts, including Reginald Dwayne Betts, Kenneth Mack, Richard Banks, Vesla Weaver, David Sklansky, Kim Ford-Mazrui, Lisa Miller, Jeff Fagan, Risa Golubuff, Heather Gerken, Dan Richman, Bernard Harcourt, Don Herzog, Robert Post, Randall Kennedy, Aziz Rana, Frank Zimring, Lisa Daugaard, Dorothy Zellner, Christopher Muller, and Andrew Wise. Tracey Meares pushed me to produce drafts for our summer writers' lunches, reminding me that before anything could be good, it first had to be. John Witt read multiple drafts, offered wonderful suggestions, and was endlessly encouraging.

Arthur Evenchik read every word of every chapter, dozens of times. Arthur's eyes were the first to see a draft, and the last to review any changes. In between, we spent hundreds of hours discussing and debating the ideas and arguments that appear in these pages. I am forever in his debt.

I received generous feedback from faculty workshops at the University of Michigan, Georgetown, Cornell, Berkeley, Yale, Columbia, Harvard, Temple, the University of Virginia, and Stanford. I also appreciate the probing questions from students in Sharon Dolovich's After Guilt class at NYU Law School, Vesla Weaver's Race and Politics of Punishment seminar at Yale College, Michael Leo Owen's Politics and Punishment seminar at Emory University, and Fordham Law School's Seminar Series on Advanced Criminal Law and Criminal Procedure hosted by Deborah Denno. The research was supported by Lenny Bernardo and a fellowship from the Open Society Foundations, as well as by my hosts at OSF's New York, Baltimore, and Washington, D.C., offices.

If there are better librarians than those at the Yale Law Library, I have yet to meet them. Jordan Jefferson and Julie Krishnaswami in particular worked wonders, resolutely tracking down elusive material. Deb Tropiano handled thousands of details graciously. I also benefited from spectacular seminar students and research assistants, including Aaron Littman, Tina Thomas, Cynthia Liao, Haran Tae, Meghan McCormack, Tamar Lerer, Cal Soto, Wendy Zupac, Sarah Tallman, Kristen Lang, Silvia Ibrahim, Marbre Stahly-Butts, Irina Vaynerman, Michelle Mangan, Kate Mollison, Tian Huang, Alexandra van Nievelt, Megan Hauptman, Anna Arons, Katherine Demby, Tyler Hill, Jackie Delligatti, Allan Bradley, Olivia Schwob, Micah Jones, Ashley Dalton, Rebecca Ojserkis, Rachel Baker, Jerelyn Luther, Andrea Katz, Asli Bashir, Rakim Brooks, Christopher Pagliarella, Elisabeth Ford, Dvora Toren, Erica James, Hillary Vedvig, Brandon Thompson, Kelley Schiffman, Jonas Wang, Alexandra Barlowe, Marian Messing, Ravi Bhalla, Julie Hutchinson, Sam Brill, Rachel Luban, Carolyn Lipp, Aubrey Jones, the students at the Inside-Out Prison Exchange Program at Manson Youth Institution, and, above all, Matthew Lee, Renagh O'Leary, and Jesse Schreck.

I relied on terrific librarians and staff at Howard University's Moorland-Spingarn Research Center, the Special Collections Research Center at the George Washington University Library, the Legislative Services Office of the Washington, D.C., City Council, and the Washingtoniana Collection at the Martin Luther King Jr. Memorial Library, the central facility of the D.C. Public Library.

Many people agreed to be interviewed for this book, and I couldn't have completed the project without them: Roger Wilkins, Angela Davis, Nkechi Taifa, Clifford Alexander, Cynthia Jones, Don Braman, June Jeffries, Jack Evans, Greg Mize, Kathy Patterson, Keith Stroup, Kim Taylor-Thompson, Laurie Robinson, Pat Wald, Lenese Herbert, Ronald Sullivan, Ron Weich, Hallem Williams, Ted Gest, Brenda Smith, Albert Herring, Charity Tolliver, John Bess, Carol Thompson Cole, Esi Mathis, Frank Smith, Julie Stewart, Ron Weitzer, and Harold Brazil.

Others helped indirectly, but just as essentially. My colleagues at the Public Defender Service in D.C. taught me how to be a lawyer. Owen Fiss, Akhil Amar, Catharine MacKinnon, Harold Koh, Jeffrey Lehman, Randy Hertz, and Adolph Reed, Jr., guided me into the academy. Charles Lawrence, Mari Matsuda, and Kimberlé Crenshaw convinced me, and many others, that legal scholarship could include our stories. Amy Chua and Jed Rubenfeld believed in this book before I did, and their enthusiasm persuaded me.

David Domenici and Cheryl Mills put me up during research trips to Washington, D.C., and Lucca and Indigo Domenici-Mills filled the evenings with laughter, break dancing, and Forbidden Island. When the going got tough, I could count on Sharon Brooks, Elizabeth Alexander and Ficre Ghebreyesus, Miriam Gohara and Marcus McFerren, Vesla Weaver and Chris Lebron, and the entire Black Family Dinner posse. Murray Zimiles lent an artist's eye at a crucial juncture. Abby Rezneck and Miles Ehrlich offered encouragement, Peet's Coffee, and gelato.

Writing this book was a family journey. My mother, Constancia Romilly, and my stepfather, Terry Weber, came to New Haven countless times to offer child care when I needed "just one more weekend to write." My wife, Ifeoma Nwokoye, sustained us, all while completing a grueling graduate school program and launching her own career as a nurse practitioner. My grandmother Jessica Mitford died two decades ago, but she left behind *Kind and Usual Punishment*, a powerful indictment of American prisons that I consult regularly. Published in 1973, before the mass incarceration era had arrived, her book is a reminder of how entrenched the crisis described on these pages truly is.

This book would not exist if not for my father, James Forman. He gave every ounce of his being to the black freedom struggle. He taught me that African American history is American history, and that it is worth writing about. Not a day goes by that I don't think of him, and miss him.

# Index

Names in quotes indicate pseudonyms. Page numbers in *italics* indicate illustrations.

Abner, Velencia, 53
ACLU, 140, 205, 281n34, 285n17
Adams, Eric, 277n80
addiction, 44, 273n16; treatment for, 26–28, 122–24, 139, 147–48, 150, 169, 173, 236, 246n39, 277n73; *see also* drug dealers; drugs; War on Drugs
affirmative action, 158, 266n147; in D.C. police force, 99, 112, 266n147
African Americans: Africans' struggle parallel to, 34; as agents of criminal justice system, 9–11, 13–14, 242n19; class divisions among, *see* class; crime feared by, 10–11, 12–13, 26, 32, 35, 51–60, 125–26, 194–95, 202, 224, 242n19, 245n35, 252nn21, 23, 268n13; drug dealers demonized by, 10, 29–31, 32–33, 142, 246n47; drugs perceived as means of racial subjugation by, 27, 37, 127, 249n76, 268n18; economic opportunities for, *see* employment, barriers to; as elected officials, 10, 19, 33–46, 55–56, 62, 134, 165–66, 203, 218, 221, 242n13, 257n114; favoring both crime control measures and root-cause solutions to crime, 12–13, 29–30, 63–64, 76–77, 114, 157, 168–69, 196–97, 246n49, 272n76; federal spending priorities of, 272n76; gun ownership by, *see* black tradition of arms; growth in political power of, 19, 73, 112; homicide rates for, 57, 161–62, 194–95, 203, 218, 275n36; ministers' influence on, 39–40, 42–43, 45; as police officers, *see* police officers, black; population of, in South, 82; punitive attitudes of, 9, 272n76; seeking to protect gains of civil rights movement, 11, 127, 194–96; as vigilantes, 32–33, 64–72, 126, 136, 257n112; whites mistrusted by, 27, 35–36, 37, 45–46

*Afro, see Washington Afro-American*

Afro-American Patrolmen's League, 270n46

Alabama, 66, 86

Alaska, 21, 283n1

Alex, Nicholas, 109, 110

Alexander, Clifford, 266n142

Alexander, Michelle, 220, 279n12, 284n11

American Federation of Government Employees, 140

*Amsterdam News* (Harlem), 32, 103, 282n55

antidiscrimination laws, 272n76

Armstrong Technical High School, 81, 101

Arnold, Thomas, 159

arrest records, 186–94, 219; arbitrariness of, 190; lifelong consequences of 7, 12, 20, 23–24, 45, 173, 174, 186, 213, 215, 218–19, 236–38, 284n9; racial disparities in, 194, 213; sealing of, 186; without convictions, 186, 190–91, 193

Arrington, Marvin, 165–66

asset forfeiture, 156, 165–66, 167, 172–73, 186, 277n86

Atlanta, 18, 19, 62–63, 74–75, 83, 165–66, 258n119; black police officers in, 82–88, 85, 87, 113

*Atlanta Daily World*, 62, 84, 86, 88

bail and bail bonds, 13, 127, 129, 174, 268n19

Bailey, Ralph, Jr., 160

Baker, Ella, 73–74, 257n115

Baldwin, James, 79, 155–56

Baltimore, 165, 221, 265n130, 266n135, 275n43

Bannon, James D., 108

Barksdale, Ethelbert, 82

Barry, Marion, 35, 45, 55, 139; on drugs, 29, 45, 165; on police, 105–106, 167, 168, 172–73, 175, 177, 266n146, 278n108

BDC, *see* Blackman's Development Center

Beard, Eugene, 111

Beatty, Vander, 248n70

Bell, Eldrin, 166

Bennett, Elijah, 101–102

Bennett, William, 175, 232

Bernstein, Carl, 49

Biderman, Albert, 245n35

Bilbo, Theodore, 97

*Birth of a Nation, The* (film), 67

Black, Donald, 108

black church, 42–43; on gun control, 59–60; views on drugs of, 39–40, 42–43, 45, 220, 284nn14, 15

Black Lives Matter, precedents for, 11, 73–74, 94–97, 101–104, 171

Blackman's Development Center (BDC), 27–31, 28, 30, 33, 246nn39, 47

Blackmon, Douglas, 66

black nationalism, 33–34, 70, 104–105, 247n63, *see also* SNCC

black newspapers, 10, 83, 103; *see also* *Amsterdam News; Los Angeles Sentinel; Washington Afro-American*

black-on-black crime, 50, 51–55, 54, 57–58, 58, 63, 137–39, 138; as civil rights issue, 11, 195; heroin and, 26–27, 31–32, 44; as new threat, 72–73, 257n108; police indifference to, *see* police force: black victims neglected by; police violence as, 154; police violence vs., 11, 242n18; as suicidal, 203; as term, 137, 242n18, 270n46

Black Panther Party, 69, 246n44

Black Police Caucus, 175

Black Pride movement, 33, 58, 58, 109

*Black Silent Majority* (Fortner), 31–32

black tradition of arms, 65–70, 71–74

Black United Front (BUF), 34, 43, 70, 105

Blease, Cole, 56, 253n37

Board of Parole, 132; *see also* parole

Bond, Julian, 69, 241n7

Boston, 50, 92, 108, 275n38

Bouie, Jamelle, 279n12
Bowden, Lovinger, 37, 249n76
Bradley, Tom, 19
"Brandon," 3–8, 224
Briscoe, Curtis, 159
Brown, James, 58
Brown, Kenneth, 130
Brown, Michael, 101
Buckley, William F., 21
Bureau of Social Science Research, 42
burglary, 13, 227; defense against, 10, 26, 53, 126, 252n21, 258n120
Bush, George, 166, 272n76
Butler, Paul, 203, 282n56
buy-bust operations, 120, 144

California, 157, 221, 238; black officials in, 19, 165; drugs in, 21, 134–37, 135, 167, 281n34; guns in, 69–70, 167, 275n40, 281n34; police in, 103–104, 107–108, 167, 204; see also Los Angeles
Capitol View neighborhood (Washington, D.C.), 125, 258n120
Carmichael, Stokely, 34, 36, 37; on armed resistance, 70, 256n93; Black United Front and, 34, 105
Carson, Clayborne, 69
Carter, Arthur, 147–48
Carter, Jimmy, 21, 55, 244n19
*Challenge of Crime in a Free Society, The* (President's Commission on Law Enforcement and Justice), 104, 108
Chambliss, William, 170
Charlotte, North Carolina, 113
Chicago, 75, 92, 108, 165, 167, 270n46, 281n34
*Chocolate City* (album), 18, 19
Citizens for Safer Streets, 139
Civil Rights Commission, 98
civil rights movement, 8, 20, 33–34, 55, 69, 98; black police as disappointment to, 100–101, 106–111, 114; marijuana and, 22–24, 33–37; police integration demanded by, 79,

82–88, 85, 98, 102–106, 182–83; white activists in, 8, 20, 74; within the system, 55–56, 100
civil service exams, 90, 93–94, 110, 263n73
Clark, Daniel, 66
Clark, Georgia, 72
Clark, Kenneth B., 272n76
Clarke, David, 20, 22, 45–46, 62; Marijuana Reform Act introduced by, 17–25, 33–46, 56–57, 217, 253n39; policing and, 147–48, 171; on sentencing, 129, 131, 132, 133
class, 13, 44, 100–101, 146, 243nn21, 23, 246n49; disparities in the criminal justice system based on, 13, 35, 39, 132, 176, 223; policing based on, 108, 182, 207–11, 265n130, 266n135; see also employment, barriers to; poverty
Cleaver, James H., 137
Clem, John, 159
Cleveland, 19, 50
Clinton, Bill, 196, 279n12
Clinton, George, 18, 19
Coates, James, 250n105
Coates, Ta-Nehisi, 66, 243n21, 275n43
cocaine: crack vs. 158, 164; sentencing and 121, 124, 129, 131, 139, 164; see also crack
Cochran, Johnnie,137, 139, 270n45
Cole, Gloria, 125
Cole, Richard, 160
collateral consequences, 7, 12, 20, 23–24, 45, 173, 174, 186, 213, 215, 218–19, 236–38, 284n9
Colorado, 21, 283n1
Columbia Heights neighborhood (Washington, D.C.), 20, 124–25, 222
Comey, James B., 214
Commission on Interracial Cooperation (CIC), 83
Commission on Law Enforcement and Administration of Justice, 104, 105, 108
Committee of One Hundred Ministers, 39, 42, 43, 284n14

community policing, 180, 183
*Condemnation of Blackness, The*
  (Muhammad), 155
Congo, Democratic Republic of the, 34
Congress, 157, 196, 270n39, 279n12;
  D.C.'s status and, 18–19, 41, 45, 59,
  74, 97, 253nn44, 45, 258n117; drug
  legislation in, 21, 164, 172, 205, 221;
  gun control legislation in, 54, 59,
  62–64, 70, 71, 76
Congressional Black Caucus, 41, 205
Controlled Substances Act, 21
Conyers, John, 157; gun control
  supported by, 62–64, 72, 76, 257n108
Coombs, Orde, 32–33
Cosby, Bill, 106
court system, *see* criminal justice
  system; judges; prosecutors; Public
  Defender Service
Cox, James, 171
crack, 25, 156, 158–80; black officials'
  response to, 165–66; children and,
  153, 156, 158, 162–63, 225; cocaine vs.,
  158, 164, 204, 205, 229; compared to
  slavery, 10, 158, 163, 273n16; decline of,
  179–80, 194, 218; federal response to,
  164; homicides and, 156, 158, 159–62,
  165, 166, 174–75, 178–79
Crawford, H. R., 166, 171
crime, 25–26, 31–32, 47–60, 124–25,
  137–39, 143, 159–64, 251n8; black-
  on-black, *see* black-on-black crime;
  decline of, 217–18; deterrence of, 114,
  128, 140; drugs and, 10, 25–26, 31–32,
  44, 50, 126, 136, 145, 156, 158, 159–62,
  165, 169, 174–76, 218, 228–29, 245n35;
  1994 federal legislation against,
  196, 279n12; protection against,
  *see* self-defense; reasons for rise of,
  50; root-cause solutions to, 12–13,
  29–30, 63–64, 76–77, 114, 132, 142,
  146, 151–53, 157, 169, 197, 214, 246n49,
  272n76; white-on-black, 65–70, 72; *see
  also* African Americans, crime feared
  by; crack; guns; police forces

criminal justice system, 7, 14, 231;
  alternatives to, 236–38; central
  paradox of, 35, *see also* police
  forces: black victims neglected by;
criminal justice system: racial
  disparities in; class disparities in,
  *see* class; crack epidemic's effect on,
  156–57, 164; discretion in, 60–61,
  236; educational disparities in, 13,
  39, 76, 152, 193, 219, 226; failure of,
  as deterrent, 128, 143, 144; gender
  disparities in, 177, 241n2; in global
  perspective, 7, 18, 148, 205, 228;
  increasingly harsh sentencing in,
  75–77, *see also* sentencing; in Jim
  Crow South, 66; as local, 148, 237;
  overcrowding of, 140, 165, 176, 177;
  perception of, 9, 121; piecemeal
  nature of, 10, 13–14, 45, 148, 215,
  229, 238; police perspective on,
  129–30; prison conditions in, 5, 13,
  176–78; racial disparities in, 6–7, 8,
  17–18, 20, 21–22, 23–24, 35, 46, 61,
  76, 98, 113–14, 176, 179, 202, 205,
  206, 213–14, 218–19, 238, 249–50n86,
  277n80, 283n70; racism's role in
  creating, 11–13, 35, 155–56, 164,
  242n19; reform of, 217–22, 228–31,
  236–38; as revolving door, 127–29,
  128, 130, 131, 140; victims' roles in,
  11, 57–60, 223–24, 236, 237, 238;
  white-on-black violence unpunished
  by, 65–70, 72, 73; *see also* gun
  control; mandatory minimums;
  police forces; racial profiling;
  sentencing; War on Drugs
criminal records, *see* arrest records


*Daily Sentinel* (Raleigh, N.C.), 82
Daugaard, Lisa, 277n73
Davidson, Eugene, 95, 97, 100–101
Davis, Ed, 136
Davis, Owen, 90, 92–93
D.C., *see* Washington, D.C.

debt servitude, 66

decriminalization, *see* marijuana: decriminalization of

Dedmon, Jesse, Jr., 99

defense lawyers, 13; *see also* Public Defender Service

Democratic Republic of the Congo, 34

Dempsey, Oberia, 31–32

Department of Corrections, Washington, D.C., 10, 13, 14, 132, 166, 177

deterrence, 114, 128, 140

Detroit: black mayor of, 19, 31, 65, 165, 254n70; crime in, 31, 62, 63–64, 75, 247n53; police in, 106, 108–109, 165, 261n58

diGenova, Joseph, 175

Diggs, Charles, 41

disenfranchisement, 7, 12, 66–67, 236

*District Lawyer, The* (journal), 140

District of Columbia General Hospital (D.C. General), 162

diversion programs, 122–24, 147, 224, 227–28, 231, 235–36

Dixon, Arrington, 254n69

Domenici, David, 151–53

Donaldson, Ivanhoe, 247n63

"Dozier, Sandra," 186–94, 209, 213, 215, 220

"driving while black," 170, 204; *see also* pretext stops; racial profiling

drug dealers, 28–33, 40; addiction treatment for, 122–24, 139, 147–48, 150; crime and, 126, 136, 145; differentiated by drug, 124, 129, 131, 139, 172, 174; forfeiting assets of, 156, 165–66, 167, 172–73, 277n86; maximum sentences for, 22, 121, 124, 129, 131, 133, 134, 144, 205, 267nn2, 4; minimum sentences for, 114, 131, 134–39, 144, 164, 205, 221, 267n2, 269n33, 272n76, 282n55; as murderers, 32, 136; open-air, 125–27, 137, 141–42, 168; Operation Clean Sweep against, 167–73, 176–78, 180; other police tactics against, 120, 141, 144; as race traitors, 10, 29, 32–33, 142, 246n47; users vs., 124, 129, 143–44, 172, 174–76, 273n16; white, 18, 28–29

drugs: crime and, *see* crime: drugs and; as genocidal, 173, 249nn75, 76; nonviolent offenses involving, 145, 175, 220; overdoses of, 25, 26, 32, 36, 143, 259n75; perceived as means of racial subjugation, 27, 37, 127, 249n76, 268n18; as public health issue, 147–48; root-cause solutions to, 29–30; selling of, *see* drug dealers; war on, *see* War on Drugs; *see also* crack; heroin; marijuana

Du Bois, W.E.B., 68, 255n81

Dukakis, Michael, 166

Dulaney, W. Marvin, 82

DuPont, Robert, 24, 26–28

Dyson, Michael Eric, 228

Eastland, Jim, 92

East Side Night Club, 160

Ebenezer United Methodist Church, 59

*Ebony*, 58, *58*, 71, 137, *138*, 166, 270n46, 272n76

Emovon, Osahon Sandy, 159

employment, barriers to, 88–90, 110–11, 142, 157–58, 187, 266n136; arrest records as, 189–93, 215, 218–19, 237–38; unions as, 89, 261n46

Epp, Charles, 198, 212–13

equal protection, 65–66, 223, 236, 254n68, 259n14

Europe, 157, 167

Fauntleroy, John, 38–39, 40, 44, 249n86, 251n110

Fauntroy, Walter, 59, 139, 253nn44, 45; on gun control, 59, 60, 62, 74, 75, 76, 166–67, 254n69

FBI, 204, 214, 254n70

FedEx, 190–92, 215

Ferguson, Missouri, 188

"Fifth Avenue, Uptown" (Baldwin), 79, 155–56

Finley, Harrison F., 94, 101

Flamm, Michael, 48, *256n93*

food stamps, 157, *273n7*

Ford, Gerald, 19

Forman, James, Sr., 8, 69, *241n7*

Fortas, Abe, 131

Fortner, Michael, 31, *242n19*, *246n49*

Fourteenth Amendment, 65–66, 223, 236, *254n68*, *259n14*

Fowler, Andrew, 39–40, 42, 45, *284n14*

France, heroin from, *247n59*

Frederick Douglass Community Improvement Council, 171

Freed, Daniel, 14

Freeman, Don, 37

Fudge, Marcia, 221–22

Fulwood, Isaac, 112, 159, 160, 167–70, 172, 175–76, 178–79, 184

Fulwood, Teddy, 168, 179


"Gaffney, Pastor," 231, 237

gangs, 156, 197, 226–27, 232, *285n28*

Garner, Eric, 101, 171

Gary, Indiana, 18

Gay Activist Alliance, 140

Georgetown neighborhood (Washington, D.C.), 126, 143, 201, 210

Georgetown University, 228, *256n98*

Georgia, 62–63, 71, 72, 86; *see also* Atlanta

*Getting Guns Off the Streets of New York* (NYPD), 197

Gibson, Kenneth, 19

Girl Scouts, 173

Giuliani, Rudolph, *242n16*

Goins, William Lee, 160

Gold Coast (Washington, D.C.), 208, 210

Goldwater, Barry, 12, 48–49

Gray, Freddie, 171

Great Society programs, 13, 76–77, *258n130*, *272n76*

Green, Judge Joyce H., 172

Green, Judge June L., 176, 177

Gregory, Dick, 61

Grinspoon, Lester, 24

Gulf War, 162

gun control, 47–77; assassinations and, 59, 62; black opposition to, 63, 64–72, 68, 75, *254nn68*, 69, 70, *256nn93*, 98, *257n103*, *258n120*; black support for, 57–64, 71, 72–74, 76, *256n98*, *257nn108*, 112; impotence of on city level, 62, 65, 77, 161, *254n69*; national movement for, 62–64, 69–70, 71–72, 74–75, 76–77; 1975 D.C. legislation for, 56–62, 64–65, 70–71, 76–77; parallels with War on Drugs, 51, 75–76; racial overtones of, 48–49, 61, 66, 69–70, 71, 77; rationale for, 50–51, 167, *252n14*; as term, 51, 56; *see also* guns

guns, 47–77, 159–62, 165–67, 194; black tradition of, 65–70, 71–74; drugs vs., 204–207, *282n52*; federal charges for, 206–207; homicides caused by, *see* homicides; injuries caused by, 162, *275n40*; legislation targeting, *see* gun control; liberals on, *282n52*; mandatory minimums for, 60–61, 75, 131, 139, 145, *258nn119*, 120, *269n33*, *282n55*; Operation Ceasefire against, 197–204, 206–15, *see also* pretext stops; Rapid Deployment Unit and, 170; sentencing and, 5, 60–61, 74–75, 114, 206, *258nn117*, 119, 120; types of, 161, 166–67; white use of, 65, 66, 69–70, 213, *254n70*; youth and, 196


Hailes, Edward, 132

Halleck, Charles, 23, 24, 45

Hamer, Fannie Lou, 69

Harlem: drug war in, 31–33, 166, *247n59*; police in, 102–103, 134, 156

Harris, Kamala, 221

Harris, Kate Clark, 272n76
Harris, Ron, 204–205
Harris, Stanford, 59–60
Harris, Stanley, 140
Hartsfield, William, 87–88
Harvard University, 101
Harvey, Carrol, 29
Hassan Jeru-Ahmed, 26–31, 33, 40, 246nn39, 47
Henderson, Erma, 63–64
Henderson, Wade, 202
Herbert, Lenese, 169, 203
heroin, 10, 25–33, 149, 156; black community response to, 26–33, 44, 246nn39, 44, 47, 247n59; crime and, 26–27, 50, 126, 245n35; juveniles and, 25, 31, 245n33; marijuana and, 40, 44; methadone maintenance and, 26–27, 28, 246nn39, 44; sentencing for, 120–22, 124, 129, 131, 133–34, 139
Herring, Albert, 161, 174–75, 275n35
"Highsmith, Dante", 222–28, 231–36, 237, 238–39, 285nn27, 28
Hillary, Tony, 126, *126*
*Hilltop, The* (campus newspaper), 53, *54*, 246n47, 249n75
Hines, Samuel George, 40, 42
Holder, Eric, 9, 144, 229; Operation Ceasefire and, 194–204, 207–208, 214
Homeboy Industries, 238
Home Rule Act (1973), 19, 34, 41, 45–46, 55
homicide rates, 50, 62, 218, 251n8; in D.C., 10, 48, 142, 159–62, 166, 173, 174–75, 178–79, 194–95, 201, 218; in Detroit, 50, 62, 247n53; in New York, 50, 218; by race, 57, 161–62, 194–95, 203, 218, 275n36
House of Representatives: District Committee of, 18–19, 41, 97; Judiciary Committee of, 62–64, 70, 71, 76; Sentencing Reform Act of 2015 in, 221
Houston, 137, 165

Howard University, 70, 208, 261n46; anticrime sentiment at, 53, *54*, 61; antidrug sentiment at, 36–37, 246n47, 249nn75, 76; attendees of, 20, 34, 88, 101, 247n54

ID badges, 175, 181, 182
Illinois, 279n2; *see also* Chicago
implicit bias, 214
Indianapolis, 198, 201, 280n19
Initiative 9, 139–43, 145–46, 161
institutional racism, *see* racism
integration, *see* police officers, black; segregation
Isikoff, Michael, 204

Jackson, Clifford, 159
Jackson, Jesse, 158, 166, 195–96, 270n46
Jackson, Maynard, 19, 37, 76, 165–66, 249n75; on gun control, 62–63, 71, 72, 74–75, 76, 258n119
Jackson, Robert, 198
Jacob, John, 158
jails, 176–78, 237; overcrowding of, 140, 165, 166, 177, 278n108; pretrial, 174, 176
Jaffe, Harry, 158
Jaffe, Jerome, 26
Jarrett, Valerie, 229
Jeru-Ahmed, Hassan, *see* Hassan Jeru-Ahmed
Jefferson, Burtell, 78; as chief of police, 78, 111–14, 167–68; discrimination faced by, 80, 90–91, 93–94, 263n73; education of 81, 88, 101; on sentencing, 124, 127, 129–30, 132, 133, 139, 140, 142, 143, 145, 147, 148
*Jet*, 55
Jim Crow, 65–67, 80, 81, 82–88, 131; present as comparable to, 205, 209
job training programs, 30, 89, 157, 227, 272n76
Johnson, James Weldon, 68

Johnson, John H., 137
Johnson, Lyndon B., 48, 76, 104
Johnson, Nicholas, 65
Johnson, Robert, 206–207, 282n55
judges, 13, 192, 204, 236: black, 3–8, 14, 38, 203, 247n54; discretion of, 60–61, 122, 127–30, 130, 236, 268n21
jump-out squads, 169, 171
juries, 13, 129; racial makeup of, 9, 12, 95, 203
juvenile court, 5, 225, 232
juvenile detention facilities, 5, 222, 236
juveniles, *see* youth

Kansas City, 56; Gun Experiment in, 197–98, 199, 201, 212–13, 280nn19, 21
Katzenbach, Nicholas, 104, 108
Keith, Damon, 31, 247n54
Kelly, Ray, 277n80
Kennedy, David, 161, 163
Kennedy, John F., 62
Kennedy, Randall, 44, 72, 250n108
Kennedy, Robert F., 62
Kennedy, Ted, 127–28, 131
Kephart, William M., 91–92
Kerner Commission, 35, 104
Kick Their Assets, 165–66
King, Martin Luther, Jr., 84; assassination of, 57, 59, 70, 124–25; invoking of, 3–4, 7, 9, 194–96, 211, 224; Southern Christian Leadership Conference and, 20, 55
King, Martin Luther, Sr., 84, 86, 87, 100
Krugler, David, 67
Ku Klux Klan, 81, 86, 158

Latinos, 12, 218, 248, 285n28; pretext stops of, by police, 197, 277, 281n34
lawyers, black, 38, 203; *see also* prosecutors; Public Defender Service
Layton, John, 105
lead poisoning, 50, 218
League of Women Voters, 140

legislatures, 14; *see also* Congress; Washington D.C., city council of
Leichter, Franz, 248n70
"Leslie, Lynn," 223–24, 232, 233, 235, 238
"Lester, Bernice," 123–24, 149
Levin, Benjamin, 282n52
Lewis, John (columnist), 101–102
Lewis, Nancy, 280n26
liberals, white, 83, 282n52; black mistrust of, 35–36, 45–46
life sentences, 32, 121, 221
Lightfoot, Bill, 281n40
Linder, Tom, 86
Lipscombe, Leon, 47–48, 48, 73
Lorton Reformatory (Lorton, Va.), 24, 132, 176–77
Los Angeles, 18; black officials in, 19, 134, 165, 270n39; drugs in, 134–37, 135, 145, 158; police in, 103–104, 167, 204, 207, 208
*Los Angeles Sentinel*: on drug dealers, 145, 158; on PCP, 134–37, 135; on police, 103, 207, 208
*Los Angeles Times*, 204
Lumumba, Patrice, 34
lynching, 8, 72, 81, 195

Mafia, 28–29
Makeba, Miriam, 34
Malcolm X, 50, 69
Malcolm X College, 71
mandatory minimum sentences, 114, 119–50, 236; D.C. ballot initiative for, 114, 139–43, 145–46; D.C. council push for, 124–33, 269n34; for drug dealing, 114, 121, 131, 134–39, 144, 221, 267n2, 269n33, 272n76, 282n55; failure to reduce crime by, 143; federal, 133; for gun crimes, 60–61, 75, 131, 139, 145, 258nn119, 120, 269n33, 282n55; in L.A., 134–37; mass incarceration and, 143–44, 148; opposition to, 132–33, 139–41, 146,

148, 236; pleas and, 144; support for, 129–30, 131–32, 134–39, 140, 145–46
marijuana, 17–25, 33–46, 217–20, 285n18; arrest disparities for, 18, 20, 21–22, 23–24, 46, 219, 285n17; black opposition to decriminalization of, 33–46, 220, 248n70, 284nn14, 15; decriminalization of, 11, 20–25, 42, 76, 215, 217–20, 244n19, 283nn1, 2, 284n9, 11, 13, 285nn16, 18; found in vehicular stops, 186–93, 201–202; as gateway, 21, 40, 44–45, 220; juvenile use of, 37–41; relative safety of, 21, 24; sentencing for, 17–18, 22, 45, 121, 124, 129, 131, 139, 251n110
Marshall, George, 157
Marshall, Nelson, 94–95, 101
Marshall, Thurgood, 19
"Marshall Plan" for U.S. cities, 12–13, 157, 215; *see also* crime: root-cause solutions to
Maryland, 65, 70, 109–10, 113, 161, 202, 208, 279n2
mass incarceration, *see* criminal justice system
Massing, Michael, 244n19
Maya Angelou Public Charter School, 151–56, 163, 179, 180–84
mayors, black, 19, 165; *see also specific people*
McCrary, Justin, 266n147
McGinty, Derek, 197
McGrath, Kay Campbell, 258n119
McKinney, Billy, 71
McMillan, John L., 18–19, 41
Meek, Russ, 63, 71
Meese, Ed, 175
*Messenger, The* (magazine), 68, 68
methadone, 26–28, 44, 246n39
Metropolitan Police Department (MPD), *see* police forces
Miami, 86–87
Michigan, 75, 106; *see also* Detroit
Miller, Kelly, 261n46
Mississippi, 8, 69, 74, 82, 97

Montgomery, Alabama, 86
Moore, Douglas, 55, 105, 131, 176, 253n44; on gun control, 64–65, 70, 71, 72, 75, 254n68; on marijuana, 33–41, 42, 44, 45–46, 217, 219, 249n86
Mosby, Marilyn, 221
Moskos, Peter, 265n130, 266n135
Moultrie, H. Carl, 9
MPD (Metropolitan Police Department), *see* police forces
Muhammad, Khalil Gibran, 155, 242n16, 246n49
Mulford, Don, 70
Mumin, Ibrahim, 126–27
Murch, Donna, 279n12
Murphy, Frankie, 171
Murphy, Patrick V., 104
Murray, Robert, 91, 93, 95, 97, 99, 100

NAACP, 48, 56, 68, 158, 202; Citizens' Mobilization Against Crime, 32; police integration sought by, 84, 95, 97, 100, 103; on sentencing, 132, 139, 221
Nance, Jason P., 285n27
Narcotics Treatment Administration (NTA), 27, 147–48
National Bar Association, 137, 139
National Commission on Civil Disorders, 35, 105
National Commission on Marihuana and Drug Use, 21
National Conference of Black Lawyers, 139
National Council of Police Societies, 114
National Guard, 166
National Institute on Drug Abuse, 24, 204–205
National Lawyers Guild, 140
National Moratorium on Prison Construction, 140
National Organization of Black Police Executives (NOBLE), 114, 267n155
National Public Radio, 199, 229, 280n21

*National Review* (magazine), 21

National Rifle Association, 142–43

neighborhoods, black, 146, 208–12; black officers limited to, 86, 92, 109; death toll in, 161–62, 275n38; as decimated by drugs, 44, 169; presumption of guilt in, *see* racial profiling; riots in, 103, 124–25; Trump on, 12; violence in, *see* African Americans: crime feared by; white officers in, 56, 102, 104, 171

Newark, New Jersey, 18, 19

*New Jim Crow, The* (Alexander), 220, 284n11

New Orleans, 113

New School for Afro-American Thought, 70

New York City, 165; guns in, 206–207; heroin epidemic in, 31–33, 247n59; marijuana laws in, 248n70; police in, 102–103, 109, 110, 134, 165, 167; stop-and-frisk in, 197, 212, 277n80

*New York Times*, 127–28, 197, 280n19

Nixon, Richard M., 20, 21, 49, 76–77

nonviolent drug offenders: insufficiency of focusing on, 220–39; Obama on, 221, 228, 230; rhetoric about, 145, 175, 220; *see also* drugs; drug dealers; War on Drugs

Northwest D.C., 95, 126, 159, 160

Oak Hill (juvenile prison), 5, 222, 235

Oakland, California, 70, *105*, 165

Obama, Barack, 213, 221, 228, 230

O'Bryant, Tilmon, 93–94, 99–101, *107*, 263n73

O'Connor, Sandra Day, 7

Ogletree, Charles, 38

Ohio, 19, 21, 50, 221–22, 279n2

Operation Ceasefire, 197–204, 206–15, 280nn15, *21, 26*

Operation Clean Sweep, 167–73, 176–78, 180

Oregon, 21, 22, 283n1

Page, Jerome, 132, 146

Pan-Africanism, 34

Parker, Michael, 258n119

Parks, Bernard, 204

Parliament (band), 18, 19

parole, 14, 112, 127, 132, 205, 221

Parris, Fred, 160

Partnership for a Drug Free America, 273n16

Paul Laurence Dunbar High School, 81

PCP (phencyclidine), 134–37, *135*, 173

PDS, *see* Public Defender Service

Pettit, Becky, 219

Philadelphia, 165, 221; police in, 91–92, 106, 107–108, 165

Phillips, Charles, 178

Pinnock, Horace, 160

plea bargaining, 60, 122–24, 148–50

police forces, 13, 78–115, 153–56, 165–76, 178–84; accountability for, 171–72, 210–11, 237; affirmative action within, 99, 112, 266n147; asset forfeiture and, 156, 165–55, 167, 172–73, 277n86; aggressive tactics of, 7, 11, 23, 79, 83, 94–97, *96*, 98, 101–106, 108, 109, 113, 154–56, 165–73, 180–84, 219, 267n155; black officers on, *see* police officers, black; blacks protected by, 73–74, 210, 211, 257n114; black victims neglected by, 30–31, 56, 64–74, 79, 83, 126, 254n68, 257nn103, 108, 114, 253n37, 267n155, 270n46; cooperation with, 30, 52, 79, 99, 183; disrespect by, 83, 96–97, 99, 171; Gun Recovery Unit of Washington, D.C., 212, 283n63; guns of, 166–67; implicit bias of, 214; ineffectiveness of, 178, 179; juveniles and, 153–56, 171, 178, 180–84; misconduct settlements by, 171; presumption of guilt by, 153–56, 181–82; pretext stops by, *see* pretext stops; problem-oriented, 277n73; racial profiling by, *see* racial profiling; racist origins of, 79, 81–82, 155–56, 181; residency of, 102, 266n146; on sentencing, 129–30; special powers of, 167; stop-and-frisk used by, *see* stop-and-frisk; tactics against drug dealers by, 120, 141, 144, 169–73; Trump and, 12; as unrestricted by the Constitution, 153, 200, 212, 283*n63*; warrior mind-set of, 154–56, 165–73, 180–84, 219

police officers, black, 71, 78–88, 90–94, 95, 97, 98–115, 154, 165–66, 167–68, 175–76, 181, 182, 270*n46*, 282*n56*; Atlanta's fight for, 82–88, *85, 87*, 96–97; as chiefs, in D.C., 9, 78, 111–13, 168, 169, 178; as chiefs, nationally, 10, 79, 112–13, 115, 165, 204, 206; conflicting goals for, 79–80; limited impact of, 106–11, 113–15, 265*n130*, 266*n135*; motivation of, 90, 110–11, 112, 266*n136*; promotion of, 92–94, 99, 103–104, 105, 110, 111–13, 263*n73*; rationale for, 79–80, 83–84, 95, 102, 106, 107, 182–83; second-class status of, 80, 86–87, 90–94, 95, 97, 103–105, 112, 167–68, 261*n58*; white resistance to, 79, 81–82, 86, 92; *see also* police forces

politics of respectability, 44, 250–51*n108*

Portland, 281*n34*

possession with intent to distribute, *see* PWID

Poussaint, Alvin, 53

poverty: drugs and, 147; enforced by segregation, 88–89, 261*n46*; increased under Reagan, 157–58, 273*n7*; as root cause of crime, 12, 63–64, 76–77, 132, 146, 214; *see also* class

Powell, Adam Clayton, Jr., 103

Powell, James, 102

Powers, Tyrone, 254*n70*

presumption of innocence, 153–56, 181–82

pretext stops, 170, 186–94, 197–204, 208–215; consent for, 188–89, 199–200, 212, 279*n2*, 281*nn29, 34*; damage done by, 213, 215; lack of objection to, 202–204, 206–11; minor crimes found during, 201–202, 213, 281*n34*; nationally, 197–98, 280*nn19, 20, 21*; of pedestrians, *see* stop-and-frisk; rationales for, 188, 280*nn19, 26*; success rates of, 200–201; traffic regulations and, 198, 199, 212–13; *see also* asset forfeiture; Latinos: pretext stops of, by police; racial profiling

pretrial diversion programs, 236

pretrial service agencies, 13; *see also* bail and bail bonds

Price, Blanche, 95

Prince George's County, Maryland, 70, 106, 109–10, 113, 158, 208

Pringle, George, 160

prisoners, reentry into society of, 236–38

prisons: conditions in, 5, 13, 176–78; construction of, 196; education in, 236; organizing within, 35, 176

probable cause, 153, 212; *see also* pretext stops; stop-and-frisk

probation, 3, 5, 7, 14, 60, 121, 127, 129, 131, 145, 191, 205

prosecutors, 13, 23, 149, 174–75, 192, 198; black, 194, 203, 207, 221, 223–24; discretion of, 60–61, 123, 133, 190; plea bargaining and, 122–24, 144, 148–49

prostitution, 35, 186

protective custody, 177

Public Defender Service (PDS, Washington, D.C.), 38, 119–20, 202, 209, 267*n1*; as civil rights organization, 7–8, 120; duty days at, 185–94; failure to hire black lawyers, 38; funding of, 236; juvenile clients of, 3–8, 222–28, 231–36, 237, 238–39; promotion within, 119

public health, 147–48

public housing, 186, 215

*Punished* (Rios), 285*n28*

PWID (possession with intent to distribute), 144

Quander, Paul, 37

race riots, 67–68, 70, 102–104, 124–25;
  *see also* whites: antiblack violence by
racial profiling, 197, 201–202, *208*,
  280*n26*, 281*n40*, 282*n56*; class and, 13,
  207–11; consequences of, 186–93, 213;
  lack of objection to, 202–204, 206–11;
  in pretext stops, 188–94, 197–204,
  208–15, 280*n26*; traffic regulations
  and, 198, 199, 212–13
racism, 88–90, 120, 255*n81*; armed
  resistance to, 65–70, 72, 254*n70*;
  black excellence in the face of,
  93–94, 167–68, 181–82, 249*n86*; in
  development of mass incarceration,
  11–13, 35, 61, 155–56, 164, 242*n19*;
  drugs in black communities as
  manifestation of, 27, 37, 127, 249*n76*,
  268*n18*; in employment, 88–90,
  110–11, 261*n46*, 266*n136*; implicit
  bias vs., 214; as root cause of crime,
  63–64, 76–77, 146; in schools, 12,
  38, 81, 90, 262*n59*; *see also* criminal
  justice system, racial disparities in;
  police forces; racial profiling
Raleigh, North Carolina, 82
Ramsey, Charles (Chuck), 204, 213
Randolph, A. Philip, 68, 256*n84*
Rangel, Charles, 166, 247*n59*
rape, 72, 160, 177, 253*n37*, 268*n13*
Rapid Deployment Unit (RDU),
  170–71
Raspberry, William, 27, 33, 60, 94, 176
Ray, John, 124, 130–34, 139–42, 145, 147,
  269*n34*
Reagan, Ronald, 69, 166, 244*n19*;
  appointees of, 140, 175; social services
  cut by, 12–13, 157–58, 272*n76*, 273*n7*
Reagon, Bernice Johnson, 257*n115*
reasonable suspicion, 212; *see also*
  pretext stops
Reconstruction, 65–67, 81–82, 259*n14*
Redfield, Sarah E., 285*n27*

Reiss, Albert, 108
responsibility politics, 44, 250–51*n108*
revolving door justice, 127–29, *128*, *130*,
  131, 140
Richmond, Virginia, 206
Rios, Victor, 285
riots, 67–68, 70, 102–104, 124–25
Rizzo, Frank, 106
robbery, armed, 47–48, 49, 75, 227, 230,
  237; guns and, 50–51, 252*n14*
Robert H. Terrell Law School, 38
Roberts, David, 101
Robinson, Jackie, 87–88
Robinson, Spottswood, W., III, 131
Rock, Chris, 53
Rolark, Calvin, 101, 173
Roux, Vincent, 23
Rowan, Carl, 128, 145
Ruff, Charles, 132–33, 140, 269*n30*
Ruiz, Israel, Jr., 248*n70*
Russia, 205

San Diego, 107–108
Saunders, Michael, 159
Saunders, William, 258*n119*
Savannah, Georgia, 86
schools: for court-involved youth, 151–56,
  163, 179, 180–84; as dangerous, 125,
  146, 162, 181; federal spending on,
  272*n76*; incarceration and, 5, 13, 24,
  39, 219, 236; racial disparities in, 12,
  34, 38, 81, 88, 90, 193, 262*n59*; as root-
  cause solution, 29, 76, 151–53, 157,
  169, 236; suspensions from, 224–26,
  285*n27*
*School-to-Prison Pipeline* (Redfield and
  Nance), 285*n27*
Scott, C. A., 84, 86
Scott, Gwendolyn, 159
Scott-Heron, Gil, 36
Sealy, Lloyd, 103
search and seizure, *see* asset forfeiture;
  pretext stops
Seattle, 277*n73*

segregation, 88–90, 91, 263n59; in police departments, 80, 86–87, 90–94, 95, 97, 103–105, 112, 265n58; residential, 162, 207–11, 275n38; in Wilson administration, 67, 255n81

self-defense, 64–70; guns for, 5, 63, 64–72, 68, 75, 126, 254n68, 69, 70, 256nn93, 98, 257n103, 258n120; other strategies for, 53, 125, 163, 245n35; 252n21; for women, 72

sentencing, 7, 119–50; arbitrariness of, 150; class and, 13, 35, 132, 176, 223; and crack, 164, 205; discriminatory, 133, 134, 164; disproportionate, 121, 173, 221; diversion vs., 122–24, 147, 224, 227–28, 231, 235–36; judicial discretion and, 60–61, 122, 127–30, 130, 236, 268n21; lengthening of, 32, 75–77, 114, 127, see also mandatory minimums; for life, 32, 121, 221; for marijuana, 17–22, 45, 251n110; maximums, 22, 121, 124, 129, 131, 133, 134, 144, 205, 267nn2, 4; plea bargaining and, 122–24, 144, 148–49; with prior convictions, 121, 267nn2, 4; rationale for, 140

Sentencing Project, 6, 9, 205

sexual abuse, in prisons, 177

Shaw neighborhood (Washington, D.C.), 20, 124–25, 126–27, 151–54

Sherrill, Robert, 70

Sherwood, Tom, 158

Shipler, David, 211–12

Silbert, Earl, 60

Simon, David, 230

Sims, Water A., 86

Sklansky, David, 164

slave patrols, 81, 181

slavery: crack compared to, 10, 158, 163, 273n16; criminal justice system compared to, 205

Small, Reginald, 160

Smith, Bernard, 159

Smith, Frank, 125

SNCC, see Student Nonviolent Coordinating Committee

social services, 227–28; cut by Reagan, 12–13, 157–58, 272n76, 273n7; see also addiction treatment

solitary confinement, 177

South Africa, 181, 205

South Carolina, 18, 56, 62, 66–67, 82, 253n37

Southeast D.C., 125, 159, 160, 187, 193

Southern Christian Leadership Conference, 20, 33, 55

Spaulding, William, 250n105

Special Action Office for Drug Abuse Prevention, 26

State Department, segregation in, 89

Stennis, John, 49

Sterling, Eric, 164

Stevenson, Bryan, 231

Stokes, Carl, 19

Stone, Chuck, 99, 100–101

stop-and-frisk, 12, 169, 171, 198, 280n21, 282n56; in NYC, 197, 212, 277n80; students subject to, 153–55, 180–84; see also pretext stops

stop and search, see pretext stops

Stoughton, Seth, 154

Student Nonviolent Coordinating Committee (SNCC), 73–74, 247n63, 257n115; armed resistance by, 69, 70; author's parents in, 8, 69, 120, 241n7; D.C. leaders in, 34, 55, 105, 112

Students for a Democratic Society, 36

super-predators, 232

suspensions from school: 225–26, 285n27

Sweet Honey in the Rock, 257–58n115

Taifa, Nkechi, 205

Talmadge, Herman, 86

Task Force on 21st Century Policing, 213

"Thomas, Jeremy," 223–24, 232–39

Thomas, Pierre, 170

Thompson, Beverly Anita, 159–60
Thompson, Steven, 160
Thompson, Tracy, 204
Tidwell, Mike, 161
Tillman, Ben "Pitchfork," 66
tinted windows, 187, 193–94, 199, 212, 280n26
Tonry, Michael, 17, 250n107
traffic stops, 188, 198, 199, 212; *see also* pretext stops; racial profiling
trauma, 153, 162–63, 225
Trotter, Monroe, 67
Truman, Harry S., 88
Trump, Donald, 12, 237
Tucker, Sterling, 42–43, 97, 105, 250n105
Turner, Maurice T., Jr., 167, 168
Tuskegee Institute, 83

unions, 89, 111, 261n46
United Moorish Republic, 27
Urban League, 43, 97, 132, 146, 158, 251n110; on crime, 53, 146; on racial disparities, 23, 139
U.S. Attorney's office, 132–33, 140, 161, 175, 194, 203, 269n30
U.S. Department of Justice, 131, 133, 188, 194–95, 229, 230
*U.S. News and World Report*, 127
U.S. Parole Commission, 112
U.S. Sentencing Commission, 144
U Street neighborhood (Washington, D.C.), 20, 124–25

veterans, 67–68, 94, 256n84
victims: equal protection for, 223–24, 236; punishment desired by, 57–60, 232
Vietnam, police recruiting in, 106
violence, 11, 242n16; drugs and, 145; masculinity and, 59, 102; *see also* crime; guns
violent offenders, lack of compassion for, 220–39;

Viorst, Milton, 49–50
voting rights, 7, 10, 12, 66–67, 236

Wagner, Robert F., Jr., 103
"Walker, Curtis," 3–8, 14, 224, 231, 233, 236, 238
Wallace, George, 12, 76
Ward, James, 160
Ward, Willis F., 261n58
Ware, Richard, 57–59, 62, 73
War on Drugs, 17–46, 119–50, 153–84; African American attitudes toward, 25–46, 124–27, 134–43, 165–66, 173; beginning of, 20, 45; black church on, 39–40, 42–43, 220; crack epidemic and, 25; declining support for, 204–206, 217–22, 228–31, 236–38, 283n1, 284nn11, 13, 285n16; drug dealers targeted by, *see* drug dealers; federal role in, 164, 172, 205; heroin epidemic and, 25–33, 40, 44; ineffectiveness of, 178, 179; invisibility of black victims in debates about, 46, 56–57, 253n39; mandatory minimum sentences used in, *see* mandatory minimum sentences; marijuana decriminalization during, 20–25, 33–46, 244n19; Operation Clean Sweep in, 167–73, 176–78, 180; parallels with gun control, 51, 75–76; police powers for, 166–67; racial disparities in, 17–18, 20, 21–22, 23–24, 25, 46, 164, 204–205, 219, 250n107, 285n17; racializing of, 164; support by black officers for, 114, 267n155; as term, 51; users targeted by, 174–76; *see also* drugs; drug dealers; *specific drugs*
Washington (state), 277n73, 283n1
Washington, Booker T., 68, 81, 83
Washington, D.C.: armed resistance in, 67–68, 70; asset forfeiture in, 172–73; ballot measures in, 139–43, 145–46;

black men under supervision in, 6; black middle class in, 97, 101, 139, 208–11; Board of Commissioners of, 95–97; Chamber of Commerce of, 99; city council of, *see* Washington, D.C., city council of; Civilian Complaint Review Board in, 172; Corporation Counsel for, 132; crime epidemic in, 47–55, 143, 159–60; Federation of Civil Associations, 268*n19*; General Hospital of, *see* District of Columbia General Hospital; gun control in, 51–62, 64–65, 70–77, 161; heroin epidemic in, 25–33, 245*n33*; homicide rate in, 10, 48, 142, 159–62, 166, 173, 174–75, 178–79, 194–95, 201, 218; jail in, 25, 35, 176, 177–78, 186; as majority-black jurisdiction, 9, 18, 19–20, 34, 55, 62, 247*n63*; marijuana arrests in, 18, 20, 21–22, *22*, 23, 46, 186–93, 201–202; marijuana decriminalization in, 17–25, 33–46, 217–20, 283*n1*; mayor of, 19, 165; police force of, *see* police forces; segregation in, 88–90, 162; self-determination of, 18–19, 34, 41, 45–46, 55, 59, 74, 97, 253*nn44*, *45*, 258*n117*; U.S. Attorney for, 132–33, 140, 161, 175, 194, 203, 269*n30*; Year of Shame in, 159–60

Washington, D.C., city council of, 19–20: on gun control, 51, 55–62, 64–65, 70–75; on mandatory minimum sentences, 124–33, 269*n34*; on marijuana decriminalization, 20, 22–25, 33–46, 56, 215, 217–20, 283*n2*, 284*n9*, 285*n16*; prison conditions for inmates from, 177

Washington, Kenneth, 54, 56
Washington, Ricardo, 159
Washington, Walter E., 19, 22, 41, 43, 52, 111, 266*n142*
*Washington Afro-American*, 89, *206*; on crime, 47, *48*, 51, *52*, 53, 55, 61, 64, 252*n21*; on drugs, 147–48, 173, 176,

268*n18*, 273*n16*; on police, 92, 94, 97, 98–101, 127
*Washington Bee*, 113
*Washington Informer*, 101
*Washington Post*, 27, 34, 49, 54; on crime, 49, 60, *126*; on drugs, 21, 23, 27, 41, 141, 145, 204; on police, 94, 170, 280*n26*
*Washington Star*, 49
Washington Urban League, *see* Urban League
Waters, Maxine, 134, 136, 270*n39*
Watts, 103–104
Weaver, Vesla, 251*n8*
Weitzer, Ronald, 209–11
welfare, 12–13, 76–77, 157–58, 258*n130*, 272*n76*, 273*n7*, 284*n9*
Wells, Ida B., 69, 73
Wells, Tommy, 217, 284*n9*, 285*n16*
whites: antiblack violence by, 65–70, 72, 73, 81, 82, 98, 254*n70*; black mistrust of allied, 35–36, 45–46; decriminalization supported by, 284*n13*; drug dealing by, 28–29, 214; drug use by, 17, 23, 39, 132, 164, 176, 202, 205, 213, 248*n70*, 281*n34*; exempted from Operation Ceasefire, 201, 213; fear of crime by, 49–50, 53, 61, 195; punitive attitudes of, 9; resistance to black police by, 79, 81–82, 86, 92; role of, in development of mass incarceration, 11–13, 242*n19*; stereotyping of blacks by, 92, 155, *see also* racial profiling; suspected of promoting black addiction, 27, 37, 127, 249*n76*, 268*n18*; *see also* police forces; racism
white supremacy, 18–19, 66, 82, 92, 254*n70*
*Why Blacks Kill Blacks* (Poussaint), 53
Wilkins, Robert, 202, 207
Wilkins, Roy, 49, 56, 103
Wilkinson, Monty, 198
Williams, Isaac, Jr., 96, *96*
Williams, Joseph, 159
Williams, Juan, 141, 145

Williams, Seth, 221
"Willis, Tasha," 119–24, 141, 144,
    148–50, 151, 267nn1, 2
Wilson, James Q., 197
Wilson, John, 55–56, 69, 73, 112; on
    drug dealing, 125; on guns, 56,
    60–61, 64, 69, 71, 257n112
Wilson, Woodrow, 67, 255n81
Wilt, G. Marie, 108
Winter, Nadine, 166, 269n34
*Wire, The* (TV series), 230
World War I, 67–68, 256n84
World War II, 50, 157

York, Michael, 170
Young, Coleman, 19, 31; on gun
    control, 65, 75, 254n70
Young, Whitney, 25
youth: drug use by, 3–8, 25, 31, 37–41,
    125, 196, 245n33; appeal of gangs for,
    222–28, 231–36, 237, 238–39, 285n28;
    gun use by, 5, 196; racial profiling of,
    151–56, 163, 179, 180–84, 285n27;
    traumatizing of, 153, 162–63, 225

Zimring, Franklin, 217–18